THEATRE AND WAR 1933–1945

D1343534

To my father, for his support, generosity and love over the years

THEATRE AND WAR 1933–1945

PERFORMANCE IN EXTREMIS

EDITED BY MICHAEL BALFOUR

Berghahn Books
New York • Oxford

First published in 2001 by

Berghahn Books

www.BerghahnBooks.com

© 2001 Michael Balfour

792.
94
BAL

02781963

Library of Congress Cataloging-in-Publication Data

Theatre and War, 1933–1945 : performance in extremis / edited by Michael Balfour.
p. cm.
A Collection of essays originally published in various publications,
1946–1996.
Includes bibliographical references and index.
Contents: The adventures of Mother Cartridge-Pouch / Jeffrey T. Schnapp –
Theatre and politics of the Mussolini regime / Pietro Cavallo – Towards an
aesthetic of fascist opera / Erik Levi – Hitler's theatre / Bruce Zortman – The war
years / Andrew Davis – The role of Joan of Arc on the stage of occupied Paris /
Gabriel Jacobs – German refugee theatre in British internment / Alan Clarke –
Thespis behind the wire : a personal recollection / George Brandt – The muses in
Gulag / Alexander Solzhenitsyn – Cabaret in concentration camps / Peter
Jelavich – Brigades at the front / Joseph Macleod.
ISBN 1-57181-762-X (hbk. : alk. paper) ISBN 1-57181-497-3 (pbk. : alk. paper)
1. Performing arts – Europe – History – 20th century. 2. World War,
1939–1945 – Theater and the war. I. Balfour, Michael.

PN2570.T389 2000
7911.094'09043–dc21   00-046734

British Library Cataloguing in Publication Data
A catalogue record for this book is available
from the British Library.

Printed in the United States on acid-free paper.
ISBN 1-57181-762-X hardback
ISBN 1-57181-497-3 paperback

CONTENTS

Introduction   1

Part I: The Aesthetics of Fascism

1. The Adventures of Mother Cartridge-Pouch   11
   Jeffrey T. Schnapp

2. Theatre and Politics of the Mussolini Regime   21
   Pietro Cavallo

3. Towards an Aesthetic of Fascist Opera   32
   Erik Levi

4. Hitler's Theatre   46
   Bruce Zortman

Part II: Theatre, Occupation and Curfew

5. The War Years   54
   Andrew Davies

6. The Role of Joan of Arc on the Stage of Occupied Paris   65
   Gabriel Jacobs

Part III: Theatre Behind Barbed Wire

7. German Refugee Theatre in British Internment   83
   Alan Clarke

8. Thespis Behind the Wire – A Personal Recollection   117
   George Brandt

9. The Muses in Gulag   124
    Alexander Solzhenitsyn

10. Cabaret in Concentration Camps   137
    Peter Jelavich

Part IV: Theatre at the Front

11. Brigades at the Front   165
    Joseph Macleod

Index   188

THE CONTRIBUTORS

George W. Brandt, MA, PhD, Professor Emeritus of Radio, Film and Television Studies at Bristol University, emigrated from Berlin to England in 1934. After graduating in Modern Languages at University College London during the War, was interned and deported to Canada. Worked in the Bristol Drama Department from 1951 until 1986. Publications include a verse translation of Calderon's *The Great Stage of the World* (Manchester, 1976) *British Television Drama* (Cambridge, 1981) Memories and Inventions (Piccolo, 1983) *German and Dutch Theatre, 1600–1848* (Cambridge, 1993) *British Television Drama in the 1980s* (Cambridge, 1993) *and Modern Theories of Drama* (Oxford, 1998). 'Thespis Behind the Wire' was originally published in *Theatre and Film in Exile*, edited by Günter Berghaus and Oswald Wolff (Berg Publishers, 1989).

Pietro Cavallo is an Assistant Professor of Contemporary History at the University of Salerno, where he teaches history of political parties. His research and publications have been concerned with Fascism, the Second World War, the Communist movement and the American Myth. His books include *Immaginario e rappresentazione: Il teatro fascista di propaganda* and *Riso amaro: Radio, teatro e propaganda nel secondo conflitto mondiale*. 'Theatre and Politics of the Mussolini Regime' was originally published in *Fascism and Theatre*, edited by Günter Berghaus (Berghahn Books, 1996).

Alan Clarke trained as an actor at the Central School of Speech and Drama, worked in a number of repertory theatres and made an educational television series in the GDR. He read Theatre Studies at the Humboldt University in Berlin, where he also completed his Ph.D. He has continued to lecture in theatre and media studies in both further and higher education. He has written, directed and translated a wide range of plays for the theatre and radio. 'German Refugee Theatre in British Internment' was first published in *Theatre and Film in Exile* edited by Günter Berghaus and Oswald Wolff (Berg Publishers, 1989).

Andrew Davis is the author of several books and a part-time tutor for the Extra-Mural Departments at Cambridge and London Universities, the City University and the Workers' Educational Association. 'The War Years' was first published as a chapter in *Other Theatres* (Macmillan Books, 1987).

Gabriel Jacobs is a lecturer in French at University College Swansea. Current research is on the language of propaganda in occupied France. Author of *The Antigone of the Resistance* (AUMLA) and other publications. 'The Role of Joan of Arc on the Stage of Occupied Paris' first appeared in *Vichy France and the Resistance; Culture and Ideology*, edited by Roderick Kedward and Roger Austin (Croom Helm, 1985).

Peter Jelavich has written extensively on German theatre, including *Berlin Cabaret* (Harvard University Press, 1993) and *Munich and Theatrical Modernism – Politics, Performance and Playwrights 1890–1914* (Harvard University Press, 1985). 'Cabaret in Concentration Camps' originally appeared as an epilogue in *Berlin Cabaret*.

Erik Levi is currently Senior Lecturer in Music at Royal Holloway University of London. He is the author of *Music in the Third Reich* (Macmillan, 1994) and several chapters and articles dealing with aspects of German Music from the Weimar Republic and the Nazi era. An active performer and broadcaster, he is also an experienced music critic writing regularly for the BBC Music Magazine, The Strad and Classic CD. 'Towards an Aesthetic of Fascist Opera' was originally published in *Fascism and Theatre*, edited by Günter Berghaus (Berghahn Books, 1996).

Joseph Macleod wrote extensively about Russian Theatre. His books included *New Soviet Theatre* (Allen and Unwin, 1943) and *Actors Across the Volga* (Allen and Unwin, 1946). He also published novels. 'Brigades at the Front' originally appeared in *Actors Across the Volga*.

Jeffrey T. Schnapp holds the Pierotti Chair in Italian Literature at Stanford University. He is the author of *18 BL and the Theater of Masses for Masses* (Stanford University Press, 1996) and *The Transfiguration of History at the Center of Dante's Paradise.* Among his forthcoming books are *Italian Fascism. A Primer* (Nebraska) and *Verso la chiara scienza. Gaetano Ciocca, architetto-ingegnere tra fascismo e democrazia* (Skira). 'The Adventures of Mother Cartridge-Pouch' was originally published in *Staging Fascism: 18 BL and the Theater of Masses for Masses.*

Alexander Solzhenitsyn is one of Russia's most influential writers. He was born at Rostoy-on-Don in 1918, the son of an office worker and a schoolteacher. During the Second World War he served continuously at the front as a gunner and artillery officer, was twice decorated, and reached the rank of captain. In early 1945 he was arrested and charged with making derogatory remarks about Stalin. For the next eight years he was in labour camps. When his book *One Day in the Life of Ivan Denisovich* was published in 1953, on Stalin's death, Solzhenitsyn had to remain in exile for three years, although his wife was allowed to join him. After the publication in Europe of his book *The Gulag Archipelago,* he was arrested by the authorities and deported. His other works include *The First Circle, The Love-girl and the Innocent* and *Cancer Ward.* In 1970 Solzhenitsyn was awarded the Nobel Prize for Literature. 'The Muses in Gulag' was first published in *The Gulag Archipelago.*

Bruce Zortman's interest in German Theatre dates from his years as a Taussig Fellow at the Free University of Berlin. The author interrupted his own study to collaborate with Charles Laughton on the anthology The Fabulous Country. Other work includes *In a Land that is not yours,* a play about a young victim of Holocaust filmed for television by Warner Communications, and a suspense novel *The Fifth Criterion* (FB, 1980). The essay was first published in *Hitler's Theatre – Ideological Drama in Nazi Germany* (Firestein Books, 1984)

Acknowledgements

This book came about by accident. It was a result of the inevitable post-traumatic period after finishing my doctorate and finding that I did not have a reason to be lurking in the library, skulking in bookshops and scouring second hand book-sellers for specialist publications. In other words I had to find a new excuse for my bookish habits, and to my surprise and delight I did.

I owe debts and gratitude, both personal and professional, to many people over the year it took me to select and edit these essays. I need to thank all the contributors who not only allowed me to put this collection together, but who offered support, advice and encouragement along the way. I owe much to Günter Berghaus – who has done a great deal of important work in this area already – and who was incredibly generous and supportive of this project. Thanks also to Baz Kershaw, for stimulating and challenging me over the years, and to Marion Berghahn for all her electronic encouragement via e-mail. This book could not have been completed without my wife's unceasing support – and her tactful late night yawns as I blabbed on about the intricacies of Russian footnotes. To her I owe everything.

Introduction

All art brings a message into the world, but it is not the message of morality or of philosophy, nor of discourse and law-giving. It is the message of life, of life itself . . . And where there is no reverence, or respect, for the creative impulse of art there can be no civilised society. Civilisation exists only where conscience exists.[1]

The theme of this book is the many different forms theatre took during the extreme political and social turmoil of the Second World War. It is my hope that underlying the accounts is a contemporary relevance to exploring the radical potential of theatre, and of exploring forms of resistance against dominant structures of authority and power in ways that are not just negatively against a regime but positively for some human value or ideal that lies well beyond ideological territory.

The essays in this collection demonstrate that in the midst of mass killing, starvation, degradation, disease and continual fear, the theatre flourished. They have been selected and edited from a wide range of publications dating from the 1940s to the 1990s. The authors are academics, cultural historians, and theatre practitioners – some with direct experience of the harsh conditions of Europe during the war. Each author critically assesses the function of theatre in a time of crisis, exploring themes of Fascist aesthetic propaganda in Italy and Germany, of theatre re-education programmes in the Gulags of Russia, of cultural 'sustenance' for the troops at the front and interned German refugees in the UK, or simply cabaret as a currency for survival in Jewish concentration camps.

Attempting to understand theatre practices during the chaos and decimation wrought by the war is somewhat of a problem. The problem is not just our inability to understand the historical context in experiential terms, not just the helplessness of the mind before a destructiveness beyond imagining, but it is that no historical, philosophical or metaphysical explanation can possibly cope with the complex questions it raises about human nature.

If we take, for example, the context of the Jewish concentration camps it is hard to imagine how conditions could have been less conducive to performance. The physical dimensions in the camps included constant torture, mass executions, labour so exhausting that the worker was expected to live for only a matter of months, and rations so meagre that, even after the camps were liberated, victims by the thousands died from irreversible malnutrition. One would expect such an atmosphere to lead to complete disintegration of all will to survive. Nazi's instituted policies aimed at severing the connection between one's self and one's surrounding.

> The prisoners mind, the moral and philosophical decisions that had formed identity, were no longer of use. All they could rely on was the animal need to survive. In short, the Nazis aimed to create a victim who was nothing more than a beast. All human value was extirpated. Only the power to work, the fear of pain, the ability to obey, and the will to live survived.[2]

Testimonies from survivors of the Jewish ghettos also suggest that there was too much fear, too much suffering for there to be even a consideration of cultural life. The houses were hideously overcrowded, with an average of nine to a room in Warsaw.[3] Disease was rampant, food and money were very scarce; education, and very often reading were forbidden. There were arbitrary killings by the Germans, and regular deportations to the labour and concentration camps. The streets would be full of beggars, orphans and often corpses. Ben Helfgott, a survivor from the Polish ghetto of Piotrkow and Buchenwald concentration camp, provides testimony of the conditions.

> Your energy went into surviving and it was so much a matter of luck. A sadistic SS officer might see you on the street. And they had dogs trained to go for a man's testicles. And then there were the knocks on the door in the night when they rounded up people for deportation.[4]

Under normal peaceful conditions, the artist's struggle begins when he/she is faced with the task of transforming his/her ideas and writing through rehearsal into performance. A wartime theatre artist's problems (whether in a ghetto or camp) started at the very beginning of the artistic process with the acquisition of writing materials, lack of space for rehearsal and performance, the difficulty of persuading an audience to come to an illegal event, and the everpresent threat that if caught they would be deported, arrested or even killed.

In an environment established for the purpose of destruction rather than creation, artists needed great ingenuity to plan, rehearse and perform. The theatre that was finally created was affected by all these circumstances. In his published diaries of those years, the actor Jonas Turkow reveals what lengths performers and audiences had to go to in order to mount a production.

> The theatre was located in an attic, where a stage and curtain were set up . . . In order to reach the house you had to pass many court-yards and mountains of ruins. In various spots pickets were posted who had the double task of showing theatre-goers the way and of watching to see that an unwanted guest – a German – did not sneak in. If one did, each picket passed a code word to the next and then the audience, together with the artists, left through a side door and hid amid the ruins.[5]

Given the risks, why did artists and audiences risk their lives for these performances? It would be easy to give facile answers – the artists' need to create, the unquenchable human spirit. But we must remember the difficulty these theatre performers had in putting on a show. The most innocuous works were illegal. If discovered by an SS officer they could be sentenced to death. Perhaps foremost, we must recall the abuses to which these people were subjected; they do not fall within the range of any normal human experience. No matter how strong an artist's urge to create had been before the war, the absolute brutality of ghetto or camp life might naturally have dimmed it. The performance must have had extraordinary value for their creators, or they would not have been created. Helfgott

> To have art was another way of fighting the Germans. The arts were illegal and so it was a form of defiance. If the SS had found out the organisers would have been sent away or a few people shot. I remember that performances were usually full. There were never any announcements or posters. The news just spread by word of mouth. We were starved of any kind of culture, learning or studies, and it took your mind away from the turmoil. [6]

The whole question of civic resistance, the use of theatre as defiance, is very important. The cultural manifestations were an attempt to affirm human values, to deny dehumanisation. Jacob Gens, a leader of the Vilna Jewish Council, wrote in his diary nine months before he was arrested and shot by the Gestapo, 'We wanted to give people the opportunity to free themselves from the ghetto for several hours, and this we achieved. Our bodies are in the ghetto, but our spirit has not been enslaved'.[7]

One of the tangible reasons for performance in these extreme circumstances, and a theme which emerges from a number of chapters in this book, is that artists, in creating performances, experienced an element of control in their work. They alone were responsible for the form and style of their creations, their focus and occasionally their subject matter; they made decisions for themselves. Whether the decisions were motivated by a sense of history, a sense of aesthetics, or both, through their performances they were able to create a dramatic space in which they commanded power denied them in reality. A sense of dignity and self-worth was thereby momentarily preserved. Furthermore, the process of creating helped the theatre-makers evade the painful reality of prison camp life and establish an illusion of normality, at least while they were engrossed in their work. Then they could think of something normal, something that did not hurt. This need to divorce themselves from the gruesome aspects of 'a world gone mad' may also explain the 'neutral' themes of the productions – in which we see camp events chronicled, but minus the horrifying aspects with which the camps were fraught.

However the war-time performances also highlighted another issue – which will be critically addressed in this book – of theatre as a politically and socially malleable medium for cultural expression, as conducive to supporting the structures and ideologies of power as to challenging and overthrowing them. Any potential of theatre to produce resistances and hope against oppressive power structures has to be balanced with its inverse ability to be exploited by dominant ideologies for the (perceived) benefit and deception of the public.

The relationship between theatre and art to propaganda is not at all straightforward. George Orwell's statement that 'all art is to some extent propaganda'[8] was probably closer to the truth than Hitler, who on one occasion was heard echoing the popular view that 'art has nothing to do with propaganda'.[9] Not the least of the ironies contained in these seemingly contradictory statements is the fact that Hitler's remarks were addressed to Josef Goebbels who, as head of the Reich Ministry for Popular Enlightenment and Propaganda, had attempted to create a state apparatus for thought control which could have served as a model for the perfect totalitarian state depicted in Orwell's novel *Nineteen- Eighty-Four.*

Goebbels's Ministry moreover, despite Hitler's apparent claim for art's privileged status, concerned itself intensively and in intricate detail with the production and dissemination of cultural works. The more spectacular moments of this activity, especially the scenes of students publicly burning the works of Heine, Thomas Mann, Brecht etc., were recorded on newsreel and are now housed in film and TV archives around the world. That they are periodically slipped into various documentaries dealing with the Third Reich has no doubt contributed to the widespread belief that Nazi Germany is to be identified with the very essence of twentieth-century propaganda, and that by witnessing and condemning such scenes we will somehow strengthen our resistance to propagandistic messages which may be aimed directly at us by sinister forces within our own society.

Propaganda does not often come marching towards us waving swastikas and chanting 'Sieg Heil'. In reality, propaganda is much more subtle. It conceals itself in an attempt to coalesce completely and invisibly with the values and accepted power symbols of a given society. When Hitler claimed that art had nothing to do with propaganda he was anticipating a perfectly integrated National Socialist Germany whose art would spontaneously and unthinkingly reproduce the desired images and perceptions.

Several of the writers in this collection are careful to distinguish their readings of fascist culture from the tendencies of early post-war histories of the Third Reich: the first presents Fascism as simply opposed to culture, whether traditional or modernist, the second as merely instrumental in relation to it. These tendencies have not been helped by Göring's alleged statements on art: 'Every time I hear the word culture I reach for my gun . . .'. In reality the Fascists embarked on an ambitious schedule of opera and the building of huge outdoor 'art' stadiums to house mass spectacles in Germany and Italy. The Fascists' desire to reinvent the arts in the name of their ideology represents, perhaps, one of the most ambitious periods of State subsidy in Western Europe this century. These performances were not intended to be crude, didactic and overt propaganda pieces, indeed Goebbels was contemptuous of such exercises, like Alfred Rosenberg's *Myth of the Twentieth Century*, which he described as an 'ideological belch'.[10] Shortly after the Nazis assumed power he explained that there were two ways of making a revolution: 'You can go on shooting up the opposition with machine-guns until they acknowledge the superiority of the gunners. That is the simple way. But you can also transform the nation by mental revolution and thus win over the opposition instead of annihilating them. We National Socialists have adopted the second way and intend to pursue it'.[11] Goebbels continued:

> So I must simplify reality, omitting here, adding there. It is the same with an artist, whose picture can diverge a long way from the objective truth. What matters is that my political perception should, like the artist's aesthetic one, be genuine and true, that is to say beneficial to society. Detail doesn't matter. Truth consists in what benefits my country.[12]

But these statements need to be regarded as both contentious and contradictory. Despite these notions of an invisible 'mental revolution', many of the Nazi's experiments in mass theatre performances *were* actually crude and didactic if not downright artistic failures. As several of the writers in this book observe, the performances were jingoistic pieces, none of which particularly impressed. Solzhenitsyn's essay on the re-education camps in Russia makes the point about propaganda very clear, 'if anybody should ever try to tell you with shining eyes that someone was re-educated by government means through the KVCh – the Cultural and Educational Section – you can reply with total conviction: Nonsense!'[13] At the same time in Occupied France, and perhaps even amongst the operatic artists in Germany, the constraints of having to produce overtly pro-fascist pieces were circumvented by practitioners determined to produce plays under close scrutiny and censorship. Nor should it be forgotten that propaganda in the form of 'light-hearted' shows designed to boost the morale of the troops at the Front, or of civilians sheltering from an air raid, can serve a useful function. The point about all these examples is that the extreme societal conflict of the Second World War highlights the complexity of theatre and its relationship to authority and power; its ability to resist and transcend, as well as to be incorporated into the ideological machinery, in a way that is both revealing and significant for contemporary culture.

The book has been divided into four sections: *The Aesthetics of Fascism; Theatre, Occupation and Curfew; Theatre Behind Barbed Wire;* and *Theatre at the Front*.

The Aesthetics of Fascism begins with Jeffrey Schnapp's detailed reconstruction of the 18 BL spectacle, a performance that was a direct response to Mussolini's call for 'a distinctive fascist theatre for twenty thousand spectators'. The spectacle was set outside Florence on a site the size of six football fields and its cast included an air squadron, an infantry, a cavalry brigade, fifty trucks, four field and machine gun batteries, ten field radio stations, six photoelectric units, and over two thousand amateur actors performing before an audience of twenty thousand. Named after the first truck to be mass-produced by Fiat, 18 BL was 'conceived as a dramatic crucible. . . . in technique and effect somewhere between a theatre of war and a film production of epic proportions . . .'[14]. Schnapp's article is a fascinating cultural reconstruction of this forgotten event and serves as a springboard for three other essays which develop the inquiry into the place of the arts in the Fascist imagination. Pietro Cavallo contextualises the wider cultural concerns of the Mussolini regime, offering insights into Fascist models of narrative, historiography and the spectacle; while Erik Levi explodes the myth that culture under the Third Reich suffered. In particular he points to the commissioning of an astonishing 170 new operas between 1933–44 as testimony to the Nazi's creative energies. Levi's revealing essay discusses the Nazi's search for what Goebbels described as an art that has a 'romanticism of steel' and deconstructs the National Socialists aesthetic to glean clues of ideological relevance and hints of subversive undercurrents, arguing that some of the most significant challenges to Nazi cultural authority occurred in the Opera Houses of the post-Weimar period. In Bruce Zortman's essay, 'Hitler's Theatre', the author documents the 'destruction that is wrought by the imposition of totalitarian precepts on the theatre'.[15] He argues that an energetically subsidised theatre does not necessarily produce a creative one, and that the artistic quality of a theatrical production declines in direct proportion to its mass appeal specifically when it is designed to further political or ideological ambitions.

The *Theatre, Occupation and Curfew* section contains two essays. The first details the remarkable transformation of British theatre during the war years. Andrew Davis's essay remarks on a war-time trend which for the first time since the nineteenth century diminished the dominance of London West End stage productions. An amusing and representative anecdote from this essay is of a melodramatic actress responding to the forced re-location of a West End theatre company to 'the provinces' with a shocked: 'Burnley. Where's Burnley?'. Not only were theatre companies forced to vacate their London buildings but performances were created in makeshift 'non-theatrical' locations: evacuation centres, war hostels, factory canteens, army camps, gun sites and even tube stations (with the occasional trains roaring through) – and in front of audiences the majority of whom had never been inside a theatre. The second essay documents the French theatre during the German Occupation and reveals a surprising fact that attendance's rose dramatically during the period (1940–44). Audiences were undeterred by the difficulties of getting to and from the theatre under black-out conditions, by the ban on heating or by the constant interruptions caused by air-raid sirens. Gabriel Jacobs's essay argues that the French theatre was able, at times, to subtly survive the extensive censorship. This was despite the large crew of German Propaganda-staff who attempted to sway French public opinion towards 'collaboration' in the Nazi New Order; and the subtle use of a cultural structure with which the French were already familiar, rather than the superimposed German production of books, films, theatre etc. The one character that could be relied upon to please everybody was Joan of Arc. She pleased the Germans because, in her life and by her death, she showed up both the frailty and the perfidy of Albion. She pleased the French because she could be presented as the symbol of a humiliated France fighting to regain her stained honour and self-respect.

In 1940 25,000 German and Austrian refugees who had fled Hitler's Germany were detained for indefinite internment in the U.K. The majority were Jews, leftists, liberals, anti-fascists, intellectuals and artists who has sought refuge in Britain, only to be arrested and sent to camps with cramped and basic conditions. Several committed suicide, either out of desperation, or from fear that they would suffer similar atrocities encountered in German camps. In one English camp there were three Nobel prize-winners, twenty Oxford professors, a dozen scientists and many world-renowned actors, musicians and artists. In order to fight the sense of abandonment and dislocation the internees formed cultural and education groups, which included topical revues, original plays dealing with prison life, and performances of works by Aristotle and Thomas Mann. *Theatre Behind Barbed Wire* contains five fascinating stories dealing with theatre in the most unexpected of situations – the wartime prison. Two essays recount the experiences of German refugees in British internment; Alan Clarke's essay documents the story, while George Brandt provides a personal testimony illustrating the tale with insightful knowledge. *Theatre Behind Barbed Wire* also deals with the more sinister application of the arts in prisons, with extracts from Alexander Solzhenitsyn's memoirs of the Gulag Archipelago in Soviet Russia. The section concludes with the unique story of cabaret in the concentration camps of Westerbork, Dachau and Theresienstadt. Peter Jelavich's unsettling account of elaborate shows put on with the encouragement and active support of the SS commandants. Some of those who performed for the German officers were granted the privilege of living in private cottages and the promise of exemption from deportation. In other words becoming a member of the cast was a life-or-death matter. Many prisoners boycotted the revues because they considered them tasteless at best, and sacrilegious at worst. This is not surprising when one learns that the wood for the stage at Westerbork had been taken from the demolished synagogue of a nearby town. However for some inmates the performances were a 'valuable component of inner resistance' to the extent that inmates believed the shows provided not only short-term diversion but also gave them the mental strength to carry on. Moreover, some revues tried to achieve concrete, practical goals. Certain scenes probably attempted to be conduits between the inmates and the camp commandants, by appealing for good treatment. Performers were even able to express defiance, and evoked the brutal conditions – the barbed wire, the armed guards, the cynicism of the promises while offering a vision of eventual freedom. While the cabaret offered hope, it was for many a short-term hope, as the shows did not alter the fate of most inmates. This powerful essay documents the context of cabaret's 'light music and performance beside an open grave' arguing that the genre was strained to the limits in the concentration camps, and it was there that cabaret died.

The last essay in the book charts the remarkable achievements of Russian theatre 'brigades' taking entire classical and contemporary works to the front-lines. By February 1945 no fewer than 800,000 performances had been given by 900 brigades composed of 15,000 artists, including companies which entertained the guerrillas *behind enemy lines*. The stages were lorry platforms, warship decks, forest clearings; and the scenery was tents and sheets. There was hardly a first-class theatre in the Soviet Union which did not organise a theatre brigade. Nor was this considered a mere act of 'cheering up the boys'. High profile Moscow directors prepared brigade programmes in the same way they prepared first nights '. . . and were bound to show the front line real high art'; *Anna Karenina* and *The Three Sisters* were performed to an audience of anti-aircraft gunners in a dug-out trench. The touring brigades, dressed in camouflage capes, often under fire, toured the front-lines in any manner they could, on foot, on horseback, hitch-hiking or boarding munitions trains, and performed at night sometimes within 500 yards of the enemy. Joseph Macleod's essay was written shortly after the war, and describes the bravery and ingenuity of theatre artists, circus performers, opera stars and puppeteers who endured and shared the conditions of the front-line with their countrymen – on an astonishing scale never before witnessed in any other war.

I have deliberately included essays with a range of styles and varying levels of analysis, reflection and documentation. Some essays are meticulously researched academic pieces, others are personal insights into wartime experiences; some were written shortly after the war, others were written a few years ago. The reason for this is that theatre history, or any kind of history, is dependent on diverse interpretations and readings. The intention was to present a selection of work which not only analysed theatre practice during the war, but humanised and personalised it. I hope this makes this collection a richer sourcebook, one that deepens understanding as well as knowledge of this unique period. History will always demonstrate a variety of interpretations of the past, and a tolerance of this diversity, whether temporal or cultural, personal or analytical, is the absolute base of any considered exploration of the past.

Notes

1. Collins, Cecil (1944) *The Vision of the Fool*, London, Penguin, p.4
2. Blatter, J. (1982) *Art of the Holocaust*, London, Orbis, p.9
3. Lister, David (1989) *Independent*, 9 November, p.17
4. ibid, p.17
5. Turkow, J. in *Independent*, David Lister, 9 November 1989, p.17
6. Lister, David (1989) *The Independent*, 9 November, p.17
7. ibid., p.17
8. Orwell, George (1970) *The Collected Essays, Journalism and Letters, vol.2*, Sonia Orwell and Ian Angus (eds.), Middlesex, Penguin, p.276
9. Balfour, Michael (1979) *Propaganda in War 1939–1945*, London, p.41
10. ibid., p.43
11. ibid., p.48
12. ibid., p.431
13. Solzhenitsyn, A. (1975) *The Gulag Archipelago*, London, Collins and Harvill Press, p.469
14. Foster, H. (1996) Foreword to *Staging Fascism: 18 BL and the Theatre of Masses for Masses*, Jeffrey T. Schnapp, California, Stanford University Press.
15. Zortman, Bruce (1984) *Hitler's Theatre – Ideological Drama in Nazi Germany*, Texas, Firestein Books.

PART I

THE AESTHETICS OF FASCISM

CHAPTER 1

THE ADVENTURES OF MOTHER CARTRIDGE-POUCH

JEFFREY T. SCHNAPP

18 BL was originally scheduled to be performed on 22 April as the crowning event of opening-day ceremonies at the 1934 Littoriali, but logistical difficulties – including, it would appear, a noticeable lack of zeal on the part of his young cast of actors – led Blasetti to seek a one-week delay as early as the middle of March; to which Pavolini objected on the grounds that 'the human material (young fascists) could not be so well employed . . . and news of postponement would be demoralising'.[1] Several weeks of torrential rains ensured that Blasetti had his way. Expectations had been raised to fever pitch by a month of press coverage in such newspapers and reviews as La Stampa, L'Ambrosiano, Corriere della Sera, Il Giornale d'Italia, La Tribuna, La Nazione, Il Nuovo Giornale, Il Lavoro Fascita and Il Cantiere; and the delay hardly diminished the public's conviction that 'the good success of 18 BL is something that, in these times of impassioned discussion of collective art, individualistic art, etc., etc., transcends in importance even the Lictorial Games themselves'.[2]

  It was the organisers who contributed the lion's share of hyperbole, however, and what had once been billed as a mere experiment soon began to take on an air of permanence. By mid-April, a scriptwriting contest for future spectacles had already been announced, with prize monies of 17,000 lire: 10,000 for the first-place winner, 5,000 for second, and 2,000 for third.[3] These future spectacles would grant 'maximum prominence to scenes of mass movement sustained by technical resources unavailable on the ordinary stage (lights, searchlights, loudspeakers, motor vehicles, etc.)

while dialogue is to be kept to a minimum. Historical revocations are not to be excluded, even if the spirit of the Littoriali discourages the pursuit of actual choreographic effects and timeworn common-places (pageants in period costume, etc.).'[4]

In order to guarantee that 18 BL (and not historical pageants) would become the absolute point of reference, a call was issued to all artists: 'The organising committee of the Littoriali attributes great importance to the participation of Italian artists in this first mass spectacle (i.e. 18 BL), so that the experiment and successes of tomorrow may be guided by this particular experience. The event will make it clear how the war scenes included in the spectacle (artillery in action, columns of trucks, troop movements, etc.) could be of special interest to all artists participating in the contest.'[5] In the meantime, Pavolini and Blasetti were already envisaging the Isolotto theatre as a permanent structure, predicting that it would be the crucible within which the first genuinely fascist art form would be forged, a school for the directors of the future, and an academy where, 'If one experiment follows another and a tradition forms, there is no reason why a new Aristophanes or Aeschylus cannot arise tomorrow.'[6] The exuberance of the moment is best captured by the Florentine theatre critic Cipriano Giachetti, writing on the eve of the performance:

> Today it is war, revolution, reconstruction. Tomorrow it could well be the great events of history, reconstructed along essential lines, lines whose veracity exceeds that of the cinema, where artifice prevails over reality. Tomorrow it will be the most celebrated poems (a few days ago Blasetti suggested (Giosue) Carducci's 'Song of Legano') and perhaps fantastic creations. Because nothing that speaks to spectators' sensory organs and emotions is precluded in this new theatre.[7]

It was against the backdrop of such lavish expectations that the first 'theatre of masses' opened its doors on 29 April, exactly one week after the inauguration of the Lictorial games and one year after Mussolini's SIAE speech. The sell-out audience assembled according to plan, if one exempts the persistence of certain high-bourgeois theatregoing habit: 'ladies in evening dresses, dancing shoes, coats made of young and delicate fur, gold and silver jewellery'.[8] Despite (or indeed, because of) such affections, this portion of the spectacle would be judged a success by all. As intended by the organisers, the bridge, the various massing points, and the back-lit auditorium, all seem to have infused the assembled spectators with the sense that they themselves were the protagonists of Mussolini's mass theatre. [9] There were 'not 3,000 actors', observed many audience members, 'but 23,000.'[10] To this extent, 18 BL can be said to have fulfilled Robespierre's dream of a theatre in which the

spectator himself is the principal source of spectacle: 'the most magnificent of spectacles is that of a great people assembled'. [11]

The two-hour performance commenced with the entire landscape as well as much of the seating area veiled in a curtain of white
smoke. At the appointed hour, a call to order sounded over the public address system, the lights were extinguished, and the smoke
dissipated, exposing to view the immense stage, the surrounding
landscape, and the night sky. The first of the play's three acts began
with the trumpet calls from the solemn opening bars of maestro
Renzo Massarani's orchestral score: 'Trumpet Calls and Dances for
18 BL'.[12] Then came the broadcast of the spectacle's leitmotif, 'The
Captain's Testament': a First World War hymn associated with the
daredevil Alpine brigades instrumental in Italy's victory over Austria in the battle of the Piave river and, later, in the rise of fascism.
The action may be summarised as follows:

Act 1, Scene 1. The location and volume of the chorus of singing
voices oscillates as a searchlight scans the right portion of the stage,
finding bodies, networks of barbed wire, running soldiers, sand-
bags, galloping horses, artillery being hauled into position.[13]
Suddenly the rumble of an 18 BL Fiat truck is heard, and as it
crosses over the horizon line, artillery barrages light up the night
sky. A spotlight reveals the truck's destination: a troop of several
hundred second-line Italian soldiers, to whom its jovial Tuscan driver, Ugo Ceseri, delivers good humour, rations, and mail. The
truck's nickname, 'Mother Cartridge-Pouch'(Mamma Giberna) is
repeatedly shouted out in the course of a brief dialogue between
Ceseri and the soldiers.[14]

Scene 2. New volleys of rockets are fired in the distance by the
enemy forces, and a spotlight points to the middle hilltop, where a
fierce machine-gun battle has front-line Italian soldiers pinned
against the barbed wire. The truck now rumbles up the slope, its
armoured shield (borrowed from a 75-millimetre artillery battery)
riddled by bullets. A firestorm rages as it clears the crest of the hill.
Snippets of dialogue and song can be heard, interwoven with
mechanical sounds and explosions. The driver heaves two sacks of
food into a communications trench and continues down the back
side of the slope out of the public's view. An Austrian artillery shell
explodes where it has disappeared.

Scene 3. Confused voices are heard in the dark. The truck reappears
around the corner of the third hill, its roar resounding with redoubled force. The twilight reveals that it is brimming over with young
soldiers being transported to the front. Several dozen 18 BLs follow

in its wake and unload their soldiers, who join in the assault across the top of the ridge. Searchlights scan the horizon. Artillery and machine-gun battles start and stop until, at last, victory is at hand. Far behind the top of the first hill, an Italian flag is hoisted against the brilliant white light of a sign announcing the conquest of Italian Trento and Trieste. Ceseri's truck, buried under a collapsed wall in the middle of the stage, re-emerges from the rubble to lead a parade of 18 BLs over the horizon towards the flag, accompanied by triumphal shouting and song. End of Act 1. The stage lights are extinguished, the stadium lights turned on.

The transition between First World War and the labour strikes of 1922 is marked by a fade out of the cannonades and by a fireworks display designed by Blasetti and pictured as follows in his notes:

> After the victorious cries and chants will come an original pyrotechnic show, festive in its frequency, its showers, and its bright colours (white, yellow, blue, pink) to be fired in rapid alternation from the left and right sides of the stage. Lasting as long as needed to complete all requisite set changes, this display will gradually diminish in frequency and in the festiveness of its colours and sounds to the point where it becomes, in the end, an isolated but abundant rain of deep blood-red hue, echoed by a howl issuing from the stage.[15]

The intermission was carried out precisely as described, so when Act 2, Scene 1 begins and the stadium lights are turned off, the public finds itself beneath a fiery curtain and assailed by the electronic growl of a howling mob. Beyond the red rain, the repositioned stage lights reveal a new landscape on the lower left-hand side of the stage. Strewn across it are abandoned work implements, battered haystacks, rotting produce. Factory sirens sound, but their wail is soon distorted into the squawk of rusty gears. Ceseri and his mechanic are attempting to unload their 18 BL's cargo. They preach against the strike and call out for help. But they become the target of a roving mob of grey strikers, brandishing pickets and a bright red flag. The mob's 'mechanical howl' – the phrase belongs to the script – increases to deafening proportions as the strikers surround the truck (symbol of the First World War) and batter it with sticks and stones, leaving the mechanic unconscious. At this very instant, the truck's engine starts up and begins to roar above the chorus of shouts. The circle of strikers opens up, and if cesari can be overheard crying for revenge as the truck escapes into the gully.

Scene 2. An immense banquet table bearing the word PARLIA-MENT appears atop the central hillock bathed in red light. Seated at the table is a group of geriatric politicians representing the liberal, socialist, and popular parties, as well as the Freemasons. Some are elegantly dressed in black tuxedos. They wear oversized top hats, which hang down over their eyes, and are engaged in conspiratorial whispering. Others are fat, sloppily but brightly dressed, and full of rhetorical bluster. The strikers gather around them, remaining silent except for the occasional chorus of 'Long live the people's representatives!' and 'Down with the army!' Soon all conversation has ceased and the only noises that can be heard are those of the banquet. Knives and forks clang on plates; the old men chew, belch and cackle. A few minutes later, applause rings out. A socialist policeman has stood up to begin a speech. Instead of a voice, however, the sound of a barrel organ issues from his mouth: a wind-up barrel organ, like that employed by beggars with monkeys, playing the 'Dance of the Seven Veils' from Richard Strauss's opera *Salome*. Behind him, hundreds of slogan-bearing multi-coloured balloons rise up into the sky filled with empty promises. The barrel organ churns away for several minutes, after which it begins to wind down as a newsboy cries out headlines announcing the foundation of fascist groups. The balloons vanish and the music stops. One of the elders croaks loudly the fateful words of Luigi Facta before the March on Rome: 'But what do these fascists want?' At this precise instant, Mother Cartridge-Pouch, loaded with young fascists, appears unexpectedly over the hilltop and sends everyone scampering. She thunders down the hill and overturns the table of parliament. In the aftermath of her intrusion Ceseri harangues the mob: 'Seven million paycheques lost due to the railway strike! One hundred and thirty million in damages to farming thanks to the socialist dictatorship in the Bologna region! Everywhere dead men sacrificed to the demagogic beast! Workers, when will you be free yourselves from your mystifying leaders? Italians, your salvation lies in your daring!'[16]

Scene 3. Fire alarms ring out. Fascist hymns are sung by choruses far away and nearby. Ceseri's admonitions have failed, evidently, since a factory is ablaze in the left corner of the landscape. His 18 BL, filled with black-shirts, goes to the rescue but is ambushed by an armed socialist mob, from which issues the usual mechanical howl. Bullets fly in all directions. Other fascist brigades douse the fire. When the ambush is over, darkness descends again, and in the twilight one can see the fascist dead and wounded being heaped onto the platform of Ceseri's truck, as if on an altar. The truck rolls up to the summit of the stage's central crest, and 200 fascists converge upon it, arranging themselves in a square formation and standing mutually at attention. Over the horizon, a bright white light glows with increasing intensity. Projected from out of the light, a 'metallic and clear voice' (Mussolini's) interrupts the funeral silence, calling out: 'Heroes of the war and martyrs of the revolution!' 'Present' they respond. 'To whom does Italy belong, to whom Rome?' continues the metallic voice. 'To us! – To us! – To us!' they respond.[17] But the chorus of voices is no longer isolated. From all sides of the auditorium and stage, 1,000 blackshirts, including members of the audience, shout out, 'To us!' Led by a convoy of several dozen trucks, they parade out across the landscape and converge over the horizon line, where their silhouettes vanish into the white light. Act 2 has ended; fascism's putative revolution, the March on Rome, has begun.

The final act of 18 BL concerns one of the centrepieces of fascist domestic policy and perhaps the most revealing of fascism's redemptive myths: the draining of the Pontine marshes, the reclamation of marshland for purposes of agriculture, and the construction there, always at breakneck speed, of fascist new towns.[18] Since these events project the action of 18 BL ten years forward, Blasetti devised a second interlude to mark the transition from the early 1920s to 1932. First, as the sounds of the March on Rome begin to taper off, the stage's searchlights turn away from the marchers towards the night sky, which they scan nervously. Suddenly several aeroplanes – doubtless in formation, according to the conventions of the contemporary mass flight – appear and repeatedly swoop down over the stadium, showering the crowd with broadsheets from Il Popolo d'Italia proclaiming Mussolini's seizure of power and celebrating the principal phases and accomplishments of fascist rule. At the same time, young fascists dressed like newspaper boys run up and down the aisles, shouting out the headlines and distributing newspapers. Once the time allocated to carry out set changes has elapsed, the newspaper boys vanish and the aeroplanes peel off to the right and left of the stage.[19]

Act 3, Scene 1. The lights drop, and Massarani's heroic dance music sounds. The stage is a swarm with hundreds of near-naked children, who wend their way up over the horizon following furrows cut into the land by a handful of peasants, whose wagons and tools are in view. The children are followed by 100 athletes in formation, who perform a gymnastic dance with lances and bows: emblems of the 'human reclamation' accomplished by fascist education.

Scene 2. Off in a hollow to the left of the stage, a swamp comes into view under a faint greenish spotlight. Filled with reeds and bubbling mud, it emanates steam and frog-like croakings intermingled with voices of rumour, calumny, and doubt.[20] As the gymnasts depart, one of the frogs mutters, 'Billions and billions spent to uglify the race! Violent and ignorant generations are being fashioned, hungry for war, slaughter, and excess'. 'They tell me the holy youth of Milan have risen up in the name of pagan tyranny', croaks another. 'How true, how true! In Naples too,' responds a third.[21] The rumour mongering continues until, above them on the stage, a monumental figure on horseback (identical to the Garibaldi of 1860) appears in profile against intersecting beams of light: the Commander. He utters only two steely words: 'Here...landfill'(Qui. Colmanta). A legion of trucks roars up alongside the centre-right lip and begins to fill in the swamp. The Commander rotates 180 degrees and issues a command to a squadron of bulldozers on the right side of the stage: 'In three days, the road to Littoria will cross this void. We shall work all night.'[22]

Scene 3. The entire stage is lit. On the left, the filling operation continues; on the right the bulldozers carve out a highway. Here and there packs of workers can be seen plowing and planting the land. Trucks criss-cross in the background. The agitation continues until a factory whistle sounds, marking the end of the night shift. Tools are abandoned, the trucks head back to their sheds, songs of war and revolution are sung. The stage is left empty, except for a few stragglers whose banter is overheard as they await a ride from Mother Cartridge-Pouch, now re-baptised Old Cartridge-Pouch. Still driven by Ceseri, she arrives from offstage right, battered and torn. Although she is able to transport them halfway across the stage, her motor is blown and soon begins spewing steam and smoke. All efforts to revive her fail, and, instead of abandoning her, they decide to push her right up to the lip of the first swamp. As she wobbles towards the precipice, two columns of trucks filled with workers arrive on the scene. They surround her and shut off their engines. The left hillock is now ablaze 'in the mode of dazzling transfigurations or the head of Moses'; there is a dead silence.[23] Ceseri stands at the centre of this funereal composition and proclaims in a mournful tone: 'She has fought the war, the revolution, and the battle of land reclamation. Now she will eagerly support the highway to Littoria'.

The old truck is pushed over the precipice into the swamp and buried in the mud, as Ceseri prophesies her return (with a characteristically fascist, not to mention blasphemous, conflation of the secular and sacred orders): 'in three days she will return to her duties anew, my old lady. Forever!' [24] The lights darken and focus on her carcass. The double column of trucks departs and passes above her, barely visible. The sound of marching drums is heard, blended with music. White buildings flicker in the distance as Italy marches off towards the city of the future: Littoria (now renamed Latina), first of the fascist new towns. A heroic trumpet call is heard far off in the distance and echoes back with redoubled force. The stadium lights come on.

Notes

1. Pavolini to Blasetti, postcard, dated 11 April 1934, BA.
2. Anon., 'Fatti e argomenti,' *Il Cantiere: Settimanale di Cultura Politica* 1.7 (14 April 1934): 1.
3. This information was diffused via numerous newspapers, including *Il Popolo d'Italia* and *La Nazione* (see the 13 April 1934 issue).
4. 'I Littoriali di Cultura e d'Arte: Concorsi per soggetti di spettacoli di masse,' *Il Nuovo Giornale*, 13 April 1934, 4.
5. ibid.
6. Alessandro Pavolini, 'Fascisti giovani al lavora: Lo spettacolo di masse,' *Il Bargello*, 1 April 1934, 3. Cf. Blasetti: 'It is to be hoped that this mass theatre will become a school for shaping the young directors of tomorrow, who will have to ensure its vitality and continuation' (quoted in Cipriano G[iachetti], 'I preparativi del teatro di masse: Alessandro Blasetti all'opera,' LN, 12 April 1934, 5). Sofia would later accuse Blasetti of having aspired to a state pension: 'The fact of the matter is that Blasetti was yearning for a state pension, thinking that he had ensured for himself the permanent directorship of this theater' (Corrado Sofia, 'Il corago immaginario,' *Quadrivio* 2.29 [13 May 1934]: 2).
7. Cipriano Giachetti, 'La rappresentazione del *18 BL* ha luogo stasera,' LN, 29–30 April 1934, 5.
8. The full passage from Marcello Gallian's sometimes mocking description reads: 'But as soon as one reached the river's edge, an unheard-of spectacle greeted the eye: ladies dressed to the nines, wearing dancing shoes, young [*sic*] and delicate furs, and gold and silver baubles, marched in single file across a boat bridge extending from one bank to the other. The legendary audience of opening nights [at the opera], apparelled in its usual manner, but heading out into the open fields under a sky enshrouded in darkness' ('Una notte d'aprile,' *Quadrivio*, 6 May 1934, 3).
9. The two best descriptions of the pre-spectacle spectacle are those of Guido Piovene ('Dalla gloria della trincea al tempo di Mussolini: Lo spettacolo di masse a Firenze con duemila attori e ventimila spettatori,' *L'Ambrosiano*, 30 Apr. 1934, 1) and Gallian ('Una notte d'aprile'). All accounts emphasise the audience's sense that it was participating in a mass rally.
10. Raffaello Franchi, '*18 BL* spettacolo di masse,' LIL, 6 May 1934, 1. The point is repeated by Piovene in 'Dalla gloria della trincea al tempo di Mussolini,' 1: 'The audience felt that it was the protagonist, the protagonist of an event dear to the heart of all Italians and of solemn significance'.
11. Maximilien de Robespierre, 'Man Is the Greatest Object,' quoted in Frederick Brown, *Theater and Revolution: The Culture of the French Stage*, New York: Viking, 1980, 76.
12. The opening movement of *Squilli e danze per il 18 BL* is designated as *solenne*, consisting of a series of trumpet calls accompanied by tam-tams and slow drumming. Massarani's score was published in 1937 by Edizioni G. Ricordi in Milan.

A transcription for bands was produced by Salvatore Pappalardo and published by Ricordi in 1938.

13. This opening scene must have been nearly identical to the opening scene of *1860*, with its crosscut scenes of cavalry, ruined buildings, running figures, and blazing fires.

14. In Blasetti's script, published as '*18 BL: Spettacolo di masse per ii popolo*,' *Gioventu Fascista* 4.8 (15 April 1934): 12–14, the truck was named Mother Glory *(Mamma Gloria)* and not Mother *Cartridge~Pouch (Mamma Giberna)*. Some time in April, Blasetti must have decided to switch to the latter name, which is not found in any of the scripts in BA.

15. Alessandro Blasetti, 'Prime considerazioni e proposte: Tempi della rappresentazione,' 1, BA.

16. Cited from the second part of Corrado Sofia's typescript entitled 'Mistero in 9 quadri,' in BA. Sofia was the principal author of Act 2, scenes 2 and 3, and seems to have selected most of the songs.

17. Blasetti, '*18 BL: Spettacolo di masse per il popolo*,' 13.

18. On Littoria, see Tommaso Stabile, *Latina una volta Littoria: Storia di una citta* (Latina: Arti Grafiche Archivio, 1982), and Silvana Cardosi, 'Il mito di Littoria durante il Fascismo' (diss., Magistero Maria SS.Annunziata, Rome, 1973). On the fascist new towns, see Diane Ghirardo, *Building New Communities: New Deal and Fascist Italy,* Princeton, Princeton Univ. Press, 1989 and Riccardo Mariani, *Fascismo e 'citta nuove'* , Milan, Feltrinelli, 1976.

19. The original plan was for two entire air squadrons to overfly the crowd. For reasons that may have to do with the one-week postponement of the performance, these two squadrons were reduced, according to some accounts, to a few airplanes; according to others, to a single one: 'Vasco Magrini's airplane – the only one that appeared, despite the two squadrons that had been promised – performed three extremely brief laps around the stadium. Young fascists then began moving about the audience announcing Mussolini's seizure of power while distributing copies of the 28 October 1922, issue of *Il Popolo d'Italia*' (Giuseppe Longo, '*18 BL* a Firenze: Non è nato il teatro di masse,' *Gazzetta di Messina, 4* May, 1934, 3). The original plan had been described in Blasetti's notes as follows: 'Crisscrossed by the multicolored beams of the searchlights, the aeroplanes will drop broadsheets from *Il Popolo d'Italia*. . . . After they have flown over the audience for the proper amount of time, they will vanish to the right and left sides of the auditorium. When they are far enough removed, the auditorium lights go off and, accompanied by a lively orchestral prelude, the stage lights illuminate the athletes who mark the beginning of the third act or moment of the spectacle' ('Prime considerazioni,' 2, BA).

20. Another element borrowed from Blasetti's film *Sole.*

21. Blasetti, '*18 BL: Spettacolo di masse per il popolo*,' 14.

22. Ibid.

23. 'A hilltop pushes forward against the horizon all lit up in the ode of dazzling transfigurations or of Moses's head' (Gallian, 'Una notte d'aprile,' 4).

24. Blasetti, '*18 BL: Spettacolo di masse per il popolo*,' 14. This messianic portrayal of Mother Cartridge-Pouch relies upon the christomimetic components that make up the cult of the Virgin Mary.

CHAPTER 2

THEATRE POLITICS OF THE MUSSOLINI REGIME AND THEIR INFLUENCE ON FASCIST DRAMA

PIETRO CAVALLO
Translated by Erminia Passannanti and Günter Berghaus

Fascism and Theatre

During the years of Fascism, Italian theatre was characterised by complex and contradictory factors. Against all expectations, the 'official' theatre of the time avoided subject matters inspired by the 'new time' and 'new spirit' of Fascist Italy. This lack of commitment was often commented on and condemned by intellectuals close to the regime, by Ministers of the *Cultural Popolare*, and of course the Duce himself. Mussolini had complete faith in the educational power of the stage: 'Theatre is one of the most direct means of reaching the heart of the people'.[1] In 1933, he coined the ambiguous expression *teatro di massa* (theatre of the masses), which implied that the traditional theatre, due to its limited seating capacity and antiquated repertory, was inadequate to rally the people under the banner of Fascism. Soon, the expression became the object of (often contradictory) interpretations. On 28 April 1933, on the occasion of the fiftieth anniversary of the Societa Italiana Autori ed Editori, Mussolini delivered a speech at the Teatro Argentina and declared:

> I've heard that theatre is going through a crisis. This crisis does exist, but it is mistaken to believe that it is any way connected to the rising popularity of cinema. We must take into account both the spiritual and the material aspects of this crisis. The first concerns the authors,

the second the number of seats. We have to make plans for a theatre of the masses, a theatre capacity of 15,000–20,000 seats (..). The art work of the stage has to possess the wide-ranging appeal that people are asking for. It must stir great collective passions and must be imbued with a sense of vivid and deep humanity. It has to present matters that truly count in people's spiritual life and that reflect their aspirations. We have had enough of the obsession with this ill-famed 'theatre of adultery'! The spectrum of these 'triangular' complications has at last been exhausted. Allow the collective passions to find dramatic representation, and you'll see the stalls crowded with people again.[2]

And yet, the Duce's warning went unheard. Italian dramatists remained ultimately deaf to the appeal, despite their respect for a government that seemed to hold them in great esteem and, for the first time in Italian history, showed an interest in promoting the theatrical arts. Throughout the years of the Fascist regime and even during the Second World War, they clung to innocuous themes, especially to that 'ill-famed triangle' the Duce had castigated and rebuked.

Although there is clear evidence that many people in show business endorsed Fascism, they made little attempt to deal with subject matters directly related to Fascist myths and ideology. Throughout the Fascist era there were few signs of a truly Fascist theatre as envisaged by intellectuals and students close to the regime. At several congresses they demanded a theatre that would give expression to the 'new spiritual climate' Italy was experiencing, a theatre innovative in form and content, capable of revealing both the ideals and ethics that were already inspiring the 'faith' and behaviour of the masses.[3] However, a theatre of this kind would have implied an overcoming of Fascism itself; or, to be more precise, the superseding of the traditional and reassuring values, which for large strata of the Italian society – especially the petit and middle bourgeoisie in urban centres, who formed the social basis of the regime – represented the main reason for lending their support to Fascism. It was, in other words, an overcoming of the tranquility and certainties so effectively summed up in a popular song of 1937 that spoke of 'one thousand lira a month', the 'modest job', the 'little cottage in the suburbs' and the 'pretty young wife'.[4]

There was a general tendency for dramatists to comply with the taste of their audiences (who showed no interest in experiments with new themes and forms of presentation). Therefore, playwrights continued to deal with traditional topics and employ popular formats. In addition, when a first attempt was made to create a theatre for the masses (with 18 BL on 29 April 1934 at the opening of the Littoriali del Teatro[5]), it failed abysmally. The same 'catastrophic'[6] results – to quote an expression used by the stage censor, Leopoldo Zurlo – could be observed at the premiere, given at the Teatro Lirico in Milan, of *Simma*, a drama in which Francesco Pastonchi outlined the conflict between spirit and materialism so dear to the regime. Despite Mussolini's support for the production, and in fact, for several others to follow, little popular enthusiasm could be generated for spectacles of this kind. There was even active opposition in Fascist circles to such plays. For example, between February and March 1935 the Compagnia del Nuovo Teatro of Fernando de Cruicati staged two of the most emotionally charged Fascist plays in Rome: *La lunga marcia di ritorno*, by Mario Federici, and *I tre atti*, by Marcello Gallian. The message behind the first play was that because the First World War had not lived up to expectations, the soldiers' 'march' had to be taken up again,[7] whereas the author of the second play exalted the revolutionary spirit of the early Fascists and contrasted this with the petty quibbles and narrow horizons of the middle-classes.[8] The productions of these two plays were organised under the auspices of the *Ispetorato del Teatro* with the aim of promoting a Fascist youth culture.[9] However, the reactions were so violent that Zurlo felt bound to intervene, noting that the opposition to the production 'seemed to be organised by someone who either had not viewed the plays or had done so with a deplorable lack of attention'.[10]

However, there was another form of Fascist theatre, mainly produced by amateurs (teachers, journalists, lawyers, but also workers, housewives, unemployed people). Their plays hinged upon situations, characters, plots, and slogans more or less dear to the regime. These dramas were far more popular than one would imagine: thousands of scripts were submitted to the censor; who with unrelenting dedication sifted through every piece of dramatic writing to be performed on stage (irrespective of whether the boards were erected in a rural hamlet, a small parish, a *Casa del Fascio*, or a major playhouse). Hence, there are hundreds of files that can still be consulted in the Central State Archives in Rome, giving us a detailed insight into the dramatic aesthetics of dedicated Fascists.

Fascist theatre came into existence soon after the March on Rome. Salvattor Gotta claimed in *Comoedia* his right of primogeniture,[11] staking a claim for having written the first example of Fascist drama with *Il convegno dei martiri*. It was performed at the Teatro Argentina in Rome, on 21 April 1923, and dealt with the tragic destiny of a young Fascist, Gustavo Doglia, who had died in Turin in a clash with left-wing partisans just before the March on Rome.

The regime showed a rather ambivalent attitude towards such openly propagandist theatre. Although striving to foster new dramatic writing with competitions and prizes awarded by the Fascist organisations such as the *Dopolavoro,* it did not create any structured network of performance spaces, where the stream of new and Fascist plays could be performed. As far as the *Carri di Tespi* and the *Dopolavoro* amateur dramatic companies were concerned, they had a repertory which resembled that of the normal theatre and show business. Genuinely Fascist theatre lacked even the kind of support which the Catholic theatre movement (founded by Don Giovanni Bosco in the second half of the nineteenth century) had enjoyed during the first post-war years.[12]

Much of this was due to the fact that the regime preferred to entrust its propaganda to newspapers, magazines, cinema and radio rather than to theatre. This choice was determined, perhaps, not so much by the failure of the practical experiments made with a Fascist theatre for the masses, but rather by the unsatisfactory quality of the scripts submitted to the censor or the juries of important national competitions.

A typical example of this situation was Renata Mughini's *I figli,* a play infused with the fascist spirit of the time, which won the San Remo Prize in 1938. As Zurlo noted, this altogether mediocre work offered an ending which was 'too contradictory to be logical'.[13]

Equally tangible were the other weaknesses of the play, and they had not escaped the members of the jury, Marinetti, Rosso di San Secondo, Simoni and d'Amico, or its chairman Ettore Romagnoli. In their final verdict, they emphasised the freshness and lack of rhetoric in the play: 'Even though the play does not reach a high artistic standard, as a typical juvenile work it seems to embrace at least the spirit of our time'.[14] This episode is quite remarkable, for among the 177 competing plays there were those such as *Chilometri bianchi,* by Mario Federici – who also wrote the already mentioned, and often fiercely criticised, play *Lunga Marcia di ritorno* – which put themselves in the wrong by presenting anxieties and doubts, rather than certainties or reassuring realities. *Chilometri bianchi,* which was put on at the Teatro delle Arti in Rome and published in *Il dramma* a few months later, portrays the anguish of a survivor who, returning from the war after having wandered through half of Europe, no longer feels inside himself the old love for his Fatherland. For this reason, his wife persuades him to avoid meeting their children:

> We, who love our children so dearly, could hurt them in their purest sentiment, their unshakable faith. Even though they are good boys, they would start having doubts, they, who never had any doubts. Maybe we wouldn't even notice it immediately. It's terrible, Marco,

it's like a hidden illness for our poor children! They would start wondering how you, their hero, has been able to lose yourself. And they would start thinking that the love people feel for their country is not as absolute as they thought.[15]

In all the drama competitions, the quality of the plays which drew their inspiration from Fascist mythology fell short of expectation. Zurlo himself came to realize this when he was correcting, often at the explicit request of the author, both the grammar and syntax of the scripts submitted to him. It is probable that these dramas found their only attentive reader in this scrupulous officer!

Furthermore, Fascist theatre experienced the hostility of Silvio d'Amico, one of the high priests' of Italian theatre. He resolutely opposed didactic theatre as practised in Soviet Russia or Nazi Germany. In October 1934, at a congress organised by the Fondazione Volta on the state of Italian drama, he declared:

> A theatre with didactic aims might be expected to be all right for the working class, but it falls outside the realm of art. Posters displayed on school walls are fine to impress and move our pupils. So, in a sense, they do work, but who would dream of showing them in an exhibition among genuine works of art?[16]

The following year, d'Amico placed his ban on the theatre of propaganda, which for some authors had become their only chance to achieve popularity:

> Those who scrutinize the flow of scripts submitted to drama competitions, which succeed each other almost incessantly, know well that an increasing number of plays deal with patriotic subjects like soldiers, Fascists and so on. They are, in the best cases, nothing but mere didactic compositions with edifying endings, conventional pictures of a world inhabited by heroes and villains. If, by an absurd coincidence, these plays would ever reach the stage, propaganda would gain no profit from it and theatre itself would decline, forever deserted by its audience.[17]

Confined as he was to a logic still anchored to a canon of traditional aesthetic standards, d'Amico could not understand that the criteria he was applying to that form of theatre had to be extended. As a matter of fact, the points he objected to were indeed the key features of those plays. They tried to communicate, as efficiently as possible, a simple message which could not be misinterpreted by the audience. Such avoidance of ambiguous touches led to a rather Manichean character divided into good and evil, with a positive hero often identifiable from the very beginning of the play (even when he initially fought on the side of the enemy). As a result, the plots of these dramas were of the most predictable and elementary kind, and the dialogues full of slogans and apodeictic phraseology. ('In a work of art, nothing is more anti-fascist than irony!' Salvator Gotta rightly affirmed).[18] In short, this form of theatre was aimed at confirming and strengthening the convictions of a public that was already tuned into the author's feelings. In some plays, the dividing line between fiction and reality was entirely dismantled: the actors addressed their speeches straight to the audience, or mingled with the spectators in the auditorium. Along with this new mannerism came the habit of resorting to strongly symbolic or allegorical characters. Some scripts ended by displaying either the fascist insignia or a portrait or Mussolini. For example, M. Dorta advised in the final stage direction of his play *Ritorno* (1935): 'The scene remains in the dark – while against the sky the Duce's figure appears, surrounded by applauding young Blackshirts'.[19]

This, however, must not lead us to the conclusion that Fascist theatre was erected on the same principles as left-wing militant theatre. Formal devices such as direct addresses to the audience or symbolic characters were rarely exploited in an inventive fashion. Compared to the traditional bourgeois theatre, *agit-prop* introduced remarkable innovations in staging technique (for example when performing in the courtyards of working-class tenements, in front of factories, in the streets, or even on the tramways). [20] Fascist theatre, however, remained rooted in the schemas of nineteenth-century dramaturgy and stage design. The plays possessed a traditional beginning, a linear development of the chosen theme, a peripatetic climax and a conflict-resolving finale; the stories imitated real-life events; the characters embodied, except in some rare cases, real people. Left-wing *agit-prop*, on the other hand, turned 'characters' into 'stereotypes' that schematised some fundamental characteristics of the various social classes.[21] It must be emphasised that *agit-prop* theatre made its 'debut' in a revolutionary period during which the cultural patterns of the nineteenth century were breaking down and a fruitful dialectic relationship was established between political innovators and creative intellectuals. Fascist theatre, on the other hand, appeared on the scene after the March on Rome, when the 'revolution' had already taken place; therefore, its task was not so much to mobilise the masses against the constituted order, but rather to reinforce an already established system.

The Second World War

The lack of victories (at the outbreak of the Second World War) that could be exploited for war propaganda forced dramatists to indulge in episodes which epitomised singular feats of civil or military heroism. Already during the second year of war, episodes which were actually defeats began to proliferate in the plays, marking in this way the wretched conditions of both the soldiers and the civilians. No wonder the censors judged these plays to be counter-productive in terms of propaganda.[22]

By reading these plays, one gets the impression that, initially, the armed conflict was no traumatic experience for the Italians. People continued to treat it as a remote event which did not interfere with the 'normal' course of their daily lives. In 1940, the censors recorded a dearth of suitable plays based on war topics. The following year, the percentage of 'performable' scripts had increased considerably, but they progressively lost their peculiar ideological features and, step-by-step, revealed the intrinsic horrors of war. This is not to say that there was a linear progression from enthusiasm to condemnation of the war. Public opinion oscillated just as much as the viewpoints expressed in the plays, although by winter 1942–43 eloquent signs of disapproval could be heard everywhere in Italian public life.[23]

From the scripts preserved in the censorship archives one indisputable fact emerges: for a large number of Italians, the war was gradually causing serious disruption to the fixed pattern of everyday life. The plays I have been able to analyse display a considerable variety of attitudes and dramatic narratives, and such heterogeneity was more pronounced than one would normally expect to find in this type of theatre. In short, clear and authoritative patterns that could be used to interpret the war events were vanishing. The images of armed conflict conveyed by the authors (mourning and suffering caused by the bombings, food shortages, restrictions of every kind that were imposed on the civilians) were more and more often based on real-life experiences rather than on the official war propaganda.

From 1942 onwards, the stage functioned as more than a medium to broadcast phrases and slogans imposed from 'above'. It turned into one of the few channels authors could employ to express personal anxieties, even to question the reasons for fighting the war. Although some of these doubts may have been purely rhetorical and were ultimately aimed at reinforcing the official Party line, they nevertheless offered unexpected answers to the questions civilians and soldiers were asking themselves during those years.

Let us take, for example, *Sulla Manica visibilita discreta*, a play by a young student of the Genoese GUF[24] in Florence. The main character is a war pilot, Mietti, who does not have enough courage to face the enemy. Mocked by his comrades, he finds in the captain of the squadron his only friend and confidante. Having understood the drama of the young pilot, the officer comes to his aid, explaining that to be brave does not necessarily mean to be reckless, but to be capable of overcoming one's fear. Mietti does find the strength to hurl himself on the enemy, but only after seeing his captain's airplane being shot down. Only then does he find an answer to his skeptical self-questioning: 'Why must I kill other men and be killed by them?'[25] So, Mietti fights and dies as a hero, not for ideological, but purely personal reasons. The human sentiment of pity and compassion pushes the ideological world of propaganda into second place.

It is of some significance that only a few of the plays produced after 1942 were concerned with the actual front-line battles (and it must be underlined that the Russian front, which alone amounted to a large-scale tragedy, completely disappeared out of sight), but with the soldiers' return to their family and home towns. The scripts were crowded with survivors, exhausted, wounded, blind, at times proud of having sacrificed themselves in the name of their country, but more often utterly distressed because of their disablement. For example, the main character in *Famiglie eroiche* cries out: 'No! – Don't uncover my eyes! I could horrify you. Make me strong enough to bear my misfortune, my God! Oh, unlucky mother of mine! (. . .) Why didn't I die? Much better to die hundreds of times than to live such a disgraceful life.'[26] In a way, this play can be regarded as emblematic of the Fascist stage during the last years of the war. That which in this play started off with unbounded enthusiasm for Italy's entry into the war, progressed in the third act to 'palpable sadness'[27] and ended in the last act with a gloomy air of despair.

Plays of this last period were increasingly characterised by a dreary and agonising atmosphere, which emphasized the gap between the author's purpose and the effect the play actually had on the audience. Zurlo was more and more often compelled to forbid these performances which could cause 'bitter thoughts provoked by the display of innocent victims', and he felt obliged to ask: 'How can it be desirable for a play that purports to exalt war to show at its beginning an ambulance out of which the desperate cries of both the mothers and the wounded can be heard?'[28] In a letter to Pavolini he stated: 'I can't deny that I fully support a glorification of war; however I also find it most inopportune to offer a realistic reproduction of it. Too many hearts in the audience would bleed when the dangers, sufferings and pains of war are demonstrated on stage'.[29]

Zurlo's remarks reflected the vision of the war that was, albeit often unintentionally, projected by the scripts submitted to his office. In *La rinuncia*, for example, the author relates an ordinary day in a girl's school. The pupils talk about their innocent dreams, their elevated hopes, their love affairs, etc. They discuss their like or dislike for this or that teacher, but this garrulous atmosphere soon comes to an end, and the uncertain life in wartime rises to the surface. Erminia, one of the students, learns that her fiancé has been killed at the front. In order to avoid reminding her of her sorrow, the other girls ask their boyfriends not to come and meet them by the school gates. The 'renouncement' is suggested by an old spinster, who went through the same pain in her youth: 'I can still remember them happily walking off with their boyfriends, and me, alone, standing in the middle of the road and feeling so bewildered and unhappy. I could have died staring at the house from which he was never to appear again. I would have given anything to escape looking at their happiness, which only multiplied my torments'.[30]

Fascist theatre concluded its trajectory by giving evidence to needs that hardly corresponded to the imperatives of the regime (it is no coincidence that the shows promoted by the Dopolavoro delle Forze Armate [the Armed Forces Recreational Service] were primarily escapist comedies and music-hall entertainment). While the regime's propaganda machinery continued to deal with war topics, promising more justice, a new redistribution of wealth among people and nations, and a new social and moral order, the playwrights confronted the burning emotional issues that were on people's minds. Initially they interspersed them with official ideological rhetoric, but eventually these slogans were almost completely supplanted by evocative descriptions of the soldiers' experiences in the trenches and those of their brides, mothers and children suffering at home.

This is to say that the war, depicted in the early stages of Fascist drama as a collective event, had slowly been transfigured into a merely individual and private matter. The symbolic system of signification, on which Fascist theatre and drama of the 1920s and 1930s relied so heavily, had entirely collapsed. The supremacy of Fascist ethics over the real and existential needs of the people had collapsed. The events of the war had underlined the fact that human values, such as the courage and the strength to endure sacrifices and suffering (i.e., the 'blood' which the regime had always placed in opposition to the forces of 'money'), could no longer suffice to triumph over the enemy's (i.e., the plutocracy's) indisputable technological superiority.

This situation caused dramatists to change direction in their plays written after 1942. The authors had basically two choices: the first was to base their works on values alien to both Fascist culture and propaganda. In this case, the word 'faith', having lost its poly-semous significance, assumed again a merely religious connotation and re-established prayer – especially the one addressed to the 'Madonnina' – as the only possible medium to escape the atrocities of war and to instil hope for a better future.[31] The alternative was – in a desperate attempt at re-affirming the natural desire to live – to operate with common values even though they had by now learned that these values were by no means the engine of history, nor could they lead to victory: 'It's wonderful to fight like this', it is started in *Il labirinto*, a script dated 1942, 'with no hope of escaping: no hope of winning. The only thing we can do is to hold out, to hold out to the last'.[32]

Notes

1. Mussolini in a letter to the actor Gastone Monaldi, founder and director of the company *Il teatro del popolo*, dated 22 June 1927. ACS, SPD, c.o., b.1018, f. 509.103/1

2. See Roberto Forges Davanzati, 'Mussolini parla agli scrittori', Nuova Antologia, no.1468, 16 May 1933, p.191.

3. See Pietro Cavallo, *Immaginario e rappresentazione*: Il teatro fascista di propaganda, Rome, 1990, pp. 15–38.

4. C.Innocenzi, S. Innocenzi-Sopranzi, 'Mille lire al mese', *Il canzoniere della radio*, n.5, p.13. The song was taken from the homonymous film, directed by Massimilano Neufeld.

5. See G. Salvini, Spettacoli di masse e 18BL', *Scenario*, no.5, May 1934, pp. 253ff

6. L. Zurlo, *Memorie inutili: La censura teatrale nel ventennio*, Rome, 1952, p.22

7. M. Federici, *Lunga marcia di ritorno*, ACS, MCP, cens.teatr., f.8214, 1935

8. M. Gallion, *I tre atti*, ACS, MCP, cens. Teatr., f. 6591, 1935.

9. See *Rapporto dell'Ispettorato del Teatro per S.E. il Sottosegretario di Stato*, 11 March 1936, ACS, MCP, cens. Teatr., f. 6591 as well as *Relazione di Zurlo sulle rappresentazioni della compagnia De Cruciati al Teatro Eliseo nel Febbraio-Marzo XIV*, in the same file.

10. *Relazione di Zurlo sulle rappresentazioni della compagnia De Cruciati al Teatro Eliseo*.

11. S. Gotta, 'Teatro fascista', *Comoedia*, no.5, May 1934, p.6

12. S. Pivato, *Il treatro di parrocchia: Mondo cattolico e organizzazione del consenso durante il fascismo*, Rome, 1979, p.7

13. Zurlo, *Memorie inutili*, p.186.

14. The report is enclosed in Renata Mughini, *I figli*, ACS, MCP, cens. Teatr., f.9960, 1938.

15. M. Federici, 'Chilometri bianchi', in *Il Dramma*, no.319, 1 December 1939, p.17.

16. Reale Academia d'Italia, Fondazione Alessandro Volta, *Convegno di Lettere. 8–14 ottobre 1934: Il teatro drammatico*, Rome, 1935, p.323.

17. S. d'Amico, *Invito al teatro*, Brescia, 1935, p.16

18. Gotta, 'Teatro fascista', p.7.

19. M. Dorta, *Rotorno*, ACS, MCP, cens. Teatr., f. 11074, 1935, p.24

20. See G. Buonfino, 'Agitprop e "controcultura" operaia nella repubblica di Weimer', *Primo maggio*, nos. 3–4, February – September 1974, pp. 100–101, 114–15.

21. E. Casini-Ropa, *La danza e l'agit-prop: I teatri-non-teatrali nella cultura tedesca del primo Novecento*, Bologna, 1988, p.151; C. Hamon, 'Formes dramaturgiques et sceniques du theatre d'agit-prop', in D. Bablet (ed.) *Le theatre d'agit-prop de 1917 a 1932, vol. 2: L'URSS – Recherches*, Lausanne, 1977, pp. 62–71; B, Lupi, 'L'agit-prop: Une culture politique vecue', *ibid.*, vol.3: *Allemagne, France, U.S.A, Pologne, Roumanie – recherches*, pp. 40ff.

22. 'Should I, in my role as censor, pretend not to recognise the depressing effect your script produces on the audience? Your play is undoubtedly full of noble and impartial sentiments, but it also presents all the dark nuances of the war.' Thus was Zurlo's charge in a letter to Sergio Motroni, who was the author of Vento del Nord, a play that was meant to show, according to the author's Foreword, the 'Italians as they really are', devoid of any 'vain rhetoric'. Zurlo to Montroni, 18 August 1942, ACS, MCP, cens. Teatr., f.2693.

23. See A. Lepre, *Le illusioni la paura la rabbia: Il fronte interno, 1940–43*, Naples, 1989; A. Lepre, *L'occhio del duce: Gli italiani e la censura di guerra 1940–43*, Milan, 1992; S.Colarizi, *L'opinione degli Italiani sotto il regime*, 1929–43, Rome, 1991.

24. GUF was the Fascist student organisation, the *Gruppi universitari fascisti*.

25. F. Pescetto, *Sulla Manica visibilita discreta*, ACS, MCP, cens. Teatr., f.6451, 1941, p.56

26. G.M. Giuliani, *Famiglie eroiche*, ACS, MCP, cens. Teatr., f. 9711, Act III, p.1.

27. Stage direction to the third act of Giuliani, *Famiglie eroiche*.

28. Report by Zurlo, s.d., attached to the script by C. Magliulo, Ritorneranno, ACS, MCP, cens. Teatr., f.9977, 1943.

29. Zurlo to Pavolini, 6 February 1942, ACS, MCP cens. Teatr., f.3993. The answer given by the Minister is of some interest: 'Your observations are right, especially those about the bombings (indeed, in a work of art they are more touching than in reality). It is all a question of the right measure. Generally speaking, I do not object to the fact that war is given a direct representation in the play. One must take into account that the audience, especially after having been shown the horrors of the war in those German documentary films, has become less sensitive in these matters. In a way, everyone has become accustomed to them.' Pavolini to Zurlo, 9 February 1942, *ibidem*.

30. G. Ammirata-L.Capece, *La rinuncia*, ACS, MCP, cens. Teatr., f.5048, 21941, p.20.

31. This play by a front-line soldier who had fought in the African War employed the form of a prayer as a medium to connect civilians and soldiers. It was meaningfully dedicated 'To the Virgin Mary, so that she may protect all soldiers' (see C.Basilico, *La preghiera dei piccoli*, ACS, MCP, cens. Teatr., f.5271, 1943)

32. A. Angeli Coarelli, *Il labirinto*, ACS, MCP, cens. Teatr., f. 2831, p.46.

CHAPTER 3

TOWARDS AN AESTHETIC OF
FASCIST OPERA

ERIK LEVI

Introduction

Ascribing a specific political significance to such a composite art form or music-theatre can pose particular problems for the cultural historian. Whilst examination of the composer's choice of subject matter and libretto may reveal a more or less clearly stated political objective, analysis of the musical setting can produce a more ambiguous interpretation of such intentions. This may simply be a question of differing aesthetic positions occupied by drama and music – words and action appearing to present a more concrete reflection of political reality than the seeming abstractions of musical language. Yet to make a distinction between the political functions of drama and music may also seem artificial. Certainly when libretto and text are so well integrated, as in Mozart's *Le Nozze di Figaro*, Beethoven's *Fidelio*, or Wagner's *Die Meistersinger*, the broad political message of each opera appears to be unequivocal and was perfectly understood by first-night audiences.

Whether such clear political messages can be discerned in the operas composed during the era of fascism in Germany or Italy is more debatable.[1] For ideologues and critics, the stylistic pluralism of music of the 1920s and 1930s proved intractable. At issue was the degree to which composers should repudiate modernism, and whether such a move necessitated a return to an older tradition of Romanticism. Few theorists offered a cogently argued solution to this problem, preferring instead to talk in the broadest terms of what was commonly termed 'a reclamation of national musical values'. How this was effected depended, of course, on the specific characteristics of each country's national traditions, and in this instance there were contrasting modes of development in Germany and Italy.

If the musical idioms employed by the most significant operatic composers working in Germany and Italy expressed a variety of aesthetic standpoints, thus compounding the difficulties of equating political ideology with artistic intent, a more useful line of enquiry may be to determine any general features which were common to the repertoire of this period. Of paramount importance is the extent to which operas of the fascist era represented a reaction against the immediate past, and whether performing traditions, reception and taste altered as a result of political influence. In the following discussion these questions will be examined alongside issues of text and musical style.

Operatic Developments in Nazi Germany

Between 1933 and 1944, over 170 new operas by German-speaking composers were premiered in the Third Reich, an impressive statistic which belies the notion that the period was bereft of creative energies in this area.[2] To a certain extent, the composition of new operas was encouraged. Under the auspices of the Reichsdramaturg, Rainer Schlösser, the Nazi regime evolved a co-ordinated plan in which the major opera houses were encouraged to commission and perform at least one novelty per season.[3] At a local level, numerous state prizes were awarded to composers of operas. Another important forum for performance of new opera was the music festival circuit which enjoyed an increasingly hallowed status in German musical life during this period.

Yet for all this degree of activity, opera was never deemed the ideal medium for overt political propaganda. No opera was staged in which characters appeared on stage wearing Nazi uniforms. Neither did operatic composers attempt to weave well-known political songs into the musical fabric. One possible explanation for the avoidance of such overtly political elements lies in a belief that opera represents a higher and more pure art form than drama and the spoken theatre, and as such its subject and musical matter should be divorced from contemporary realities. This argument was expounded by the Dresden critic Eugen Schmitz in 1939. Writing in the *Zeitschrift für Musik*, Schmitz claimed that whilst a spoken drama based upon the life of Horst Wessel might have gained public acceptance, an operatic setting of the same theme, depicting the

protagonist as a heroic tenor in conflict against baritone Communist agitators, would easily degenerate into the kind of nationalist
kitsch that was denounced by the regime.[4]

In surveying the subject matter favoured by operatic composers
during the Third Reich, the general avoidance of contemporary
themes is striking. Without doubt, this represents a conscious reaction against artistic trends that evolved during the Weimer
Republic. Amongst the most significant features of that period were
the promotion of experimental music-theatre which flourished in
state-subsidised theatres, and the growth in popularity of the
zeitoper (topical opera) which reached wide audiences through the
enormous success of Krenek's *Jonny spielt auf!* Yet during the Third
Reich, composers not only avoided experimental music-theatre and
the *zeitoper,* but also largely refrained from setting contemporary
dramas or collaborating with the playwrights that were most
favoured by the regime. Censorship of chosen texts never became
an important issue. Not once did the *Reichsdramaturg* withhold
approval of an opera that had already been accepted for performance by a provincial opera house. Only changes in political
circumstance, particularly during the Second World War, caused
opera houses to withdraw certain established works after their subjects were deemed inappropriate by the Ministry of Propaganda.

Given the repressive cultural environment, it is hardly surprising
that operatic texts during the Third Reich manifested the conservative   cultural   attitudes   of   the   regime.   Having   rejected
experimentation and topicality, composers turned instead to safer
themes – myths drawn from either classical antiquity or Nordic legend, settings of the established classics of German literature
(Goethe, Kleist, E.T.A. Hoffmann and Schiller), dramas that chronicle glorious episodes of German history, portrayals of simple village
life and, perhaps most frequently of all, the fairy tale. Within these
areas, it was possible to glean messages of ideological relevance –
the heroism and strength of the classical warrior, the self-sacrifice
for a higher ideal, intimations of racial superiority, and a strong
identification with the upright values of a peasant community. It is
significant, however, that the operas that gained the most public
esteem eschewed even such vague political issues, and simply
offered escapist entertainment to their audiences.[5] The emphasis on
escapism, or on depicting episodes from the very distant past, is
indicative of a broader artistic development – that of the resurgence
of the volksoper, a genre much cultivated during the nineteenth century, whose subject matter encompassed both light-hearted comedy
and romantic legend. During the first years of the Nazi regime, the
volksoper revival was strongly demanded by the Nazi musical press

as an antidote to what was termed 'negativism' and 'cultural bolshevism' of the operas of Kurt Weill, Paul Hindemith and Ernst Krenek. In order to educate younger composers to appreciate the values of the volksoper, significant changes to the repertoire were proposed for the 1933–34 season, including the resurrection of a number of operas by minor romantic composers that had fallen into oblivion over the previous twenty years. Few of the works, however, survived more than a few performances, and later attempts to salvage minor operas by Albert Lortzing, Heinrich Marschner and Otto Nicolai proved rather unsuccessful.

During the early years of the regime, the most prominent exponents of the *volksoper* were composers of an older generation, such as Paul Graener (1872–1944), Max von Schillings (1868–1933) and Georg Vollerthun (1876–1945). Largely neglected throughout the Weimer Republic, they joined the rank of Alfred Rosenberg's *Kampfbund für deutsche Kultur* and exerted considerable influence in 1933 in persuading opera houses to stage their neo-Wagnerian works. Yet their success was short-lived. Audience reception and critical opinion remained lukewarm, with some even arguing that their creative outlooks were too redolent of a 'petit-bourgeois' past.[6]

The real turning point for this group of composers came in March 1935 after the first performance of Graener's *Der Prinz von Homburg* at the Berlin Staatsoper. Although Graener had striven to create a work of 'national artistic significance',[7] the opera failed to make a strong impression and survived for only two seasons. In the same year, however, two operas by younger composers, *Der Günstling* by Rudolf Wagner-Régeny (Dresden) and *Die Zaubergeige* by Werner Egk (Frankfurt), achieved real success and were hailed in some quarters as the first genuinely National Socialist music-theatre works. Both Wagner-Régeny and Egk had spent their formative years under the cosmopolitan influence of the 1920s. Yet they had modified their musical idioms sufficiently to make them palatable to the more traditional cultural climate after 1933. Besides, such a compromise between modernism and accessibility accorded perfectly with Goebbels' much-quoted demand that National Socialist art should manifest 'a romanticism of steel'.

In the case of Wagner-Régeny, the authorities' enthusiastic acceptance of *Der Günstling* seems paradoxical. The libretto, based on Victor Hugo's play, *Marie Tudor*, was written by Casper Neher, who had a name for himself as Brecht's favourite designer and had three years earlier collaborated with Kurt Weill on *Die Bürgschaft*. Not surprisingly, such an association aroused considerable suspicion as to the political sympathies of both the composer and librettist. Yet despite post-war attempts to view the scenario as presenting some kind of resistance to totalitarianism, in reality the setting offers little opportunity either for irony or for oblique political criticism. More significantly, Wagner-Régeny's music, whilst rejecting the extravagant gestures of late Romanticism, is couched in a deliberately simple neo-baroque language modelled on Gluck and Handel.

Egk's opera, *Die Zaubergeige*, whose libretto is drawn from Franz Pocci's nineteenth-century fairy drama in which love and honesty triumph over the desire for material wealth, also presents a successful balance between traditionalism and modernism. With its judicious mixture of romantic and comic elements, it appears to be typically escapist *volksoper*, although anti-Semitic overtones are all too apparent in the unsympathetic portrayal of the shady merchant Guldensack. In keeping with the seemingly unproblematic nature of the story, Egk's music manifests a deliberate naivety. The most pervasive elements are a strong adherence to tonality, symmetrical melodies and a frequent recourse to Bavarian folkdances. This simplicity is however punctuated by insistent *ostinati* with a percussive edge and spiced with the occasional harsh dissonance, all of which give the music a veneer of modernity.

The degree to which composers were able to employ surface features of musical modernism, without encountering official disapproval, reflects the regime's uncertainty with regard to musical aesthetics. When the Danish-born composer Paul von Klenau (1883–1946) employed Schoenberg's twelve-tone technique in his opera *Michael Kohlhaas* (Stuutgart, 1933), critics eagerly condemned the composer for utilising a culturally degenerate method of composition. Yet Klenau denied any allegiance to Schoenberg, arguing that his utilisation of twelve-tone procedures was entirely original and claiming that his technique reflected National Socialist order and discipline. Such a defence of his compositional style, coupled with the evident acceptability of Keist's drama, ensured that *Michael Kohlhaas* never fell victim to censorship. Later the Schoenberg pupil Winifried Zillig (1905–1963) managed to camouflage his utilisation of the same technique in his one act opera, *Das Opfer* (Hamburg, 1937), based on Reinhard Goering's novel about Captain Scott's expedition to the Antarctic. Here again it was not so much the musical language that proved acceptable as the text which emphasises the heroic ideals of a man who is prepared to die for a higher cause.

Ambiguity in Intention and Reception

From examining the pragmatic reception accorded to the works of Klenau and Zillig, one might assume that composers of opera were allowed greater freedom of expression than playwrights and stage directors. Yet this was not always the case. In fact, some of the most significant challenges to Nazi cultural authority occurred in the opera house. In 1934, the conductor Wilhelm Furtwängler failed to secure Göring's approval for the planned first performance of Paul Hindemith's *Mathis der Maler* at the Berlin Staatsoper. Furtwängler's overt support for the composer and condemnation of artistic interference in matters of repertoire, expressed in an article published in the *Deutsche Allgemeine Zeitung,* set him on a collision course with the regime. It was a conflict that Furtwängler was unable to win, and he was subsequently forced to resign his official positions in German musical life. One year later, Richard Strauss endured the same fate, relinquishing his post as President of the *Reichsmusikkammer* on account of collaboration with the Jewish writer Stefan Zweig on the opera *Die schweigsame Frau* (Dresden, 1935). The work was heard only four times before the authorities banned further performances.[8]

Both Strauss and Furtwängler were far too influential as musical figures to be consigned to oblivion. To a certain extent, the regime needed their co-operation in order to maintain cultural credibility. Yet it is still a matter of conjecture as to how far these artists actually appeased their political masters. Strauss's next opera, *Friedenstag* (Munich, 1938), to a libretto by the Viennese theatre historian Joseph Gregor, is a case in point. The scenario is drawn from an episode that took place towards the end of the Thirty Years War, a departure from Strauss's normal areas of exploration, which at this time tended to encompass escapist comedy and classical mythology. Initially, the opera met with great success, securing approval from Hitler who attended a performance in Vienna. Critics of the period drew attention to the ideologically acceptable elements of the plot – the portrayals of the heroic Commandant, who refuses to surrender when his barracks are under siege, and his submissive wife. Yet the opera's pacifist conclusion – a choral hymn rejoicing in the laying down of arms – seemed at odds with the regime's belligerent foreign policy, suggesting that the work's ultimate message was somewhat ambiguous.[9]

A similar equivocality may be gleaned from Werner Egk's *Peer Gynt* (Berlin, 1938). The opera, a free adaptation of Ibsen's drama, was commissioned by the Berlin Staatsoper, where the young composer had secured a position as *Kapellmeister*. It marked a departure from the light-heartedness of Die Zaubergeige, being conceived on a far more ambitious scale. Two elements of the score disturbed critics at the premiere – first, Egk's tendency to lavish attention upon the grotesque elements of the drama at the expense of its romantic and humanistic aspects ; second, the recourse to a harsher musical style, reminiscent in places of Kurt Weill and other modernists. Egk attempted to justify his use of modernist elements in the scenes depicting the Trolls, on the grounds that the dissonance of such episodes was offset elsewhere by the use of unequivocally tonal passages that were representative of positve forces.

Further examination of the Troll Scene in Act 1 of *Peer Gynt* suggests however that Egk's claim of a clear division between good (in musical terms, tonal) and evil (atonal) was somewhat misleading. When, in the score, Egk described the Trolls as the 'lowest form of humanity' and a 'bunch of sadists and gangsters', he appeared to be making a more oblique reference to Nazi Storm Troopers, a point that was emphasised in the original Berlin staging. Moreover, the connection was reinforced through the parodying nature of the musical language, which at one moment recalls Weill, then lampoons a ritualistic Nazi hymn, and finally offers a grotesque distortion of the can-can from Offenbach's *Orphee aux enfers,* an operetta banned by the Nazis because of the racial origins of its composer. Egk's free adaptation of Ibsen's drama abounds in passages of Brechtian irony such as the following lines sung at the outset of the Harbour Scene (Act 2, Scene 1) :

> So ist's im Leben, dem Schwachen nicht,
> Dem Starken wind's gegeben !
> Und wer nicht selber tritt,
> Der wird getreten,
> Da hilft kein Jammern,
> Winseln, Bitten, Beten ![10]
> (What we doubt no longer :
> the weak will die
> the strong be even stronger.
> It's dog eat dog
> Eat or be eaten !
> Unless you beat your foe
> You will be beaten.)

Again, one can only speculate as to how far contemporary audiences perceived the subversive undercurrent in such passages. In any case, any initial misgivings about Egk's composition were silenced after Hitler attended a performance of the opera and personally congratulated its author. As a result, *Peer Gynt* was nominated for performance at the 1939 *Reichsmusiktage* held in Düsseldorf, although the opera was dropped from the repertory of many theatres after the outbreak of war.

The year 1940 marked something of a watershed in terms of

German operatic development. On the one hand, the Ministry of Propaganda appeared to exercise even greater control over the kind of opera that was to be performed. The banning of works by composers from enemy countries was rigidly enforced, as was the requirement to alter libretti in the light of changing political circumstances.[11] Yet at the same time, the notion of opera as entertainment that should divert the public from the realities of war was being actively promoted. This may well explain why relatively few contemporary operas exploited avowedly patriotic themes.[12] Instead, composers turned with increasing frequency to fairy tale, romance and comedy. For instance, one of the most popular escapist operas of the period was Heinrich Sutermeister's *Romeo und Julia* (Dresden, 1940), a work which attempted to reclaim a *belcanto* style reminiscent of nineteenth-century Italian opera. Another typical example was Strauss's *Capriccio*, first performed in Munich in October 1942 with financial support from the Ministry of Propaganda. Set in eighteenth-century Paris, its initial scenario amounts to nothing more than a witty, though masterful, divertissement on the nature of opera.

This vein of 'apolitical' comedy had already been exploited with great success by Carl Orff in his opera *Der Mond* (Munich, 1939), based on a fairy tale by the brothers Grimm. Orff's musical style, which reached maturity during the 1930s, offered a striking alternative to the more conventional romanticism of many of his contemporaries. As some of its roots lay outside German music i.e., in the work of Debussey and the neo-primitive Stravinsky (in particular, the ballet *Les Noces*), Nazi critics were initially suspicious of the composer's national credentials. At issue was Orff's fondness for percussive *ostinati* and his desire to strip his musical material to the barest essentials. Yet with the gradual acceptance of his most popular work, *Carmina Burana*, first staged at the Frankfurt Opera House in 1937, but subsequently better known in the concert hall, such objections evaporated. Besides, *Carmina Burana* revealed another more palatable aspect of Orff's style – a strong absorption of Bavarian folk music – and it was this element that profoundly influenced the idiom of *Der Mond*.

Orff returned to Grimm for his opera *Die Kluge* (Frankfurt, 1943). With its judicious mixture of closed forms and spoken dialogue, the work represents a further example of Orff's musical primitivism, although the instrumentation is much harsher here than in *Der Mond*. A number of post-war commentators have intimated that Orff was making a veiled attack against fascism in the unsympathetic portrayal of the despotic King. Yet such an intention appears to be purely speculative, for despite the fact that *Die Kluge* aroused a more mixed reception than _Der Mond_, the opera was staged at twenty-one theatres until 1944.[13]

Continuity or Change – the Historical Context

Analysing the nature of contemporary opera in a totalitarian society provides an obvious starting point for the definition of a fascist cultural aesthetic in the musical field. However, other considerations must also be discussed. One area which has already been mentioned is the question of performing traditions, and whether these changed as a result of political pressure. When the Nazis came to power, they were determined to sweep aside what they considered to be the cultural excesses of the Weimer Republic. To this end, they instigated a purge of German opera houses which resulted in the dismissal and emigration of numerous composers, conductors, directors, stage designers, singers and orchestral musicians. However, whilst much attention has been drawn to the effects of this exodus, it must be emphasised that the vast majority of remaining artists stayed in Germany, and that high standards of performance were maintained and even enhanced in the metropolitan opera houses. The most significant changes occurred in the composition of the repertoire which was subject to censorship by the Nazi authorities. It was no longer possible to perform works either by Jewish or 'degenerate' composers,[14] and during the war the staging of non-German works was subject to political expediency.

Yet it would be misleading to suggest that the exercise of a tighter control by Rainer Schlösser's office, the _Reichsdramaturgie_, necessarily resulted in a monolithic approach throughout Germany. Despite severe curbs on individual artistic freedom, many theatres retained some of the musical traditions that were characteristic of the 1920s. Thus whilst the Frankfurt Opera House no longer preserved its earlier reputation of promoting the avant-garde, it still proved to be one of the more adventurous of German theatres, both in the number of new operas that were staged, and in the employment of such controversial figures as Walter Felsenstein and Casper Neher. In Berlin there were clear differences of approach and outlook with regard to the two major opera houses, since political control of the Berlin Staatsoper rested with Göring, whilst that of the Deutsche Oper (formerly Städtische Oper) was under the supervision of Goebbels. As a consequence, the artistic policy of the Berlin Staatsoper remained somewhat insulated from the strictures of the Ministry of Propaganda and appeared to be more cosmopolitan.

It is difficult to estimate the degree to which the actual performances and staging of operas were influenced by the unique political climate. In terms of singing and playing techniques, nothing really changed, since the craft of vocal and instrumental production was dependent upon solid training which had been readily available at Germany's Music Academies for many years. In any case, the major singers of the era, who included such figures as Maria Cebotari, Helge Rosvaenge, Peter Anders and Vioica Ursuleac, commanded reputations that transcended national considerations through commercial recordings and broadcasts. A more open-ended question is the nature of stage productions and the re-interpretation of the classical repertoire. Thus the abstract and experimental interpretations of Wagner as manifested in the controversial Jürgen Fehling productions of *Die Fleigende Holländer* (1929, Kroll Oper) and *Tannhäuser* (1933, Staatsoper) were supplanted by stagings that were more overtly naturalistic and conformed to the conservative production style that had been preserved in Bayreuth.[15] Similar tendencies can be perceived in productions of other standard nineteenth-century operas, where conventionally romantic elements were generally emphasised. Probably the most overtly politicised operatic production of the era was Benno von Arent's *Die Meistersinger*, presented in Berlin during the late 1930s.

Whilst contemporary propaganda emphasised the historical significance of Wagner for National Socialism, it is interesting to note that the number of performances of the composer's music-dramas actually declined between 1933 and 1945. How far such a statistic was a genuine reflection of public taste is open to conjecture, since economic factors certainly precluded the regular presentation of Wagner at smaller opera houses. Perhaps more significant is the rapid increase in popularity of the works of Albert Lortzing (1801–1851), whose light-hearted romantic operas both managed to fill a void left by the expurgation of the operettas of Offenbach, and to satisfy the regime's ideological allegiance to the *volksoper*. However, apart from the Lortzing revival, German opera audiences maintained a strong preference for the same handful of works, irrespective of the changed political climate.[16]

Operatic Developments in Fascist Italy

Similar trends in audience taste could be perceived in Italy throughout the same period. Nonetheless, the organisation of operatic policy was far more disparate. Whereas in Germany Goebbels erected the necessary bureaucracy for the regimentation of culture within a matter of a year, the whole process was more prolonged under Mussolini. During the 1920s, the goal was the establishment of an Italian musicians' union based on the principals of Fascist corporatism, made up of composers, librettists, performers, teachers and lecturers. Yet in reality a plethora of different organisations emerged in the following years, many of them undergoing several transformations, modifications and changes of nomenclature. Only in 1935 did the regime present a more centralised approach with the founding of the Ministry of Popular Culture, which in turn created a Theatre Inspectorate for the purpose of controlling all aspects of theatrical and musical activity.

One of the main functions of the Theatre Inspectorate was to promote the performance of contemporary Italian opera. To this end, a few experimental opera companies were established and a permanent committee for the examination of new opera scores was convened in 1936. Then, in 1938, the Ministry of Popular Culture commissioned ten operas by well-known Italian composers in an effort to persuade the nation's opera houses to follow suit. Statistics published in Fiamma Nicolodi's book, *Musica e musicisti nel ventennio fascista*, suggest that as a result of such propaganda a slightly larger number of productions by living Italian composers were given in comparison to those by deceased masters.[17]

Examination of the contemporary Italian repertoire most favoured by the regime in the 1930s suggests a conservative bias similar to that established in Nazi Germany. Yet prior to this, many Italian composers had embraced modernism, following a similar pattern of developments in Germany. During the 1920s, for example, composers in both countries were engaged in a reaction against nineteenth-century romanticism. In Italy, this movement was spearheaded by such figures as Alfredo Casella (1882–1973), both of whom owed much to the 'neo-classicism' of Stravinsky.

Yet, during the following decade, composers were forced to modify their creative outlooks in the face of political pressure. The first signs of a backlash came in 1932 with the simultaneous publication of a 'Manifesto of Italian Musicians for the Tradition of Nineteenth-Century Romantic Art' in three of the country's leading newspapers (*Il Popolo d'Italia, Il Corriere della Sera* and *La Stampa*). This document, signed by a number of significant composers, declared opposition towards 'so-called objective music, which as such can only represent sound in itself, without the living expression caused by the animating breath that creates it' and 'which does not wish to have and does not have any human content'.[18]

The impact of these statements, which manifest a clear rejection of the musical outlooks of Casella and Malipiero, was to polarise attitudes amongst Italian composers. Although the regime refrained from taking a direct stand in favour of the conservatives at this stage, the following years were to witness a growing censorship of musical activity. The first tangible repercussions were to be felt in 1934, when Mussolini banned further performances of Malipiero's opera, *La favola del figlo cambiato*, because he disapproved of the moral implications surrounding Pirandello's fantastic and bizarre libretto. As a result, Malipiero's subsequent ventures in the operatic field were confined to more traditional dramatic models, from Shakespeare (*Guilio Cesare* [1935] and *Antonio e Cleopatra* [1937]), Euripides (*Ecuba* [1940]), Calderon (*La vita e sogno* [1941]) and E.T.A. Hoffmann (*I capricci di Callot* [1942]). Moreover, Malipiero's musical style was modified to include more lyrical (and by implication, romantic) elements, and in the final C-major section of *Guilio Cesare* with its 'Hymn to Rome', a monumental glorification of Fascism.

Generally speaking, the 1930s represented a decade of conservatism in which composers, who had previously explored more adventurous styles, retreated to the safety of more conventional models. To a certain extent, Mussolini's alliance with Nazi Germany strengthened such a trend, since both countries established a regular and reciprocal arrangement for the performance of each other's most representative contemporary operas. The links were obvious – in both countries composers had been obliged to reject theatrical experimentation and had returned to setting literary classics. Nationalistic fervour became a central theme manifested through the glorification of historical events in an earlier epoch. Musical audacity was rejected and replaced by a more overtly diatonic idiom. One can even argue that 'neo-classicism', which in both countries was reflected through an increasing absorption of the musical idioms stemming from the Renaissance and Baroque eras, was in itself a further manifestation of staunch musical nationalism directly inspired by the prevailing political climate.

Yet for all the parallels that existed between operatic developments in Nazi Germany and Fascist Italy, there were also some striking differences. Despite the promulgation of race laws in Italy during the late 1930s, the cultural environment remained far more cosmopolitan in outlook than did the deliberately isolationist approach adopted in Nazi Germany. This explains why composers such as Bartok, Hindemith, Berg and Stravinsky were performed in Italy long after their work had been proscribed by the Nazis. In the case of opera, it is remarkable to note that Berg's expressionist opera Wozzeck was performed at La Scala as late as 1942 without encountering official opposition, and that after the anti-Semitic prohibitions of 1938, Lodovico Rocca's immensely successful opera *Il Dibuk* (Milan, 1934) remained in the repertoire despite its Jewish subject matter.

Notes

1. Examination of operatic developments in Franco's Spain is excluded from the present discussion for the reason that the regime made little effort to stimulate Spanish composers to write operas, and nor were there enough theatres in which such works could be performed.

2. A complete list of these operas is published in Hans-Günter Klein, 'Viel Konformität und wenig Verweigerung: Zur Komposition neuer Opern 1933–1944' in Hanns-Werner Heister and Hans-Günter Klein (eds), *Musik und Musikpolitik im faschistischen Deutschland*, Frankfurt am Main, 1984, pp. 154–62.

3. In practice, such aspirations were only accomplished in a few centres. In Stuttgart, for example, the Württemberg State Theatre mounted only one new opera between 1935 and 1944.

4. See Eugen Schmitz, 'oper im Aufbau', *Zeitschrift für Musik*, April 1939, pp. 380–2, quoted in Joseph Wulf, *Musik im dritten Reich*, Gütersloh, 1963/1966, pp. 308–9. Schmitz's pronouncements demonstrate considerable ignorance of developments in contemporary Nazi drama, since no major playwright contemplated basing a play around the life of Horst Wessel.

5. Richard Strauss *Arabella* (1933) and Norbert Schultze's *Schwarzer Peter* (1936) were the two contemporary operas that received the highest number of performances between 1933 and 1944. Both works bear little, if any, relationship to political themes.

6. See, for example, Hans Költzsch's damning criticism of these composers' works in 'Der neue deutsche Opernspielplan', *Zeitschrift für Musik*, October 1933, p.97.

7. See Graener's letter to Hitler, dated 19 February 1936, inviting him to attend a performance of *Der Prinz von Homburg*; it is quoted in Wulf, *Musik im Dritten Reich*, p.97.

8. Artistic collaboration between Aryans and Jews was officially outlawed by the Nazi regime. Yet such a policy was never implemented with complete consistency as far as the operatic repertoire was concerned. For example, the authorities never contemplated proscribing Mozart's *Don Giovanni*, despite the fact that the librettist Lorenzo Da Ponte was a baptised Jew.

9. For a comprehensive examination of the pacifist elements in Strauss's *Friedenstag* see Pamela Potter, 'Richard Strauss's *Friedenstag*: A Pacifistic Attempt at Political Resistance', *Musical Quarterly*, vol.69, 1983, p.408.

10. Werner Egk, *Peer Gynt*, Mainz, 1938, p.130.

11. Amongst the casualties of the latter policies were Klenau's *Elisabeth von England* (Kassel, 1939), whose title was changed to *Die Königin*, and Wagner-Regeny's *Johanna Balk* (Vienna, 1941), an opera whose subject matter takes place against the background of a popular uprising against the Hungarian tyrant Prince Báthory. Before this work could be staged, the authorities in Berlin demanded that the main characters and place of action were altered from seventeenth-century Transylvania so as not to offend Germany's loyal allies.

12. Exceptions such as Marc-André Souchay's Kampfwerk 39 (Stuttgart, 1939) and Ernst Schliepe's Marienburg (Danzig, 1942), whose scenario is concerned with the Teutonic Knights' successful defence of a fortress in the face of attacks from Slavs and tartars, failed to gain more than a handful of performances.

13. Hans-Günter Klein, 'Viel Konformität und wenig Verweigerung', p.157.

14. In the light of his modernist proclivities, the 1938 German premiere of Stravinsky's *Persephone* in Brunswick seems extraordinary given the repressive cultural climate during that year.

15. During the Third Reich, the artistic alliance between Berlin and Bayreuth was further sealed after Heinz Tietjen, Intendant at the Berlin Staatsoper, was appointed director of the Bayreuth Festival in 1933.

16. Amongst the most frequently performed operas during the 1932–33 season and the 1938–39 season were Bizet's *Carmen*; Verdi's *Il travatore*, Puccini's *La Bohème*, Wagner's *Lohengrin* and Weber's *Der Freischüt*.

17. Fiamma Nicolodi, *Musica e musicisti nel ventennio fascista*, Fiesole, 1984, pp. 23–24.

18. Harvey Sachs, *Music in Fascist Italy*, London, 1987, pp. 24–25.

CHAPTER 4

HITLER'S THEATRE

BRUCE ZORTMAN

National Socialism is now part of Germany's past, but the devastating effect it had on the vital development of the theatre is still being felt. Since 30 January 1933, the creativity of its theatre and its drama has declined; a situation caused primarily by the sudden and irreversible blow the dictatorship dealt to the playwrights, actors, directors and all the artists of the theatre when they were forced either to flee or subvert their creative activity to the new policy. Max Reinhardt, Leopold Jessner, Bertolt Brecht, Elizabeth Bergner, Kurt Weill, Albert Bassermann, Ernst Toller, Fritch von Unruh, Stefan Zweig, Henry Schnitzler, Erwin Piscator, Carl Zuckmayer, Lion Feuchtwanger, and Georg Kaiser comprise an inadequate list of those who were forced to emigrate. With them they took their talent and genius, or to be more exact, their Geist, their grand spirit, and departed, most of them forever.

To be sure, in the broad spectrum of history there have been many periods in which a creative theatre has languished due to a gradual or sudden reaction against it; in this regard the history of Germany is not peculiar. The Nazis, however, did not close or eradicate the theatre they had conscripted. After immediately suppressing the humanistic creativity and the infusion of 'foreign' ideas on what they regarded as Germany's 'pure' and 'genuine' culture, they strove to supplant these vital qualities with the ideology of National Socialism; their objective was to transform the theatre and use it for their own purposes.

Though their reaction appeared sudden, their ambitious cultural program was not haphazard nor an emergency means of filling a vacuum. On the contrary, it was a well-planned program of Kuntspolitik, or cultural policy, that began years before the seizure of power. When Alfred Rosenberg founded what was to be known as Der Kampfbund für deutsche Kultur (German Cultural League) in Munich in August 1927, the National Socialist Party began influencing and controlling the exposure of art in various districts of the country.

One of the spokesmen for this organisation and a professor at the University of Vienna, Dr Othmar Spann, attacked the 'present status' of the arts in his presentation to a large group of students and guests at the University of Munich on 23 February 1929. 'If we are to think about Dada,' he charged, 'Futurism or Atonalism and so forth; if we are to think about the intruding cinema and revue, then we see. . . . in what a bad state they [the arts] are.' He further asserted that the first step towards 'cultural health' could not be taken without the help of an 'authoritarian state', and that democracy had proved itself the 'ruination of culture', for 'think what horrors occur in a democracy! Every little newcomer can enter and make himself a leader.'[1]

In March 1929, the Cultural League reported that twenty-five of its district groups were prepared to assume their duties. The groups in Weimer[2] and Munich were the first to become active while those in Dresden and Bonn commenced activity in the fall and those in Düsseldorf and Karlsruhe in early 1930; resembling armed units, they were poised and ready for infiltration. Immediately, the avant-garde artists were denounced as 'breeders of the proletarian world revolution'. This particular means of agitation, Alfred Rosenberg's favourite, offered not only a pretext to brand all undesirable works as simply 'Bolshevistic art', but created many fertile ideological objects on which to exemplify the categories of 'friend' and 'foe'. According to historian Hildegard Brenner: 'Modern art, understood in the broad sense of the term, was considered the seat of revolutionary infection at the very heart of the nation and the centre of political activity beyond the limits of 'Moscow".[3]

The West was also a target of the Cultural League. Similar to the attitude of the Communists, the League embarked upon a vigorous campaign to repudiate the West and its economic basis: capitalism. In short, it sought to be totally anti-foreign, and in doing so censured such artists as Rilke, Hofmannsthal and Liebermann for their 'un-German' attitude. Simultaneously, it intensified its anti-Semitic propaganda while wooing the 'people' as the epitome of the hard-kernel, mystic and indestructible cult. And it impelled the 'people' to search for their art in the 'blood-saturated soil' of Germany.

On 8 December, 1929, the National Socialists, then Germany's smallest party, had a decisive victory in the local election in Thuringia. Hitler moved in quickly and saw that his party's candidate, Dr Wilhelm Frick, was installed as Minister of Education. Shortly thereafter the entire administration was reorganised to fit Nazi policies: 'Protective employees' were placed within the police force, educational policies were 'adjusted', and 'undesirable' faculty were summarily replaced. Dr Hans Severus Ziegler, District Leader of the Party, was put in charge of the theatre, for which he acted as supreme censor.

Immediately, the new ministry mounted its cultural policies campaign by presenting 'art programmes' such as 'Why Negro Culture Is Contrary to German Customs' to 'prove' that jazz has deleterious effects on the German 'spirit'. Certain authors and books like Remarque's *All Quiet on the Western Front* were outlawed, while special lists of 'National Socialist Literature' were distributed. In the cinema, the films of Eisenstein and, in particular, Pabst's *The Threepenny Opera* were prohibited; in the theatre no importations, especially Piscator or Brecht, were allowed; and the works of Hindemith and Stravinsky were stricken from the concert programmes. The low point of the 'clean up' came when the ministry ordered that the frescoes on the walls and staircases of the Staatliche Bauhochschule (State School of Architecture) in Weimer, painted by Oscar Schlemmer, an artist the Nazis considered a Bolshevist, be destroyed by whitewash.[4]

On 22 September 1933, the new government passed a law creating a Reichskulturkammer (National Cultural Board) and as Minister für Volksaufklärung Und Propaganda (Minister for Public Information and Propaganda) Dr Joseph Goebbels named himself president of the board, thus becoming in title the chief of all cultural matters in the new regime. Within the structure of his board he created chambers to regulate the press, radio, literature, music, painting and film. Virtually all theatre, including private, subsidised and open air, were placed under the aegis of Goebbels' Cultural Board.

Though the Cultural Board were in full agreement regarding the National Socialists' Jewish policy, the tenuous political situation forced them to postpone their proposed reign of terror, expulsion and annihilation. In the meantime, the Jewish communities were isolated and allowed only limited access to German affairs. In an attempt to 'closet' what had, only weeks before, been the focus of German cultural activity, the Nazis placed stringent controls on these alienated communities while at the same time forcing them to continue 'normal' existence. One of the consequences of this aberrant situation was the creation of a Jewish cultural organisation that produced theatre and other arts under incredibly adverse conditions until well after the outbreak of war. Hans Hinkel, advisor

for morals on Goebbels' Cultural Board, became the supreme over-
seer of the new organisation, indiscriminately censoring its activities
while mercilessly goading it to produce.[5]

Origins of a Cult Theatre

Over 20,000 spectators stood in the stone amphitheatre on the
Heilige Berg near Heidelberg singing 'Germany Awaken!' Nearly a
thousand Hitler Youth, each carrying a flaming torch, responded to
the last note of the anthem with an exultant roar. Silhouetted
against the twilight, trumpeters in close order blared a strident fanfare, while a company of drummers filed through the Hitler Youth,
beating forth the cadence. A 450-voice Chorus of Warriors, Workers and Women flanked the highest playing areas to declare: 'Rise
up! Rise up you German nation'.

The action culminated when the Hitler Youth presented the flaming torches to the Chorus of Warriors, who raised them high amid
a muffled drum beat. Simultaneously, three fire urns around the
amphitheatre were lit. The entire ensemble then exclaimed: 'Germany! Germany above all else! Above all else in the world!'

And so ended the premiere of Kurt Heynicke's *Der Weg ins Reich*
(The Road to the Third Reich) on the summer solstice of 1935.
Much the same as any rite, this cult play, termed a Thingspiel by the
Nazis, had a rigid structure and content that was easily repeatable
by merely substituting a new title and different names for the characters. The theme was constant, the characters and their conflict
were readily distinguishable, the dialogue was exhortative, con-
trived and prosaic, and the plot was thin, ingenuous and
unimaginative. Dramaturgically speaking, it offered little or nothing
of value.

The spectacle, the pageantry and the military ornamentation,
however, had a coercive, fascinating and narcotic effect on the audience. Flaming torches, richly braided uniforms, thousands of voices
chanting in unison, and a drummed cadence interwoven with
medieval fanfare created the illusion that the power concentrated in
the auditorium and on the playing areas transcended the amphitheatre's limits and pervaded the real world outside. Massed into a
gigantic auditorium, singing national anthems repetitively, the performers and the audience became one, and any individual drives
were paralysed by this cloying unanimity. For obviously the primary purpose of this cult theatre was to create an atmosphere of
absolute uniformity, the method by which National Socialism could
function most efficiently. The individual became important only in

relation to the mass. His racial purity, as well as his ability to work, to sacrifice and to become a hero were all measured against the national standard, and, as these cult plays repeatedly expressed, individual excellence had to be absorbed by the whole. Likewise, individual thought was anathema; the fascistic government not only offered but indeed demanded that it do the thinking for its people.

The architecture and the physical setting of the amphitheatres, known as Thingplätze, produced another powerful effect. The word Thing itself refers to the pre-Christian councils that were held on sacred ground in wooded areas on and near the graves of great warriors. The Nazis proclaimed that the 400 proposed amphitheatres would be built on these sites even though there were no ruins or other archaeological evidence to identify them. The intent, however, was to create another illusion based on medieval Romanticism, Teutonic mythology, atavism, hero worship, and a return to nature, where the blonde, blue-eyed Aryan held sway; he became the image of mass identification, while the symbols of sun and universe mirrored the nation. Within these new shrines the Nazis intended to remove the people totally from reality.

Nevertheless, they did not produce this cult theatre without referring to some tested models or critical thought regarding a national theatre in the form of the Thingspiel. In its formation they used insupportable distillations of classical theatre, mythological acts of Teutonic heroism, speculative significances of hoary relics of prehistoric age, vague interpretations of medieval drama and, in particular, the culled dramatic theories of both Wagner and Nietzsche. The product, however, was essentially the fusion of an open air theatre tradition that had survived since the Middle Ages, and a decadent ideology that had surfaced during the Bismarckian expansion.

In Retrospect

The Thingspiel is an excellent example of how the quality of the arts, when inspired by extremism and regulated by government, can be reduced to stultifying mediocrity. No matter how much the völkisch artists (and the Nazis) wanted to rediscover or develop a pure German art, they failed utterly to do so, for in their search for purity they were constantly confronted with the reality of a national legacy of distinguished achievement in the arts, albeit tainted by 'foreign' influence. When Wachler discovered that the scope of Teutonic mythology and medieval mysticism were limiting, he conveniently extracted ideas from Wagner, which led him to the

Greeks, who in turn led him into the complex Nietzchean dialectic. Then, lacking the acumen to absorb these ideas and theories fully, yet attracted by their use of myth, people, religion, racism and nationalism, he was drawn into his own limbo, where he produced mediocre plays as vehicles for his fascistic ideas. He was a desecrater and distorter of the arts and philosophies that he clumsily chose for his own benefit.

The Cultural Board, demonstrating its chronic myopia, could not foresee the obvious pitfalls in their search for a place to proclaim their ideology: to ignore the changeable climate of the central European continent, to disregard the obvious ratio between the size of an auditorium and the impact of sight and sound on an audience, and to defy history by building grand theatres before a play had been written for them are all incredible. In one respect, however, their ambitious design to subvert a traditional theatre into a substitute church, a political platform and a national theatre was sound, for religion, politics and nationalism have consistently proved to be the core of the finest theatre and drama in the world; it was their method of subversion that was at fault.

The fundamental precept of the Thingspiel, to convey the Party ideology through a preponderance of 'living' symbols and not by the spoken work, was the prime and irrevocable reason for its failure. Aware of the psychological impact of a massive spectacle, the Nazis attempted to create a deceptive and illusory world in their 'non-illusary' theatre. By arguing irrationally and offering solutions in the abstract they gained a little ground. Their success, however, came when the spectacle overwhelmed the word.

But, alas, the emotional effects of spectacle are ephemeral. Parades, circuses, carnivals and grand sporting matches create an immediate and sensational response. The spectator is gripped by the narcotic effects of the extremes of sight, sound, and perhaps by extension, smell, touch, and taste, depending on the intensity of the experience. Regarding drama, however, spectacle is only one of its constituent parts; structure, intelligence and human identity are also essential.

Though shrewd and at times brilliant in their planning, the Nazis were unable to view art as anything more than functional. Assuming an 'aesthetic' polarity opposing Surrealism, they demanded that all art, particularly dramatic art (theatre, film and radio), be purposeful with clearly delineated objectives that would unquestionably further the aims of National Socialism. The artist, therefore, was never permitted to indulge himself in the type of self-gratification that alone encourages further creativity. In order to accomplish their aims, the Nazis had to generate a 'purified' group of 'artists' who would produce against a formula on demand. Quite naturally, artistic ability was disregarded, inspired talent was expelled and true quality was silenced. The arts were thoroughly degraded, reduced from excellence to mediocrity (and below) through a degenerating spiral wherein criticism, comparison and contrast were untenable, causing the cultural attitude to wither and artistic excellence to atrophy; for the values set by national leadership, or similar entity, are a predominant influence in shaping the artistic creativity of its people.

Notes

1. 'Die Kulturkrise der Gegenwart,' *Völkischer Beobachter*, 26 February 1929
2. Weimer, or course, drew particular attention since it was the home of Gropius' 'Bolshevistic' Bauhaus.
3. Hildergard Brenner, *Die Kuntspolitik des Nationalsozialismus*, Hamburg, 1963, p. 13.
4. *Die Kunstpolitik*, pp. 22–23, 32–33
5. Herbert Freeden (1956) 'A Jewish Theatre under the Swastika', *Year Book I* of the Leo Baeck Institute, London, pp. 142–62.

PART II

THEATRE, OCCUPATION AND CURFEW

CHAPTER 5

THE WAR YEARS

ANDREW DAVIES

Together with its ally France, Britain declared war on Nazi Germany on 3 September 1939. After a brief campaign during which Poland was defeated, the Germans settled down to build up their military machine undisturbed, biding their time until the spring of 1940, when they suddenly launched an attack on Belgium, Holland and France.

Although the period between September 1939 and May 1940 saw Britain engaged in no major campaigns or battles – leading some to talk of the Phoney or 'Bore War' – the social changes induced by the war were already making themselves felt. It was clear that this could only be a 'Total War' because of its enormous requirements, entailing the conscription of both the military and civilian populations. Economic demands ensured a huge expansion of the government's activities as well as the need for it to exhort its people to accept severe deprivations. But if this was to be the case, then it was recognised that the morale of the nation was all-important and the process could not be one-sided – especially when the unfulfilled promises bandied around after the First World War were recalled. The government had to give something too, and the series of White Papers issued towards the end of the war laid the foundations of the welfare state, later introduced by the Atlee administration. It was a dislocation of traditional and conservative attitudes which also affected the role and provision of theatre during the war.

The introduction of the blackout from September 1939, and more importantly the start of the Blitz in London a year later, led to massive disruption of the entertainment industry in general and the theatrical world in particular: overnight, theatres closed down, several of them never to reopen. Shaftesbury Avenue was thrown into chaos. Two theatres started up again when restrictions were eased in the middle of September 1939 after ten days. One was the Windmill, just off Shaftesbury Avenue, which offered a programme of humour, music, 'legshows' and immobile nudes; it boasted 'We never closed', and it is sometimes claimed that it was the only London theatre never to do so at this time. This is wrong: Unity Theatre likewise rapidly reopened, putting on a revue entitled *Sandbag Follies*, which had been written, rehearsed and produced within 48 hours. That Unity was so quickly in action proved symbolic of the changes which were to transform British theatre over the next few years.

This transformation revolved around two trends which contradicted the general trajectory of recent theatre history. The first was a move away from traditional venues, which people were understandably reluctant to visit when the bombing began, and a shift towards touring and mobile companies entertaining audiences at makeshift 'non-theatrical' locations: evacuation centres, war hostels, factory canteens, army camps, gun sites, tube shelters. These were places at which the 'Shaftesbury Avenue' values of proscenium arch and evening dress were obviously completely absent.

The second change followed on from the first and flew in the face of what we have seen was the growing dominance of the London West End stage since the nineteenth century. The provinces now came to the fore, especially in view of the large-scale evacuation from London. In December 1940, for example, Equity reported that of its 1500 members usually at work in London, only 26 were now employed there.[1] The veteran critic W.A. Darlington observed that 'London ceased, for the first time in her history, to be the headquarters of the English stage': 'She became a place to which theatre companies might pay fleeting visits when either the lightening of the German attacks, or the hours of performance, permitted. In stage terms, London had become a 'touring date'; and not until after the last severe bombing raid, on 10 May 1941, did she become once more the home of the long run.'[2]

An additional factor lay in the general rise in the standard of living during the war, resulting from the full employment which it brought. Real wages rose steadily and, with the shortage of consumer and luxury goods, extra money was available for the cultural activities regarded in peacetime as no more than the icing on the cake. It would be wrong to exaggerate this picture of the thriving culture stimulated by the 'People's War'; but it is undeniable that interest in the arts expanded enormously: expenditure on books doubled during the war, educational bodies found their membership numbers going up by leaps and bounds, and performers and artists in all fields were surprised and excited by the size and quality of their audiences.

As the role and scope of the government intervention grew massively, so did the old shibboleths concerning the importance of laissez-faire within the area of culture become discredited and fade away. Just as Roosevelt's New Deal in the United States had led to the Federal Theatre, so did the coalition government initiate a programme of subsidies and grants to the arts. At first it shied away from creating new institutions but instead gave a small sum of money amounting to £25,000 to the Pilgrim Trust, a private organisation headed by Dr Thomas Jones, its energetic secretary. The Trust was also given an office and the use of one of its secretaries by the Board of Education.

Disturbed by the widespread unemployment of artists and musicians arising from the outbreak of war, the Pilgrim Trust introduced the idea of 'Music Travellers': violinists, pianists and singers who were sent out to entertain listeners in temporary settings, rather like the medieval minstrels. Both performers and spectators were sceptical at first – the former having been advised to keep their programmes simple and not to annoy the irretrievably debased taste of listeners conditioned to jazz and film music, the latter suspicious that these entertainments were simply another aspect of official propaganda and doled out with the intention of 'keeping the workers happy'.

Sometimes the concerts were not a success, one musician finding that an audience which was labouring twelve hours a day, seven days a week, was apathetic. But then s/he went on to note:

> If it is necessary to balance the rather drab picture I have given of C.E.M.A. [Council for the Encouragement of Music and the Arts] concerts, let it be said that four concerts during the tour, organised publicly in mining villages, met with tremendous success and appreciation, which showed that there really is a keen and widespread demand for music among the working people of this country. My complaint is that C.E.M.A. is not really adequate in its scope or arrangement to cover one small part of this demand.[3]

The government too recognised this problem of insufficient funding, and in April 1940 CEMA was established on a permanent basis and given more money on the understanding that the government would contribute, up to £50,000, a pound for every pound donated by private sources. This turned out to be a last attempt to marry the public and private ownership of art and proved unsuccessful: in April 1942 CEMA became wholly government financed.[4] It was also reorganised so that there were Regional Offices all over the country as well as paid directorates of music, art and drama, and audition panels for local talent. This last feature was especially significant: CEMA played down the normally rigid distinction separating professionals from amateurs.

CEMA continued to organise factory concerts – to such an extent that 4,500 of them were put on in 1943 alone – but also began to widen its range of activities. In 1940 the Old Vic requested assistance in organising two tours of South Wales and County Durham, and it was the success which attended them that encouraged CEMA to support dramatic companies. The Old Vic had already transferred its headquarters away from London to Burnley ('Burnley, where's Burnley?' many of the smart London set were heard to ask), and then in 1942 they established a permanent repertory company at the Liverpool Playhouse. They also embarked upon a series of tours, deliberately visiting places ignored by the commercial drama: when the Old Vic played *Othello* in Wigan it staged that town's first straight play for twenty years.

The touring Old Vic companies had no option but to travel light; the opera company for instance had only one piano as accompaniment. But somehow this did not seem to matter. The tour to South Wales was led by Sybil Thorndike and Lewis Casson and the company's meagre scenery and costumes were transported in a single lorry with everyone travelling by bus. In such circumstances their productions had to dispense with the grandiose and formal requirements of a West End show. The major play presented during this Welsh tour was *Macbeth*, which was preceded by a 'plain clothes prologue' written in order to emphasise the contemporary nature of Shakespeare's drama with its themes of power and dictatorship. The down-to-earth and unpompous character of setting and performances achieved magnificent results, as Sybil Thorndike described in a letter of the time: 'We've never played to such audiences. None of them moved a muscle while we're playing, but at the end they go wild and lift the roof with their clapping. This is the theatre that we liked best – getting right in amongst people. Afterwards they all come round and talk to us.'[5]

Other plays toured by the Old Vic included *The Merchant of Venice*, *Medea* and Shaw's *Candida*. The ballet company could now boast two pianos when it toured and the opera company two violins, a clarinet and a violoncello.[6] By 1944 the bombing of London had largely subsided, allowing the Old Vic Repertory Company to take over the New Theatre in London. In one respect of course this was a reversion to type – the pull of London – but the Old Vic's tours had demonstrated just what could be accomplished, and the group organisation of the company's travelling plays lived on in the

repertory of their new home. Furthermore the achievements of the
Old Vic's tours prompted CEMA to fund more touring theatre companies: 14 in all by October 1942.

Another body which by and large benefited from wartime events
and moods was Unity Theatre in London. After its *Sandbag Follies*
revue of September 1939, which was revised and went through
three editions, the theatre then produced another revue, *Turn Up
the Lights*, which ran from December 1939 to February 1940. Both
revues were critical of the Chamberlain government, inspiring a
Unity fund-raising pamphlet to claim that 'We are the first theatre to
attack the war policy of a government in war time since Euripides'
Trojan Women was performed in Athens in 415 BC.'[7]

In March 1940 Unity demonstrated its continuing ambition by
mounting the first production of Sean O'Casey's *The Star Turned
Red*. It did not confine its work to its base in Goldington Street,
London, but created an Outside Shows Group during the Blitz
which specialised in performing before audiences at tube shelters
and bomb sites. One of its organisers, Ann Davies, described the
conditions surrounding one of the first shows, at a shelter in Belsize
Park underground:

> We had to ask people to squash even closer together and allow us to
> pile up on their rugs and coats. They very readily did this and off we
> went. Swanee River, John Brown's Body, Roll out the Barrel, etc., got
> them interested. . . . prepared the way for a couple of sketches, solos,
> songs and jokes. Ten minutes at one end of the platform, and ten the
> other, the same thing on another platform, and finally a show at each
> end of the lift-shafts. Even when these items had to be done sideways
> on, with occasional trains roaring through, they went over big, and
> the crowd was almost as pleased as we were.[8]

The Outside Shows Group mixed straight plays with music hall and
variety entertainment, finding a gratifying measure of audience participation. In all, Unity put on over 1000 outside performances
during the war. Early in 1944 they even ran an all-women troupe
called the Amazons Company who likewise organised outside
shows drawing upon revue material – although sadly little information has survived relating to this group, the first since the Actresses'
Franchise League to perform 'women only' plays. But not everything went well for Unity. The outbreak of war and the consequent
introduction of conscription had led to the disintegration of the
experienced collective formed during the late 1930's; the theatre
was hit four times by bombs, on one occasion blowing the roof off;
and in 1941, 1942 and 1943 the lack of writers and performers
resulted in the staging of some rather poor productions. In 1943 it
was decided to jettison the principal of anonymity in the hope that

individual recognition might attract more talented recruits. Later that year the company turned the corner, putting on Lope de Vega's *Fuente Ovejuna*, a play never seen before in London, and a music-hall history called *Winkles and Champagne*. Membership began to climb again, passing the figure of 5,000.

Older organisations such as the British Drama League found that their number of affiliated amateur groups surged upwards, reaching a record 5,000 in the winter of 1943–4. New enterprises included the People's Entertainment Society, sponsored by the Co-op, which toured a play called *The Rochdale Pioneers* about the founding of the Co-op, published other works under the title People's Plays, and hoped to finance the actual ownership of its own theatre. Another new organisation was ENSA (Entertainments National Service Association) which was set up by Basil Dean and catered primarily for troops stationed overseas, putting on cabaret and music-hall type performances which did incorporate some drama. In all, ENSA arranged two and a half million shows during the war in front of a total audience estimated at over 300 million people.[9]

Plays presented to the troops were often staged in highly unlikely settings. Bernard Miles once performed in the Orkneys in 1943, 'playing on a rough platform slung between two destroyers *Orwell* and *Opportune*, with five hundred sailors surrounding the stage and hanging on to every available projection of the two ships'.[10] Donald Wolfit organised a six-week tour of *Twelfth Night* to garrison theatres and army camps, evoking tremendous enthusiasm: 'Based at hostels, we travelled to four and sometimes five camps in a week, returning at night to the luxury of ENSA beds which seemed to be made of teak.' On only one occasion were there disturbances, when American soldiers greeted Viola with cries of 'Hello Blondie' and punctuated the performance with such remarks as 'Sez you' and 'Jesus, I don't take this at all'. Wolfit complained and the next evening the audience made not a sound. On asking for an explanation of this reversal, the commanding officer told Wolfit that he had had a talk with the men, 'and in case there was any further trouble to-night I had the military police parading the aisles with their revolvers out of their holsters'.[11]

One of the most interesting developments within non-commercial theatre during the war was also aimed primarily at the troops. By 1941 the War Office was alarmed at the succession of reports revealing low morale and boredom of the troops, most of whom had been stationed in Britain after the evacuation from Dunkirk. All too aware that this mood included widespread antagonism towards 'Blimps' and the 'officer' in general, the War Office tentatively made arrangements for lectures and talks to be part of the military routine, establishing a body called ABCA (the Army Bureau of Current Affairs) in September 1941. Certainly those in command laid down stringent guidelines, censoring pamphlets and posters and stipulating that the discussions were to be conducted by regimental officers, but nevertheless by the winter of 1943–4 over 110,000 courses, lectures and classes were taking place.

Several groups of soldiers began to organise dramatic activities: 'Penny Readings' were popular, play-reading was widespread, army groups affiliated to the British Drama League (280 had done so by July 1943), Scottish Command put on its own festival, and the garrison on the Orkneys even built its own theatre.[12] It was revealing, too, that the selection of plays by these groups indicated that light West End comedies were being ousted in favour of more serious productions: the Army Education Syllabus actually recommended Odets' *Waiting for Lefty* and some O'Casey plays as suitable material.[13]

In June 1944 a more specialised organisation called the ABCA Play Unit was formed in order to dramatise the ideas and topics discussed in the ABCA pamphlets.

The personnel of the Play Unit demonstrated just how many of the wartime dramatic experiments were built upon initiatives of the 1930s: Michael Macowan, Stephen Murray, Bridget Boland, Miles Tomalin, André van Gyseghem, Jack Lindsay and Ted Willis had all been involved in non-commercial theatre projects before the war, the last three having worked extensively with Unity Theatre in London. The Unit operated as a collective of 18 with everyone contributing suggestions and proposals for the content of the plays as well as being expected to help out with the carpentry, stage design, paperwork and other chores. As one of the members had said: 'Everyone took a turn at acting, or on the switchboard or carting rostrums or scene shifting. It was understood these jobs were done in rotation.'[14] Unit members also gave readings and lectures, and held courses for the troops on all aspects of drama.

The crucial factor influencing the work of the Unit was that it performed in a variety of 'non-theatrical' locations – nissan huts, gun sites, factory canteens – and in front of audiences the majority of whom had never been inside a theatre. In these circumstances the traditional proscenium barrier separating performers from spectators in most theatres simply did not exist and the Unit had to develop an approach which recognised this fact. It came up with a form of presentation that was almost cinematic in the speed and excitement by which it continually surprised audiences – for instance, there were speakers placed in the auditorium and even staged fights, as in *Who are the Germans?* as well as innovative lighting effects which directed the spectators' attention towards one spot and then another.

The documentary style kept scenery and costumes to a minimum, ensuring maximum concentration on the essentials of the plays, and the themes dealt with focused on contemporary issues. The ABCA Play Unit drew upon the 'Living Newspaper' format pioneered in America in the 1930s and taken up by Unity in London, but whereas Living Newspapers often became little more than 'dead history' the shock tactics used by the Unit and their willingness to combine both naturalistic and expressionistic forms continually challenged and startled the audience. As Michael Macowan wrote in January 1945: 'We have given the troops verse as two o'clock in the afternoon and heard them applaud it to the echo; we have made them leap in their seats with realistic dive bombing and listen, hushed, to a Japanese cradle song. We are still learning, and, we hope, still shaking them.'[15]

It is curious how some seasoned observers missed the significance of the novel work that the ABCA Play Unit was doing. J.B. Priestley, for example, wrote a play for the Unit called *Desert Highway*, which, whatever the merits of the piece itself, was quite unsuitable for the venue and spectators where the Unit performed. In fact *Desert Highway* was later a success on the West End stage.

The two main protagonists behind the writing of the Unit's shows were Jack Lindsay and Ted Wallis, and their plays grappled with immediate and concrete issues. In Jack Lindsay's words, 'the plays were not at all socialist . . . Anything looking remotely like party politics we excised', but in the radical context of the war years their plays chimed with the undercurrents which resulted in the substantial Labour Party victory at the 1945 election.[16] Their first production was given at the Garrison Theatre in Aldershot in July 1944 before an audience of hundreds: *It Started as Lend-lease* looked at the effects and implications of American aid to this country. *Where Do We Go From Here?* delved into the problem of post-war reconstruction.

The influential Indian novelist Mulk Raj Anand was responsible for *Famine*, and *Who are the Germans?* and *The Japanese Way* explored the nature of fascism in both these countries, but always in a way that was clear and comprehensible to the audience. The topicality of the latter play in exposing the hero-worship of the Emperor was forcibly brought home when Churchill himself ordered the play to be withdrawn. Fearing the possible political outcome of a crushing Japanese defeat, Churchill had decided that the Emperor would after all have a part to play in the post-war world. In their first six months alone the Unit gave 58 performances to a total audience of around 20,000 people, and one experienced observer noted that 'they were as responsive as any audience I have ever seen . . .'[17]. In May 1945 the ABCA Play Unit played at the Arts Theatre, London, for four very successful nights.

This upsurge of non-commercial drama continued throughout the war. All the groups and organisations were characterised by their enormous commitment and enthusiasm, bolstered by the optimism engendered by an anti-fascist war.

Long standing repertory theatres were stimulated to new efforts by the prevailing mood. Birmingham Rep, for example, despite losing all its costumes as a result of an incendiary bomb, began performing in the city's parks from 1941, a project financially guaranteed by CEMA. They continued with this outside programme every year, attracting large crowds – the 1942 season alone was seen by over 35,000.[18] Even a smaller rep company such as that in York was notching up weekly audiences of 10,000 people.[19]

CEMA was still sending touring productions around the country, each play going through an eight-week cycle. The most popular of all was Ibsen's *Hedda Gabler*, and, springing out of these visits, play-reading groups at the hostels were often set up which developed into fully-fledged drama societies. CEMA also took a few hesitant steps into the minefield of theatre ownership, managing the Lyric at Hammersmith and the Theatre Royal, Bristol; the latter in particular achieved substantial financial success. Just as crucial, CEMA was involved in the founding of the Citizens' Theatre, Glasgow, in 1943 under the chairmanship of the Scottish playwright James Birdie. As its director stated, 'it was due to CEMA's backing that this theatre was able to be started, and although their guarantee has not been touched, without such backing the whole theatre would probably not have come into existence'.[20] Older organisations thrived. The Unity Theatre of London reported its individual membership was nearing 7,000 and the Merseyside Unity was able to expand into new premises in the heart of Liverpool in 1944 as well as maintain their outdoor shows. The Co-op formed a National Association of Drama Associations. The membership of the British Drama League was now over 50,000 and by 1945 the BDL was able to claim that 5,000 societies were affiliated. The People's Theatre in Newcastle experienced a wave of enthusiasm for its productions; Toynbee Hall in London formed a touring company; and other groups giving shows included the Shelter Players and the Pilgrim Players. These were but a few of the developments taking place all over the country.[21]

This public interest in live theatre – to which ENSA contributed a great deal, giving on its own 3,000 performances each week by 1943 – was quite oblivious to the conventions and customs covering West End theatre-going behaviour and expectations, and it was a change which eventually began to be felt within London itself. Just as Dame Myra Hess's lunchtime recitals at the National Gallery were hugely popular, attracting around 800,000 people during the war despite (or because of) the makeshift surroundings, performers like Donald Wolfit began to present plays stripped bare of the usual production values thought necessary to their staging. Wolfit's 'Lunch Time Shakespeare' began in October 1940 at the Strand Theatre in London; he put on excerpts from Shakespeare's plays, songs, sonnets and prologues between one o'clock and two o'clock, changing the programme at least three times a week and continuing even when the theatre had been badly bombed. Edith Evans was another performer who presented solo shows.

In general it was noticeable that the overall quality of the West End theatre was much higher than it had been in the Fist World War. Although, naturally, musical comedies remained popular, many more thoughtful productions were staged. Amongst them were Terrence Rattigan's *Flarepath*, Peter Ustinov's satirical portrayal of the military caste, *The Banbury Nose*, Emelyn Williams' *The Morning Star* and *Watch on the Rhine*, and J.B. Priestley's *Desert Highway* and *They Came To a City*. John Gielgud also produced a highly influential series of Shakespearean plays at the Haymarket, London. With a lack of backroom staff and the normal financial trappings, the West End during the war was forced to discard many of its conventions and get closer to its audiences – a change which benefited them both. Together with this, managements such as H.M. Tennent sent companies out on tour, helped by imaginative fiscal laws which allowed such initiatives to avoid Entertainment Tax as long as they were non-profit-making. Even the government got in on the act by issuing in 1945 its White Paper on Community Centres, an important blueprint which testified to the recognised achievements of the less formal theatrical activities of the war.

As can be seen from the above, the Second World War provided a tremendous boost for non-commercial drama, especially when it is borne in mind that a League of Audiences survey of 1939 revealed that 92 percent of the British people had never been to the theatre. Many of the assumptions and conventions supported by the West End theatre – the barrier between amateur and professional and performer and spectator, the select audiences, the formalised settings, the emphasis on expensive production values, the restricted subject-matter of plays – had been challenged and weakened. For the first time since the Elizabethans, this country possessed what was virtually a national drama.

It would be wrong to overestimate the solidity of these successes.

For instance, it was entirely foreseeable that the new audiences would disperse at the end of the war and that many of the novel locations such as hostels, garrisons and gun sites would close down. It was also true that few new forms of drama had emerged: instead it was older forms like variety, music hall and the 'Living Newspaper' which were used. ENSA was criticised for having no artistic policy.[22] Finally, it was significant that most of the productions seen during the war were of the classics – Shaw, Shakespeare, Ibsen – and there were few opportunities for new writers, although few in fact displayed startling talent: when the Arts Theatre Club held a new play competition in 1943, none of the 500 entries were judged to be of merit. But despite these reservations, it is clear that the war years saw an unprecedented growth in the size and vigour of alternative and experimental theatre in Britain.

Notes

1. Robert Hewison, *Under Siege*, London, Quartet, 1979, p. 29.
2. W.A. Darlington, *The Actor and His Audience*, London, Phoenix House, 1949, p. 170.
3. 'A Violinist', 'A Tour with CEMA' in *Our Time*, No.7, September, 1941, p. 18.
4. See 'The Arts in War and Peace', in Janet Minihan, *The Nationalization of Culture*, London, Hamish Hamilton, 1977.
5. John Casson, *Lewis and Sybil*, London, Collins, 1972, p. 218.
6. Edward J. Dent, *A Theatre for Everybody*, London, Boardman, 1945, p. 125.
7. Unity Theatre leaflet held at Marx Memorial Library, London.
8. Travis, pp. 107–8.
9. Travis, op.cit., p. 130.
10. Minihan, op.cit., p. 226.
11. Bernard Miles, *The British Theatre*, London, Collins, 1948, p. 10.
12. Donald Wolfit, *First Interval*, London, Oldhams, 1954, p. 215.
13. A.C.T. White, *The Story of Army Eduction 1643–1963*, London, Harrap, 1963, p. 112
14. N. Scarlyn Wilson, *Education in the Forces*, London: Year Book of Education, 1948) p. 70; Army Education Scheme, *Arts, Crafts, Music and Drama*, London, War Office, 1945, p. 75.
15. William Harrington and Peter Young, *The 1945 Revolution*, London, Davis-Poynter, 1978, p. 51.n.
16. T.H. Hawkins and L.J.F. Brimble, *Adult Education: The Record of the British Army*, London, Macmillan, 1947, p. 172.
17. Jack Lindsay, *After the Thirties,*, London, Lawrence and Wishart, 1956, p. 61.
18. Churchill's intervention – interview with Jack Lindsay, July 1979; Ernest Sigler quoted in Robert Hewison, , op.cit., p. 163.
19. Kemp p. 112.
20. Jack Lindsay, *British Achievement in Art and Music*, London, Pilot Press, 1945, p. 21.
21. Eric Capon, 'A Citizen's Theatre is Founded', in *Million*, Glasgow, n.d., p. 37.
22. Many are detailed in Ann Lindsay, *The Theatre*, London, Bodley Head, 1948.
23. E.g. by Lindsay, op.cit., p. 45.

CHAPTER 6

THE ROLE OF JOAN OF ARC ON THE STAGE OF OCCUPIED PARIS

GABRIEL JACOBS

By 1920, when the upsurge of interest in Joan of Arc in the second half of the nineteenth century and the early years of the twentieth had resulted in her canonisation, Joan had already long represented in France a wide spectrum of nationalistic and religious ideals. In the 1920s, she symbolised the determination of a great victorious nation, and one of the forces which had made possible the flowering of its culture and genius. She was not overlooked in the 1930s when, for instance, the banners of the extreme Left proclaimed her '[la] fille du peuple, vendue par son roi, brulée per ses pretres'.[1] Her story was nevertheless perceived at that time as rather too equivocal to be taken up with much gusto by the majority of intellectuals, even when events in Spain prompted left-wing pacifists to embrace the notion of the Just War, and right-wing Catholics to support Franco's cause as a crusade against godless communism. Being identified universally as an upholder of the doctrine of non-intervention in the affairs of other nations, unless those nations tried to annex one's own, she was probably too blurred a symbol to be of decisive benefit to either faction. But given on the one hand the strength and depth of Anglophobia in many sections of pre-war French society, soon to be sharpened by Dunkirk and Mers-el-Kébir, and on the other the reality of occupation by a foreign power, it was inevitable from the outset that Joan would be an important double figure in France between 1940 and 1944.

During the Occupation, potential comparisons between the fifteenth-century France of Joan of Arc and France's predicament after the debacle of 1940 were too striking to be disregarded even by the most unpolitical of commentators. Chanoine Glorieux, in the preface to his carefully neutral biography of Joan which appeared in 1941, was at pains to point out that although his work had been all but completed before the war, the advent of the new regime had served only to enhance the importance of its subject.[2] Mareel Vioux's 1942 *Jeanne d'Arc,* intended for popular consumption, while in no way didactic, nevertheless incorporated on its title-page Pétain's pronouncement: 'Martyre de l'Unité Nationale, Jeanne d'Arc est le symbole de la France'. In more highly-coloured Vichy-orientated propaganda, from political histories to posters, the full range of possible analogies was explored. The headlines of *le Petit Parisien* of 11 May 1941[3] – 'La France célèbre aujourd'hui la fete nationals de Jeanne d'Arc, brulée vive par les Anglais..- illustrates the way in which charged language was used to arouse feelings of revenge against the English for an event separated in time from the mid-twentieth century by half a millennium. In both zones Joan was made the epitome of the Vichy ideal. 'Comme la Romde serait fière de sa fille qui s'entendait si bien aux soins du ménage!' wrote René Jeanneret in 1942 in his life of Joan officially approved for use in schools,[4] appearing to forget for a moment the rather small role played by 'les soins du ménage' in the life of the real Joan. Joan's peasant upbringing was generally extolled as an example of the solid vigour of rural virtues, while the militant partisan in her was for the most part ignored in favour of a picture of humility and obedience. But above all she was presented as the forger of political unity at a time of grave national crisis: 'Eternel sujet d'émerveillement', exlaimed Henri de Sarrau, adding, with what now seems remarkable credulity, 'comme celui qui a placé le Maréchal Pétain à la tete de l'Etat français'.[5] Some writers presented her less as the precursor of Vichy than as the embodiment of heroic grandeur, and saw her story as the Triumph of the Will. Jean Jacoby, the author of works whose titles did not hide his political colours – *Le Front Populaire en France et les égarements du socialisme moderne, Le Déclin des grandes démocraties et le retour à 1'autorité, La Race* – was drawn to a Jeanne in whom he saw a manifestation of iron resolution and fascist vitality. In his *Scénes de la vie de Jeanne d'Arc* of 1941 he rejected Anatole France's *magnum opus* on the life of Joan on account of its author's 'sordide sectarisme' (p. 16). For him, Anatole France had hidden the true Joan, whose heart had indeed been full of charity, but who in no way had sought reform or so called social justice: 'Elle ne se plonge pas dans les masses', Jacoby insisted, 'ne spécule pas sur leurs sentiments' (p. 223).

Clandestine propaganda naturally concentrated on Joan the freedom fighter, the solitary visionary who, surrounded by the lies and deceit of her own countrymen, had in the midst of defeat liberated France from foreign occupation. In such a context, the very fact that Thomas Pugey's 1943 history of Joan was published in Switzerland by the Editions de la Baconnière,[6] whose list has already included works by Eluard, Aragon and Louis Parrot, was enough to indicate that this work was to be taken as a Resistance text, despite the fact that its content was almost wholly confined to a treatise on mystical Catholicism. It seemed natural for the Resistance to adopt the Cross of Lorraine as the emblem of Free France, and parallels were frequently drawn between De Gaulle and Joan. Was not Joan, like De Gaulle, the very opposite of the *défaitistes,* who, at best, were men who had ignominiously accepted occupation in order to salvage a small corner of French existence, while the very essence of France was being dissipated? How could one fail to see in the Armistice of 1940 an image of the Treaty of Troyes, at which defeat and occupation had been legalised? 'Aux yeux dè tons les défaitistes', proclaimed an anonymous pamphlet published in Brazil, 'Jeanne est une protestation violente, acharnée . . . Jeanne nie la défaite'.[7] But the Resistance was also obliged to diminish the fact that Joan of Arc had been burned by the English. And here, the French service of the BBC in London was in an especially sensitive position. Its broadcasters chose either to overlook this feature of the story, or to meet the problem at a tangent by arguing that England was an island outpost of Free France, like Orleans, when Joan had raised her standard.[8]

Though Joan maintained a high status, then, in most forms of propaganda, particularly during the first half of the Occupation, her fate as a theatrical character was not quite as illustrious as might have been expected. It may seem surprising, and especially so given the French dramatists' predilection for myth and legend during this period (Sartre's *Les Mouches* and Anouilh's *Antigone* spring immediately to mind), but it is a fact that no Joan of Arc play written between 1940 and 1944 was produced on the stage of occupied Paris, nor, as far as professional theatre is concerned, in the provinces. Probably the most important published play on the theme of Joan of Arc written under German occupation was *Portique pour une fille de France* by Pierre Schaeffer and Pierre Barbier. Performed by amateurs in Lyons and Marseilles in the spring of 1941,[9] it was nothing more than a stylised piece of propaganda intended for use in the *Camps de Jeunesse.* It had recourse to lines like the one used – repeatedly – by an anonymous Englishman in the play: 'Les Français sont pourris, pourris, pourris', and the published version included an appendix containing chants recommended by the authors for communal performance by an entire camp: 'Comme

Jeanne, nous croyons en la resurrection de la France' (p. 111), and
the like. The play's importance as theatre, even in the eyes of its own
creators, may be judged from the following extraordinary (if eminently practical) directive: 'Il y a lieu de supprimer entièrement le
personnage de Jeanne qui pourrait etre grotesque, tenu par un
garçon' (p. 107).

In Paris, given the ever-increasing popularity of legitimate theatre, the importance of Joan as a symbol, and the wide choice of
available pre-war plays extolling her, it might have seemed that only
glitter and stardom awaited her on stage for the foreseeable future.
She made her debut in occupied Paris in Shaw's *Sainte Jeanne* in
December 1940. This was followed six months later by an appearance in Péguy's *Jeanne d'Arc*, then in Vermorel's *Jeanne avec nous*,
which opened in January 1942. But the final performance of this
play in August of that year was also virtually the end of Joan as a
character in Parisian theatres for the rest of the Occupation.

With Ludmilla Pitoeff in the title role, Shaw's *Saint Joan* had had
its French premiere in 1925, in the translation by Augustin and
Henriette Hamon. The same text was used by Raymond Rouleau's
company, with Jany Holt as Jeanne, for the production at the Théatre de l'Avenue which ran from 24 December 1940 to the end of
January 1941. Even with the play's illustrious past, and its potential
dramatic impact (theatrically it is far superior to the efforts of either
Péguy or Vermorel), it attracted relatively little critical attention.
This may have been the result of various factors difficult or impossible to evaluate: the quality of the acting, costumes and sets, even
the temperature inside the theatre in the middle of that first winter
of the Occupation. Be that as it may, the fact that reviews are com-
paratively few and far between is certainly a measure of the lack of
serious interest, in this early period, in Joan of Arc as a symbolic
character, particularly since the play closed well before the first
Occupation Joan of Arc Day of May 1941, which was to mark the
beginning of the *Pucelle* as a true cult figure. No doubt, therefore,
the performances of the play were neither deliberately didactic, nor
deliberately contentious, nor deliberately ambiguous. Historians of
propaganda (censorship boards too) are of course faced with a
peculiar difficulty when it comes to the interpretative art of theatre,
since generally only the plain text is available for examination,
while it is obvious that all manner of signals and messages can be
made to appear when actors garnish it on the stage. And, at a distance of nearly half a century from that period of chaos and
hardship, when the last thing in a theatre director's mind was the
importance of preserving the prompter's copies of a script, the problem is compounded by the impossibility of discovering which

material was deleted, or even inserted, and at which performance. However, in the case of Rouleau's production of Shaw's *Sainte Jeanne,* it may reasonably be assumed, at least, that few cuts were made. Shaw's play is not inordinately long, and with the possible exception of the Epilogue, is sufficiently compact as it stands to sustain dramatic intensity. Moreover, its strong anti-English flavour (and the fact that Shaw was Irish was emphasised in a number of reviews of the play) had considerable appeal at the end of 1940, when Albion was still exceptionally perfidious for a part of the French bourgeois theatre-going public. Shaw's numerous references to the English probably remained intact, and indeed among the few reviewers who chose to deal specifically with what they saw as the play's contemporary significance, there was unanimous agreement that its punch came from its biting and cynical treatment of British attitudes and policies. An anonymous reviewer in *Paris Soir* (24 December 1941) contended that the original 1924 London production had flopped because English audiences had preferred the Joan of Arc of Shakespeare's *Henry VI,* 'Pièce qui se termine par d'affreuses grossièretés a l'égard de Jeanne et dont le public anglais s'est fort réjoui', and Armory in *Les Nouveaux Temps* (6 January 1941) recommended the play as a cure for Anglophilia.

The vast majority of critics, however, concentrated virtually exclusively on the literary and dramatic qualities of Shaw's play. Indeed, of all the major reviewers, only the theatre critic of *l'Illustration* (R. de B., 14 January 1941) was sufficiently jostled by it as a *pièce de circonstance* to comment on its enormous latent value as propaganda beyond that of its conspicuous anti-British ethos. For him, Shaw's Joan clearly represented on stage the creation of French nationalism; for him, she was 'miraculeuse dans la mesure ou elle a galvanisé pour un idéal un pays aveuli par la défaite'. And the play does truly abound in what might have been taken as allusions to contemporary circumstances. 'Nous avons besoin de quelques fous maintenant. . . . Voyez ou nous ont menés les sages' says Poulangy to Baudricourt (p. 20)[10] – a fine briefly noted in some reviews;[11] 'Un nouvel esprit commence a se développer chez les hommes', comments l'Archeveque (p. 49); 'Si j'étais le maitre', thunders Le Chapelain, 'je ne laisserais pas un Juif vivant dans toute la chrétienté' (p. 86). Some remarks, such as Jeanne's 'rien ne comptant, en dehors de Dieu, que la France fibre et française' (p. 216), may have sounded too much like a call to arms not to have caught the attention of the censor, but little of the play would have remained if all possible topical allusions had been removed. Shaw's Joan, in the words of Ingvald Raknem is 'a sort of intractable, intolerable, sexless suffragette',[12] but she is also plainly an apostle

of national unity and a severe critic of French attitudes, both political and military. Warwick, the only important English character in
the play not portrayed as a nincompoop, is quick to see the dangers
inherent in Jeanne's idea that the rule of the king should be
absolute, since a fragmented country makes occupation and
exploitation a relatively simple matter, while for Jeanne, says Cau-
chon, 'les gens qui parlent français constituent ce que les Saintes
Ecritures décrivent comme une nation. Appelez ce coté de son
hérésie Nationalisme, si vous voulez. . . .' (p. 110). Shaw's Joan
understands that the cause of France's defeat has been its moral
and military unpreparedness. 'Notre ennemi est a nos portes et
nous sommes la sans rien faire' she exlaims (p. 73). 'Nous faisons
les imbéciles', she says to Charles, 'tandis que les godons, eux, pre-
naient la guerre an sérieux' (p. 122) (. . . .) 'A quoi sert l'armure
contre la poudre a canon?' (p. 129). Could the audiences of the
winter of 1940 have been insensitive to such patent implications,
heavy with overtones of pre-war hesitation, infighting, self-indul-
gence and low military morale, in the face of order, discipline and
blitzkrieg tactics? It would seem that Jeanne's symbolic role was as
yet too ill-defined in the national consciousness, or the critics
unsure of how far it was appropriate to press the point home –
after all, the Hero of Verdun had not yet been pronounced the
equal of the Heroine of Orleans.

By 1941, however, Pétain had crowned Joan Queen of the New
Order, and her Day was commemorated in a burst of nationalistic
enthusiasm, 'comme le signe de la réconciliation et de l'unité
nationals retrouvées', as *L'Oeuvre* (11 May 1941) put it. De Gaulle
retaliated with the idea that between 3.00 and 4.00 p.m. on Sunday
11 May, the French should take to the streets, simply to look at each
other in silence as a gesture of solidarity with Joan and the Resistance. According to the clandestine *Libération* (18 May 1941), the
demonstration was a magnificent success, the people of Paris pour-
ing into the streets at the appointed time watched by terrified and
dismayed German soldiers who did not dare to intervene – such is
the stuff of propaganda. The collaborationist press, on the other
hand, did not need to exaggerate. In the domain of the theatre
alone, Joan of Arc Day was the signal for a salvo of special occasions throughout the provinces, while in Paris the Palais de la
Mutualité and the stage of the Comédie Française saw star-studded
casts in scenes from the major *Pucelle* plays.[13] Perhaps it was this
theatrical fervour which prompted Robert Brasillach to work on his
Procès de Jeanne d'Arc, written in dialogue form, and published in
July, and Jacques Hébertot with the Compagnie du Rideau des
Jeunes to produce Péguy's *Jeanne d'Arc* at the Théatre Hébertot

(formerly the Théatre des Arts). It opened on 23 June, with Juliette Faber in the title role.

The 1941 production of Péguy's play presents a textual problem far greater than that of Shaw's *Sainte Jeanne*. A complete performance of Péguy's *Jeanne d'Arc,* in fact three plays in one, would have lasted more than eight hours. This was cut to well under three hours 'avec le respect qu'on devine' commented *Les Nouveaux Temps* (25 June 1941) by the author's son, Marcel Péguy, but it is today impossible to know which extracts were selected for inclusion. It is certain, at least, that the production was based primarily on the original three plays of 1897: Péguy's shorter *Mystère de la charitè de Jeanne d'Arc* of 1910 consists basically of a new version of two dialogues taken from only the first play of the trilogy, but most critics in 1941 give all three plays equal weight in their reviews. It is likely that Marcel Péguy's adaptation included parts of the later version, sometimes called the 'Christian Joan' as opposed to the earlier 'Socialist Joan'. But whatever his sources, after the Liberation the uncertainty led to some mystification, to which I shall return.

Partly for his numerous writings on Joan of Arc, Péguy had been seen as a luminary by the collaborationist establishment. Alexandre Marc may well have been right in his view, expressed just before the defeat of 1940, that Péguy's Jeanne was a character alien to the followers of the Führer, for whom, as he put it, 'seule la santé importe, non la sainteté'.[14] Péguy himself was nevertheless soon to become, in the words of the collaborationist author and critic Maurice Rostand (*Paris Midi, 25* June 1941), a 'grand inspiré en qui la France s'est exprimée comme en son héroine'. Péguy was recommended reading in the youth camps of Vichy France, and schools and *Chantiers de Jeunesse* were named after him.[15] Those who before the war had seen in his portrayal of Joan anything other than the future vindication of the Vichy ideal were vigorously denounced. 'Il est facheux', exlaimed Comeau in 1942, 'que les passions politiques aient pour un temps rendu suspect . . . le message de 1'héroine chantée par Péguy.[16] Not all commentators forgot that Péguy had once espoused the cause of socialism, nor that he had been Dreyfusard, but the very fact that by 1943 Jean Variot, in a general eulogy of *Jeanne d'Arc* ' felt that it was necessary to point out that the play's author had not himself been a saint, tainted as he had been by *démocratisme and philosémitisme,* is in itself some indication of the heights to which Péguy had been elevated by Vichy.[17]

It may safely be assumed that Mareel Péguy's 1941 adaptation of *Jeanne d'Arc* was a cento reflecting this official exaltation of his father. And it is evident that the play could with little difficulty be

made to fit the circumstances. Despite the fact that it differs from
nearly all other *Pucelle* dramas in ending on an unheroic and fundamentally pessimistic note, and despite the fact that Péguy was less
interested in Joan as a maker of history and the forger of a new
France than as a victim of 'le Mal universal', his heroine is of spot-
less moral rectitude, and wages an exemplary war against the forces
of social and political disorder. And the critics, who for the most
part received the 1941 production enthusiastically, were not slow to
take note of what they saw as its contemporary significance. 'Certes,
cet ouvrage vient, ou jamais, a son heure', wrote Armory in *le Matin*
(20 June 1941); '. . . si présent, si actuel', cried Jacques Berland with
astonishment *(Paris Soir,* 27 June 1941); Claude Véré *(Semaine a
Paris,* 23 June 1941) thought the success of the play assured, since
the performers were so obviously driven by the idea of a new France
embodied in the combination of Péguy and Joan of Arc. Above all,
Péguy's heroine was taken as a symbol of strong leadership emerg-
ing from simple Christian virtues. Didier Gex *(le Matin,* 28 June
1941) saw in her 'ce génie des gens simples et droits', and Armory,
in his piece for *Les Nouveaux Temps* (1 July 1941), was struck by
Péguy's desire to produce a heroic character who remained essentially *paysanne.* But no critic dealt with one of the basic themes of
Péguy's play, that charity by itself is worthless and that one is help-
less in the face of human misery unless some effort is made to
understand and eradicate its cause, in this case the imposition of the
will of one nation on another. Jeanne comes to realise that a new
war must be waged, since the peace of occupation has resulted in
only the semblance of order, which cannot be the will of God. With
so much to cut, Marcel Péguy was perhaps able to manipulate this
theme of armed revolution, or even to purge the text of it entirely,
but this would have been difficult, and it is more likely that it
remained, and that audiences associated it with the ideals of Pétain's
National Revolution.

Now a word on the mystification mentioned earlier. In 1947 a different three-hour abridgement by Marcel Péguy (how different we
are not sure) began a run at the Théatre Hébertot to mark the post-
war reopening of the theatre. It generated a proliferation of previews
and reviews, and attracted the attention of the major critics of the
day,[18] but nowhere is any mention to be found of the 1941 production. *Samedi Soir* (27 September 1947) devoted several columns to a
history of the Théatre Hébertot, based on an interview with Jacques
Hébertot himself, but for the period of the Occupation noted only
that Giraudoux, Cocteau, Passeur and Crommelynk had been produced. Marc Beigbeder *(le Parisien Libéré,* 25 September 1947) was
so impressed by Péguy's play that he thought the delay in bringing the

1897 version for the first time ever to the Paris stage was scandalous. Marcel Péguy himself, in a piece written for the 1947 programme, commented, with a certain *équivoque*, that it was surely the length of his father's original *Jeanne d'Arc* which had prevented it from ever being performed commercially.[19] The fact that the so-called premiere of 18 September 1947 was a charity affair for the benefit of La Fédération des Maquis[20] prompted P(ol) Gaillard in *l'Humanité* (26 September 1947) to point out that Marcel Péguy's past was not without stain, since the latter had contributed to *la Gerbe* and other collaborationist newspapers, and in *Les Lettres Françaises* (25 September 1947) Gaillard remembered that this ex-collaborator had for four years promoted his father as the guiding light of the 'régime hitléro-vichyssois'. One may imagine how Gaillard might have reacted if he had known of the special performance given at the Comédie Française in June 1941 'an profit des Ecrivains Combattants',[21] but he appears to have been as unaware of the first Hébertot production as his fellow critics. It is hard not to conclude that there had been a conspiracy of silence. Was Marcel Péguy's original 1941 adaptation so obviously pro-Vichy that in 1947 he thought it best forgotten? Did Jacques Hébertot simply erase the fact of the 1941 run from his memory? Did certain critics deliberately refrain from mentioning it? If such is the case, then it was perhaps in the desire to see the rapid rehabilitation of Charles Péguy.[22]

Be that as it may, the momentum created by Shaw and Péguy in 1940 and 1941 was boosted by Claudel. In July 1941, his oratorio *Jeane d'Arc au bùcher,* with music by Honegger, began a two-month Tour de France, taking in 30 towns, covering 3,000 kilometres, and involving a special train for the actors and musicians, lorries loaded with instruments, costumes and sets, and an advance guard of administrators to organise board and lodging – all in the desire to bring to the provinces, as the author himself put it, a vision of Joan of Arc surrounded by a united France.[23] Meanwhile, rehearsals were beginning in Paris for the next production on the theme of the *Pucelle,* Vermorel's *Jeanne avec nous.*[24] The venture was rather meagrely funded, and the actors of the Compagnié du Théatre d'Essais worked without pay during the rehearsal period; but their obvious enthusiasm carried them through, and the play opened to a warm reception at the Théatre des Champs-Elysées on 10 January 1942. Towards the end of February, it moved to the Théatre de l'Ambigu, and on 26 June to the Théatre Pigalle, where it ran until August. Berthe Tissen, a formerly unknown actress, played Jeanne, and in doing so made her name.[25]

Almost nothing written about *Jeanne avec nous* during the Occupation could lead one to conclude that it was taken by audiences to

be anti-Nazi or anti-Vichy. However, in contrast to the fate of
Péguy's *Jeanne d'Arc,* the post-war reprise of Vermorel's play (in
December 1945) prompted reviewers to deal almost exclusively
with the impact and meaning it had had for occupied audiences,
and moreover to brand it the first Resistance play to be performed
in Paris. Before returning, therefore, to its 1942 reception, it is
worth examining this retrospective reaction, unconstrained as it
was by the German presence.

Only the unqualified post-war acknowledgement of the clandestine message of *Les Mouches* is comparable with that accorded to
Jeanne avec nous. The vast majority of critics present at the 1945
staging saw the play as having been, in 1942, as magnificently sub-
ordinate as Joan herself. For them, the earlier production had been
'la révolte . . . contre l'ennemi de l'extérieur', 'un beau travail de
pied-de-nez', *'a la barbe des Allemands, le procès de la collboration'*
[26] They marvelled at the apparent stupidity of the German censors.
'Comment [ont-ils] su se méprendre', asked J. Van den Esch incred-
ulously *(Pays,* 22 December 1945), 'ignorer le danger de ces
répliques capables d'arracher les pavés des rues?' Jacques
Mauchemps *(Spectateur* 2 January 1946) offered his own version of
what he imagined to have been the German censors' reasoning: 'ça,
très bonne pièce. Pièce contre Anglais. Une piece pour Jeanne d'Arc,
c'est forcément une pièce pour Allemands.' But if the Germans were
dull-witted, it seems the French were not. A large number of reviewers, though with no unbiased evidence to back their claims, affirmed
with remarkable assuredness that the 1942 audiences had easily discerned Vermorel's real message, the only possible message,
according to Thierry Maulnier *(Essor,* 19 January 1946), in an
occupied country: an indictment of the occupying power. Maurice
Delarue, one of the few 1945 critics who had seen the original production, maintained that audiences had strained to see allusions to
the Occupation and Vichy in every line delivered, and that they had
unmistakably recognised Pétain and Déat in Jeanne's contemptible
judges *(Terre des Hommes,* 19 January 1946). And Simone de Beau-
voir informs us that each burst of applause was an unequivocal
demonstration against Nazi rule,[27] though Vermorel himself
(Opéra, 19 December 1945), talks of the shiver that had run down
his spine each time the silence of the audience had highlighted a daring allusion, such as his English officers clicking their heels, or his
men of the Church referring to each other as 'camarade'.

Yet some 1945 voices were not quite in harmony with the chorus. François de Roux *(Minerve,* 4 January 1946) thought that the
censors must have given *Jeanne avec nous* its visa not only because
Joan had been burned by the English, but also because of a certain

cynicism Vermorel had put in the mouths of those judging his hero-ine at her trial.

Jean Sauvenay *(Témoigtiage Chrétien,* 4 January 1946) consid-ered that one of the distinct themes of the play was the problem of the relative merits of, on the one hand, peace bought with blood-shed, and, on the other, its less costly counterpart, that of collaboration – a problem on which, in his opinion, Vermorel had rightly declined to give guidance. And Marc Beigbeder *(les Etoiles,* 1 January 1946), while recognising that it was no doubt possible in 1942 to see Vermorel's Englishmen as Germans, and his Inquisition as Vichy, thought the textual clues to these transpositions far from obvious.

How, then, is one to decide how the 1942 audiences reacted to *Jeanne avec nous?* To begin with, by this date any play treating the Joan of Arc theme, whatever the intentions of the dramatist, would have been seen in the light of pressing contemporary concerns, so that surprise at the implications of Shaw's *Sainte Jeanne* and Péguy's *Jeanne d'Arc* had now been replaced by a sense of expectation. For *les Nouveaux Temps* (20 January 1942) Vermorel's play was 'une preuve nouvelle de l'intéret que les auteurs de la génération présente trouvent, an lendemain de nos revers, a remonter le cours de notre histoire'. What is more, the title *Jeanne avec nous,* as Michel Florisoone and Raymond Cogniat noted in their survey of the 1941–2 season, was proof that the play had been written as a com-ment on contemporary problems.[28] In that hard and disheartening winter of 1941–2, it was also to be anticipated that the critical emphasis would be firmly on heroic grandeur. In the words of André Castelot *(la Gerbe* 15 January 1942), *Jeanne avec nous* was 'une pièce écrite dans le sens de la vraie grandeur, voie dans laque-lle nous aimerions tant, en cette noire époque, voir le théatre de France s'engager'. Absent are the references to Joan's simplicity. Gone is the spate of negative Anglophobic comments: only one major reviewer, Charles Quinel *(le Matin,* 21 January 1942), thought it worth mentioning that the *Pucelle* had been burned by the English. Rather, for the 1942 critics, Vermorel's Jeanne is the incarnation of positive glory and majesty, and his play has, as Georges Pioch *(l'Oeuvre,* 13 January 1942) put it, 'cet accent sobre et fort . . . lequel vaut pour toutes les époques du monde, et sin-gulièrement pour celle où nous purgeons notre peine et le morne destin qu'elle nous fait'.

In the case of *Jeanne avec nous* it is possible to ascertain precisely the relationship between this critical reaction and the text of the play, since the first published version, dated October 1942,[29] is for all practical purposes a prompter's script, with those lines which had been excluded from the Rideau des Jeunes production clearly indicated. And it is plain from this text that Vermorel's heroine does indeed symbolise self-respect, fortitude and lionheartedness.[30] 'La France, c'est l'audace, l'orgueil, la sainte brutalité, l'héroisme', she cries to Bedfort, [sic, p. 99], a line which epitomises her outlook. Bedfort himself, a mature, pragmatic and perceptive character, is the mouthpiece for moderation, and thus collaboration. It was to be expected, he explains in a selfconscious passage about the role of Joan of Arc, that a people defeated morally and physically would snatch desperately at a symbol of hope for the future (pp. 58–9), while the *reality* of that hope was there for all to see: peace and order in the unification of two great nations. 'Allons nous vivre encore pour des générations dans cet état de guerre, de crime pas-sionel, a nous entretuer tons les vingt ans . . .?', he asks with pacifist wordly wisdom (p. 141). The 1942 audiences cannot have been insensitive to such remarks, but since they came from the mouth of one of Jeanne's oppressors, the critics seem to have been at a loss as to how they should be received, and abstained from discussing them. Only Morvan Lebesque (*le Petit Parisien,* 12 January 1942) showed any willingness to come to terms with the problem, and concluded that Jeanne's opponents 'se trompent, mais de bonne foi'. In his review, Lebesque had already made his right-wing affiliations clear by disparaging the 1936 May Day celebrations, when 'Jeanne avec nous!' had been one of the rallying cries of the Front Populaire, but had commented that Vermorel's play belied the implication of its title. The 1942 critics generally ignored aspects of the play which were manifestly an incitement to revolt against imposed order. 'Ce peuple sait encore descendre dans la rue, s'ameuter contre l'injus-tice' says the kindly Lohier (p. 81); and Jeanne's response to those who argue that her cause will throw France into chaos, is pointedly explicit: 'La terre n'est pas la pour les peuples laches, on fatigués. Et le mien tout entier n'en voulait pas de votre paix de honte.' (p. 40) *Jeanne contre nous?*

It is clear that much of the play could have been interpreted to suit one's own prejudices and preoccupations. Many of Jeanne's heroic, patriotic lines could have been interpreted equally as justi-fying the National Revolution or the cause of the Resistance. Vermorel's postwar claim *(Opéra,* 19 December 1945) that Jeanne's remark about her sovereign – 'Sa France sera grande' – had had a special impact in 1942 since the King of Bourges and General de Gaulle by coincidence shared the same Christian name, may well have been true, but Vermorel's Charles is also a buffoon. In 1945, Pol Gaillard *(les Lettres Ranéaises,* 11 January 1946) was to deride 'le triste Alain Laubreaux de *Je Suis Partout* [quil prétendait meme découvrir dans la pièce des allusions anti-soviétiques et s'étonnait avec joic de voir les juges de Jeanne s'appeler inexplicablement "camarades"!' But Laubreaux's view *(Je Suis Partout,* 21 February 1942) is perfectly understandable, even justifiable, given the black picture Vermorel paints of the Church and the Inquisition, whose members use this term in addressing one another. Patrick Marsh has argued that *Jeanne avec nous* was one of only two wartime French plays (the other being Sartre's *Bariona)* unquestionably written with the specific aim of encouraging the Resistance.[31] Yet the author *of Jeanne avec nous* himself pointed out both during and after the Occupation that he put the finishing touches to it in 1938.[32] Nor must it be forgotten that Vermorel had contributed articles to the pro-Nazi newspaper *la Gerbe,* not only as a preview to the opening of his play in 1942, but also as a critic who, the year before, had strongly attacked surrealist and avant-garde theatre.[33]

Nevertheless, if it must be accepted that the claims made by critics in 1945 and 1946, though exaggerated, contained more than a germ of truth, the scales are tipped from the point of view of the text not by the confrontation of Jeanne and her judges, and even less so by that of Jeanne and Befort (a forerunner of the equilibrium maintained by Anouilh in the contest between Antigone and Creon), but by the character of Jeanne's most dangerous enemy, the Inquisitor Lemaitre. Jacques Berland's attempt (in 1942) to classify Lemaitre's position as 'l'entêtement partisan' *(Paris-Soir,* 16 January 1942) was patently strained. Lemaltre's long and detailed accounts of the physical torture inflicted by the Inquisition (pp. 60–61, 149), little of which was cut from the 1942 production, and which read like a synopsis of Sartre's *Morts sans sépulture,* were too close to reality not to have been taken as an indictment of the methods of the Gestapo or the Milice.

Jeanne is not tortured (nor was the real Joan, though Vermorel breaks with historical accuracy in having her raped by English soldiers in her cell), but she is nevertheless very clearly the victim of a system capable of bloodcurdling atrocities carried out in the name of expediency. In effect, therefore, her role has changed, partly in the way she herself is presented, but equally within the wider symbol of the unjust and sometimes brutal treatment of innocent individuals by the State, in this case itself a puppet of a ruthless foreign regime. *Jeanne avec nous* cannot have had the immediate impact as a Resistance play implied by post-war critics, since it ran almost continuously for nearly eight months without being banned by the Propaganda-staffel or its French theatrical equivalent, the Comité d'Organisation des Entreprises de Spectacle. But the fact that it was the last major theatrical Joan of Arc venture in Paris suggests either that the censors did finally consider that the subject itself had become weighted in favour of resistance to occupation as such, or that playwrights and theatre directors suspected that the censors had come to this conclusion.[34] The double meaning *of Jeanne avec nous* did not of course prevent it from being used as collaborationist propaganda. In March 1942, for example, excerpts were performed on the stage of the Théatre de la Madeleine after Pierre Champion's lecture in the series 'De Jeanne d'Arc a Philippe Pétain',[35] and the play figured prominently in the 1942 Joan of Arc Day celebrations. Fragments of it, together with other texts on the same theme, were used as interludes for a radio broadcast entitled *Noblesse musicale de Jeanne d*'Arc,[36] and it joined the *Pucelle* plays of Sclliller, Péguy, Shaw, René Bruyez, Jean Loisy, André Villiers, François Porché and Saint-Georges de Bouhélier, from all of which works scenes were performed in a gala matinée organised in honour of Joan by the Théatre National Populaire on 10 May 1942 at the Palais de Chaillot.[37] But while Gaston Denizot of *la Gerbe* (14 May 1942), in his account of yet another celebration held at the Salle Pleyel, did not hesitate almost to echo the title of Vermorel's play in exclaiming 'Jamais la grande Lorraine n'a été plus près de nous', a curt note which appeared inconspicuously in a number of newspapers[38] signified the concern of the authorities over what Joan might have come to symbolise despite their efforts. It announced that on Joan of Arc Day, celebratory rallies or meetings of any kind were strictly forbidden. To what extent did Vermorel's *Jeanne avec nous* influence official reasoning? Since the play's message was determined largely by the preformed attitudes of its audience, Vermorel's own objectives are probably rather beside the point. But *Jeanne avec nous* caught the mood of the times, and thus no doubt contributed to the growing feeling among those in power that Joan could no longer by relied upon to be a clear symbol of the New Order.

By the middle of 1942, then, Joan had little future as a theatrical character. From then until the end of the War, her sole appearance on the Parisian stage was in a *reprise* of Claudel's *Jeanne au bùcher* on 9 May 1943. This single performance at the Salle Pleyel, with the celebrated Mary Marquet reading the part of Jeanne, and Honegger himself conducting the Orchestre National, was given to a packed house, and broadcast live on radio.[39] But Claudel's oratorio, which belongs, if anything, more to the world of music than to that of theatre, in any case left little room for any variable interpretation of its message either by performers or audience, and its 1943 production was nothing more than a last flicker of limelight for Saint Joan.

Her disappearance from the stage was not wholly reflected in other forms of communication during the second two years of occupation. As late as 1944, for example, as Allied bombings increased and preparations for invasion were known to be under way, a poster showing her manacled, behind the devastated churches and cathedral of Rouen, declared: 'Les assassins reviennent toujours sur les lieux de leur crime'.[40] But posters are not live theatre, nor, like live theatre, rich in possible ambivalence. It is perfectly understandable not only that Joan's stage career should have been the first to suffer once the tide had turned, but also that in that little Golden Age of French theatre which the Occupation produced, when one might have expected her to dominate the stage, her role appears to have been somewhat restricted. Hindsight is of course of doubtful validity: in the final account we cannot know what she truly represented for individual audiences. The very fact, for instance, that virtually all theatre critics were men must certainly have distorted for us the effect she had on the women who watched her on stage. Yet it is clear that her theatrical role changed between 1940 and 1942 in a discernible way. Always a potentially fickle symbol for those who wished to promote her as the defender of the New Order, she soon became an image of the tradition of resistance. It is only natural that it should have been the theatre, as a living happening with its close dependence on the moods and emotions of the public, that paved the way for Joan's new role after the Liberation as the champion of *l'esprit de la Résistance*.

Notes

1. See Henri Guillemin, *Jeanne dite 'Jeanne d'Arc (1970)*, p. 240. For all references in text and in notes, the place of publication is Paris unless otherwise specified.
2. Chanoine P. Glorieux, *Jeanne d'Arc, fille de Dieu* (1941), p. 5.
3. Joan of Arc Day (8 May) is celebrated on the first Sunday following 7 May.
4. *Le Miracle de Jeanne* (Tours, 1 94 2), p. 59.
5. *La Leçon* de Jeanne d'Arc, no publisher, no date [1941].
6. *Traité de l'étonnement*, 'Les Cahiers du Rhone' (Neuchatel, 1943)
7. *A Jeanne d'Arc, sainte héroine de France inspiratrice de la Résistance française*, Comité Centrale de la France Combattante an Brésil (Rio de Janeiro, 1941), pp. 5, 6. The words are those of Paul Doncoeur, and taken from his pamphlet, *Quia brûlé Jeanne d'Arc? (1931)*.
8. See the text of the broadcast made by Maurice Schumann on 10 May 1941, *La Voix de la Liberté: Ici Londres, 1940–44* (1975), p. 228.
9. See the title page of the published edition, 194 1.
10. Page numbers refer to the 1925 edition of *Sainte Jeanne*.
11. For example in *Le Matin*, 22 decembre 1940 and *Les Nouveaux Temps*, 6 janvier 1941.
12. Joan of Arc in History, Legend and Literature (Oslo, 1971), p. 195.

13. See, inter alia, le Petit Parisien, 11 mai 1941; l'Oeuvre, 11 mai 1941; and le Matin, 12 mai 1941.

14. 'Héroisme et sainteté dans le message de Péguy', *Temps Présent,* 24 mai 1940.

15. See, for example, W.D. Halls, *The Youth of Vichy France* (Oxford, 1981), p. 225, and Jean Baudéan, 'Un hérétique: Charles Péguy', *La France Socialiste,* 23 octobre 1943.

16. 'Péguy et l'ame populaire', *Les Cahiers de Neuilly, 1st cahier, 1942.*

17. Péguy was not a saint, but his wartime fate was curiously akin to that of Joan of Arc, for he was claimed as a champion by both sides: for example, it was during the Vichy adulation of Péguy that the Editions de Minuit produced the booklet *Péguy-Péri* (1944).

18. For example, Thierry Maulnier, *Spectateur,* 20 septembre 1947; Robert Kemp, *le Monde,* 22 septembre 1947 and *Une Semaine dans le Monde,* 27 septembre 1947; Francis Ambriére, *Opéra,* 24 septembre 1947; and Gabriel Mareel, *les Nouvelles Littéraires,* 25 septembre 1947.

19. The programme is in the Bibliothèque de l'Arsenal, R. Supp. 2290.

20. See J.M., *Spectateur,* 9 septembre 1947.

21. See *Paris Soir,* 27 juin 1941.

22. Whatever the explanation, the misunderstanding has persisted. As recently as 1975, in the important exhibition *Jeanne au Théatre* held in Orleans, the first performance of Péguy's play, apart from some excerpts briefly seen at the Comédie Française in June 1942, was given as the post-war Hébertot adaptation; see the *Catalogue* of the exhibition, published by the Centre Jeanne d'Arc d'Orléans (Orleans, 1976), Exhibit 88. In Hervé Le Boterfs, *La Vie parisienne sous l'occupation, II, Paris la nuit (1975),* pp. 167–8, and in Patrick Marsh's 'Le Théatre a Paris sous l'occupation allemande', *Revue d'histoire du Théatre, III,* 1981 (the entire issue), pp. 287–8, the 1941 production is given as that of the *Mystère* of 1910.

23. *Comoedia,* 12 juillet 1941.

24. See Vermorel,'Avant *Jeanne avec nous', la Gerbe,* 8 janvier 1942 and *Comoedia,* 10 janvier 1942.

25. Vermorel reported on the difficulties encountered in putting on the play, and of finding an actress for the role of Jeanne, in *Comoedia,* 10 janvier 1941. See also the issues of 28 février 1942 and 20 juillet 1942 for information concerning the successive theatres involved in the production.

26. Quotations taken respectively from Georges Grégory, *Front National,* 28 decembre 1945; J. G.-R., *Arts,* and André Alter, *l'Actualité Théatrale, 30* decembre 1945.

27. *La Force de 1'age* (1960), p. 470.

28. *Un an de théatre: 1941–42* (1942), p. 8.

29. The *achevé d'imprimer* is 26 octobre 1942. Page numbers refer to this first edition.

30. This despite Le Boterf's view of Vermorel's Jeanne as, principally, 'une fille des champs, naive . . . véritable reflet de la paysannerie française', *La Vie parisienne, II,* 194.

31. Marsh, 'Le Théatre a Paris', p. 362.

32. See *la Gerbe,* 8 janvier 1942; *Comoedia,* 10 janvier 1942; and *Opéra,* 19 decembre 1945.

33. See *la Gerbe,* 8 janvier 1942 and 2 février 1941.

34. Marsh, 'Le Théatre a Paris', p. 292, suggests that the play's run was limited to only three months *(sic)* because the censors had by then understood its real message, and in the *Catalogue* of the 1975 Orleans exhibition (see note 23) the play is described as '[une pièce] qui soulignait an temps de 1'occupation allemande le

caractère "résistant" de la mission de Jeanne, et qui fut, de ce fait, rapidement interdite' (Exhibit 124).

35. See le Petit Parisien, 14 mars 1942.

36. See Paris Midi, 7 mai 1942, and the review by Honegger in Comoedia, 9 mai 1942.

37. For details of the gala see the preview in l'Oeuvre, 6 mai 1942.

38. See, for example, le Petit Parisien, 9 mai 1942.

39. See Comoedia, 15 mai 1943. There were also single radio broadcasts of René Bruyez's, Jeanize et la vie des autres, on 8 May, and a new play on the Joan of Arc theme by Marcelle Mauriette, La Servante, on 10 May; see the previews in Comoedia, 8 mai 1943.

40. See Pierre Bourget and Charles de Lacretelle, Sur les murs de Paris et de France, 1939–45 (1980), p. 166.

PART III

THEATRE BEHIND THE WIRE

CHAPTER 7

GERMAN REFUGEE THEATRE IN BRITISH INTERNMEMT

ALAN CLARKE

On 16 May 1940, the day of the dress rehearsal for *Was bringt die Zeitung?*, a topical satirical revue staged by the Kleine Bühne (Little Theatre) of the Free German League of Culture (FDKB) in London, Manfred Fürst and Margarete Hruby – two members of the cast – were arrested and sent to internment camps. They were amongst the 25,000 German and Austrian refugees who were hauled out of their beds in the middle of the night or fetched from their workplaces, or who even delivered themselves unwittingly into the hands of the police: 'The nephew of an Ealing councillor lost a pocket-book containing over £9 in Treasury notes. It was found in a neighbouring suburb by a German, who took it to the nearest police station, where he was thanked, asked his name and detained for internment.'[1]

Under the Aliens Act of 1920 most refugees entering Britain from the Continent in the late 1930s had been classified as 'enemy aliens' of varying degrees of risk, even though the majority were fleeing from Nazi oppression. Now a large proportion of them – including women and children – were rounded up and imprisoned as part of the anti-German campaign which followed the collapse of the 'phoney war'. Initially those interned were taken to transit camps in various parts of England and Scotland where they spent days and even weeks under the most primitive conditions. Many of them were then transported to the Isle of Man, the main centre of internment, where, if they were lucky, they lived in the comparative safety of converted boarding-houses until their release a year or so later. Those less fortunate amongst the male internees were shipped as

prisoners-of-war to Australia or Canada. If they arrived safely – one
Canadian-bound transport ship, the *Arandora Star,* was torpedoed
by a German U-boat resulting in the loss of many lives – those with
money or contacts, especially in the USA, had the choice of staying
there permanently; the others had to wait cut off from the rest of the
world until they could return to the British Isles. Under such circumstances it is understandable that internees in Douglas on the Isle
of Man should use this interminable waiting as the theme of an
ironical song:

> You get used to it,
> You get used to it,
> The first years are the worst years
> But you get used to it.
> You may scream and you may shout,
> They will never let you out.
> Serves you right, you so and so,
> Well, weren't you a naturalised eskimo?
> Just tell yourself it's wonderful,
> You'll get used to it more and more and more. You'll get used to
>   it,
> But when you get used to it,
> You'll find it's just as lousy as before![2]

Conditions in the Internment Camps

Although only a fifth of those arrested were shipped overseas, the
process of confinement was for all concerned an enormous physical
and psychological burden, especially since over half of them were
more than forty years old: 'The anti-Nazis suffered both mentally
and physically. They had the indignity of being treated as enemies,
and in some cases herded with Nazi civilian prisoners while at the
same time they had no news of what was happening "outside".'[3]
Those who had previously experienced the horrors of Hitler's concentration camps feared a repetition of the same fate. During the
first weeks of the internment, many committed suicide, some even
before arriving at a camp:

> . . . a former professor of Chemistry in a German University, 62 years
> old, and an international authority on dye-stuffs . . . had been
> thrown by the Nazis into a concentration camp, and got to England
> just before the war. He was engaged in research for utilising sisal
> waste in submarines. As soon as the release Orders were enacted, the
> firm applied for his exemption from internment. But no answer had
> come from the Home Office when the Police came to his home to
> take him. He begged them to wait until the Home Office replied.

They did not; and unable to face internment again, he took poison and killed himself.[4]

Even though, despite such fears, the 'English internment camps had nothing in common with the concentration camps of the Third Reich',[5] they were still extremely unpleasant places. The large number of suicide attempts during the first weeks after arrest were a result not only of the severe mental pressures on those affected but also of the inhospitable environment presented by most of these transitional camps:

> '[The internees] were pushed into any kind of available transport, and kept for days and even weeks in shocking conditions, in prisons, camps, race-horse stands, derelict factories and half-built houses, and they had to face primitive medical, sanitary and catering conditions in a Britain on which no bombs had fallen and where there was plenty of decent accommodation available.'[6]

This treatment of German refugees, even taking into consideration the panic created in this country by Hitler's advance towards the West, cannot be fully justified, especially as British Nazi supporters were being kept in normal prisons. For some time the émigrés had to contend with such conditions as existed in the winter quarters of Bertram Mills Circus or a converted cotton mill in Lancashire: 'We've been put here in an old factory building with a lot of barbed wire and no comforts. The missing window panes cause many draughts which result in colds and sore throats, but the air in the room, in which about 300 sleep, is still bad.'[7] In a camp in Prees Heath in Shropshire, which eventually had to be closed down as a result of public protest, the internees were housed in small tents with about eighteen men in each. This 'temporary' accommodation lasted for over five weeks with the residents not only living under the most basic conditions but completely cut off from the outside world. The depressing atmosphere of this abandoned existence was captured by Kurt Barthel (Kuba) in a poem written at the time:

> 08 – that is a barbed-wire square
> somewhere in England,
> somewhere amongst the heather.
> Here the sun hurts –
> here no mornings are happy
> here the wind moans so loudly –
> camp in the heather,
> no-one knows where.[8]

Another difficulty faced not only in the transit camps but in most of the internment centres was having to live in the close proximity of German Nazi sympathisers. The tense situation in a converted

Devon holiday camp was even reported in a national Sunday newspaper:

> In this camp about half the men were Nazis, the rest decided friends of our [the anti-Fascist] cause. The Nazis were organised by a Gestapo man, and behaved with deliberate arrogance and brutality. They went about singing their bloodthirsty Nazi songs, and occasionally they even beat up Jewish internees ... Life in these conditions was scarcely endurable; there was a daily civil war in the camp.[9]

Similar situations were experienced in the women's camps on the Isle of Man where about 600 to 700 Hitler sympathisers were to be found amongst the 40,000 internees. The Nazis, who were entitled to official representation through the Swiss Embassy, frequently received additional backing from the British camp authorities:

> From the official side, the comment was made that the camp was now regarded as one for Fascists and prisoners-of-war, who were granted a great war in licence so as to encourage similar freedoms for English prisoners-of-war in Germany. If they were allowed to celebrate Hitler's birthday, we could also hope that English prisoners would be allowed to celebrate the King's birthday in Germany.[10]

The Fascists were permitted to greet each other with 'Sieg Heil', to hang swastikas from their windows and to hold 'illegal' meetings on the cliffs. 'The anti-Fascists, on the other hand, were strongly forbidden from organising any kind of meeting, defined as the coming together of more than three people at any one time, and found even their attempts to form a camp newspaper thwarted by the commander's wish to please the Nazis'.[11] Occasionally the contact with the Hitler supporters was on an even more intimate, level: 'Nazis and refugee internees are housed together. There are cases where Nazi women and refugee women have to share not only their rooms but also their beds. The Nazis threaten and terrorise the refugees ...'[12] In addition, the social and hygienic conditions were appalling. The women were not permitted to use the bedrooms during the day and therefore had to spend most of their time with their children in the overcrowded lounges of the boarding-houses. Medical care was almost non-existent, and there were cases such as a pregnant woman sharing her bed with a tubercular sufferer, and a child with chicken-pox sleeping in the same room as its mother and a ten-year-old.[13]

Most hardship, though, was probably suffered by the men deported overseas to Canada, where the authorities regarded them as genuine Nazis and treated them accordingly. At the start of the war, the British government had made secret arrangements with their Australian and Canadian counterparts to take German prisoners-of-war in case Britain should be threatened by an invasion. However, by summer 1940 only three to four thousand prisoners and Nazi civilians had been taken, so that the Home Office in London – without informing its Commonwealth colleagues – 'topped up' the numbers with anti-Fascist refugees. Thus more than two and a half thousand émigrés were shipped to Canada with prisoners-of-war and Hitler sympathisers, and almost as many again were sent to Australia on their own, as the British Government had 'run out' of genuine Nazis. This did not prevent the troops accompanying the Australian voyagers on the *Dunera* from treating their prisoners like dangerous criminals:

> Our guards would have fitted well in the SS. We were 'frisked', sworn at, kicked and crammed down below in the clammy hold like galley slaves. In this floating prison we were literally treading on each others' stomachs . . . Thus we squatted in our mass coffin, abandoned, fleeced, without shaving gear, soap, towels, clean underwear, not knowing where they intended to transport us to, with the prospect of being helplessly swallowed up, if a torpedo should hit us as had happened earlier to a transport ship bound for Canada.[14]

If, when they finally landed on 'terra firma', the Australian internees were to a great extent left alone to organise their camp life as best they could, their fellow sufferers in Canada had a far more depressing situation to overcome. They were still regarded as prisoners-of-war, had to wear the regulation trousers with the broad red stripe and the coat with the red cross on the back and endured strict military discipline. Only some months after their arrival did the Canadian authorities learn that there were anti-Fascists amongst their prisoners, but even after they had been separated from the actual prisoners-of-war the refugees' treatment did not improve much. Six of them, including the Communist Wilhelm Koenen and the actor Gerhard Hintze, who had complained about the provocative behaviour of the Nazis left in the camp, were even placed in a detention centre reserved for Italian supporters of Mussolini; only a public protest in Britain and a two-day hunger strike by the other interned refugees secured their return.[15]

Although the Canadian inmates suffered more than most, all internees went through a period of extreme hardship and deprivation. The separation from family, friends and supportive organisations, the intimate cohabitation with strangers of different outlooks, political views, religious persuasions, habits and temperaments, the lack of normal comforts, the absence of social responsibilities and useful tasks, the isolation from everyday events, the lack of information about the progress of the war and the length of their confinement – all of these factors exercised a negative influence on the state of mind of the individual internee. In addition, many of them were still suffering from the shock of the apparent betrayal by their British hosts; they had seen Britain as a last bastion against the advance of Fascism and now they found themselves amongst the first victims of the British war effort against the Nazis:

> We have been Hitler's enemies
> For years before the war.
> We knew his plans of bombing and
> Invading Britain's shore,
> We warned you of his treachery
> When you believed in peace,
> And now we are His Majesty's
> Most loyal internees.[16]

This disillusionment certainly contributed to the growing sense of abandonment which conditioned the general atmosphere in many camps. How dangerous this bitterness and isolation could be is portrayed in a short story by Jan Petersen about life in Canadian internment:

> There were many in the camp who lived an empty and sad prisoner existence, letting themselves drift unresistingly. Day by day they grew more phlegmatic. Their brains stopped working. They fell into useless and purposeless brooding and fantasising ... Earlier, in an ordered life, they had gone about their tasks and duties in an honest and conscientious way. Now the constant inactivity wore them down, physically and morally. Their thoughts were sluggish and filthy like swamp bubbles. Soon they had only one topic which they varied incessantly, greedily and consummately: women.[17]

It was against such negative manifestations and outlooks that the more positively minded members of the interned community directed their efforts.

Art and Culture in the Internment Camps

The problem of poor morale amongst the internees was the most immediate concern during the first weeks of internment. Suddenly the norms of civilian life had no more validity, and it was crucial therefore to establish alternative codes of communal behaviour appropriate to the new circumstances, with set routines and collective self-discipline. At first individual, communities attempted to establish some order for themselves:

You will understand that it was only through great comradeship and understanding that the nervousness and irritability amongst the internees could be reduced to a minimum. Eight men crouching together in a small tent day and night, especially when it's raining! In my tent . . . we are at least trying to bring some order to this chaos. 2 to 3 in the afternoon is always quiet time in our tent; each of us can occupy ourselves on our own, sleep or read, or even both together; talking is strictly forbidden and visits, even the most urgent ones, are unwelcome.[18]

Later on, larger management committees were formed to establish similar routines for the whole camp. But creating calm and order 'at home' solved only a part of the internees' problem. The various social, educational and cultural needs of the prisoners also had to be satisfied, and it is interesting that a very similar process of setting up appropriate structures occurred in almost every long-term centre. Firstly, groups were established to cope with the overall organisation of the camp and the catering arrangements, closely followed by a cultural committee and the camp newspaper. A variety of such 'journals appeared – many simply as wall newspapers when the shortage of paper prevented a wider circulation such as the *Moragh Times, Onchan Pioneer* and *Frauenruf* on the Isle of Man, the *Stacheldraht* in Canada and the Australian *Camp News*. Ironically, the one aspect usually missing from these news-sheets was up-to-date information on the progress of the war outside; the general ban on news information meant that the occasional press items obtained through a sympathetic camp commander, or more usually by illegal means, were in great demand: 'In many camps the ban on newspapers was overcome by smuggling, and in one camp at least a 'black exchange' developed. A newspaper could be hired for ninepence for a quarter of an hour.'[19]

Alongside the camp journals, modest libraries were set up as well as the popular schools and 'universities'. Given the large number of middle-class intellectuals amongst the émigrés – in one English camp, for example, there were, '3 Nobel Prize winners, 20 Oxford professors and many world-renowned specialists'[20] – the staffing of these 'educational institutions' was usually of a very high standard. Courses were offered in a wide range of subjects from Darwinism to the history of the Middle Ages, the syllabus of one Canadian 'high school' including Arabic, sociology, machine construction and journalism.[21] The education of the younger internees was of particular concern, and many specialist courses and even a 'youth university' were organised to help them complete studies which had been interrupted by their arrest; some were even able to take their matriculation exams whilst still interned.[22] Even more worries were created by the young girls in the women's camps on the Isle of Man: 'They had been taken away in the middle of their training or from school. Because of a reluctance to force them to work or study, they were in real danger of frittering away their time amidst the uncontrollable influences of the peculiar atmosphere of the camp.'[23] Again the activists amongst the internees made every effort to counter such tendencies. An experienced teacher founded a school which became 'the centre of a moral and cultural social life attracting many young and not-so-young women and enabling them to develop their talents'.[24] Many girls worked in the 'kindergartens' (in one camp a deserted golf clubhouse was converted for the purpose) or took part in specially organised youth clubs.

Alongside such educational offerings, sport was also very popular in many centres, with regular competitions between teams of internees, like the football tournament in the Australian Hay Camp. Later on, as the conditions in internment gradually improved and the external restrictions on the prisoners were relaxed, possibilities of earning money arose through the sale of hand-made objects, especially toys, to the guards. In some places workshops and even factories were set up, as in Farnham Camp in Canada where camouflage nets, tables and boxes were produced for the army.[25] All these activities helped to encourage more positive attitudes within the camps and prevented the majority of the internees from becoming too introspective.

Within this process, the arts also had a crucial role to play, as Rudolf Steiner pointed out in the Australian internment newspaper, *Camp News*: 'Art is the expression of the social order from which it emerges . . . The artist's freedom is his sense of distance from this world . . . Adapting these principles to the world [of the internees] results in the artist facing up to a totally new challenge. His [old] world has ceased to exist, he must find his feet in the new one.'[26] In particular, this meant tackling the wider issues raised by a life of internment: the individual's relationship to the camp community as a whole, and the camp's attitude to the outside world. Artistic activities, both of an individual and a collective nature, were particularly suited to overcoming the most negative aspects of life in a densely populated environment. Thus, together with the other main features of camp organisation which sprang into being almost as soon as the refugees settled in, live entertainment and cultural events were soon on offer. In one Canadian camp even a Director of Entertainment Operations was appointed.[27] But if such developments were usually welcomed unreservedly by the majority of the camp population, a few negative voices were raised about whether art was of any use in the internment context. 'F.K.' in *Stacheldraht*, the news-sheet produced in Farnham camp, complained that such activities were only acceptable in a stable environment where a reasonable aesthetic *niveau* could be achieved:

> Two years of internment have led to one positive experience: culture can neither be maintained nor grow without liberty ... In consequence culture in [Farnham] was a poor worn-out and underfed lady. If you looked carefully you could even detect some resemblance to life in the Germany of today ... it soon became clear that men deprived of their liberty cannot stick together in order to live up to a standard of culture. . . .[28]

Attitudes like this not only indicated a highly elitist approach to artistic creativity which ignored the harsh conditions in which the artists had to function, but also treated culture as the *aim* of a community rather than a means of improving its spiritual and moral well-being. In contrast to such a blanket condemnation of the creative work undertaken in internment – 'the shows were poor and the last one a too, too realistic picture of the standards mingled in our camp'[29] – the editor of *Stacheldraht,* Freimut Schwarz, provided a very different assessment of the cultural life in Farnham:

> Even when you free yourself totally from the norms of the prison camp and base your judgement on the standards of normal life, the cultural activities achieved in internment must be viewed with astonishment. Despite working under the most unfavourable conditions, despite the primitive and often inadequate means at their disposal, the results do not compare unfavourably with the standards achieved 'outside'.[30]

An even more authoritative source is the artist John Heartfield, whose critical assessment of an art exhibition of works produced by those in Canadian internment emphasised how successful they were in overcoming their depressing circumstances:

> ... to be honest we are amazed. Although we were assured that this was not and could not be an art exhibition in the proper sense of the word, but rather a display of products made under the most primitive and unfavourable conditions – we would nevertheless like to comment that the majority of the works exhibited had nothing to fear from a critical appraisal.[31]

Whatever the arguments about the quality of work produced – and the proven reputations of so many of the interned artists as well as some of the poems, stories and drawings which have survived would tend to support Heartfield's evaluation – the breadth of creative output was immense. Poetry, paintings, sketches, music and sculpture were produced; concerts, theatre productions, dance performances and art exhibitions put on; and a whole range of handicrafts undertaken. In one camp Hans Joss Rehfisch formed a literary circle, in another Kurt Jooss put together a male 'corps de ballet'; Rawicz and Landauer started their famous piano partnership, and the Amadeus String Quartet first got together in internment; the former owner of a craft shop opened a weaving school; in the guest-houses of the Isle of Man pianos were 'borrowed' and an orchestra called into being; overseas, the presence of rare woods led to the production of exotic carvings.[32] If professional artists were in short supply, amateurs filled the gap, as in Wharf Mills.[33] And all this took place in an environment described as 'highly unsuitable for artistic creation'[34] where few of the normal prerequisites for such work were to be found: rehearsal spaces for drama and dance, paper, paint and tools for painting and sculpture, instruments and sheet music for the musicians, and copies of scripts for play productions and readings.

In addition, the internees often faced the discrimination and prejudice of the camp authorities, who in some cases openly sympathised with their Nazi co-prisoners. In Port Erin anti-Fascists were forbidden to view certain films which might 'provide the enemy with information', yet were allowed to see the anti-Communist movie, *Comrade X,* much to the delight of the Hitler supporters.[35] In the transit camp at Huyton, an open-air concert for the internees was stopped by the commander when his guards 'came along and listened, joined in and clapped applause'.[36] In other camps, recitals and sketches in the German language were banned by suspicious officials.

Yet despite such restrictions a colourful cultural life developed in most places, with the majority of non-Fascist internees involved as active participants or enthusiastic spectators. The effect of such events on even the most isolated of prisoners was sometimes impressive. Jan Petersen tells of a strongly built yet not especially bright sailor in Canadian internment who found it difficult to establish contact with his fellow captives:

When a 'cabaret performance' was organised in the camp to alleviate the bleakness of the camp existence for a few hours, he announced: 'I'd like to do something too!' – 'Very well, what?" he was asked. 'Bend iron!' was his answer. Heads shook in amusement and puzzlement; still, a place was found for him in the programme. When it came to his turn, he walked relaxed and quiet to the small improvised stage, placed a finger-thick iron bar between his teeth, bit on it and – bent it crooked with his huge fists. Neither before or after his feat did he say anything. But as he was thanked with laughter and handshakes, his constantly indifferent and unmoving face lit up.[37]

Even though all successes were not quite so identifiable, the consistent efforts of the committed anti-Fascists to involve their fellow sufferers in artistic activities seem to have been a crucial factor in maintaining morale. This is reflected not only in the quantity of the creative work produced in internment but also the subject matter chosen by the artists. Max Zimmering identified three main themes running through this interned art: the refugees' concern with their cultural heritage, problems relating to their confined existence, and their relationship to events 'on the other side of the camp gates'.[38]

For the émigrés the problem of their cultural background, both during internment and later, was a highly controversial subject with a wide variety of views and interpretations laid upon it: '[The concept of a German cultural heritage] can be interpreted very broadly . . . it encompassed a period stretching from German classicism to Hitler's accession to power, because for many culture had ceased to exist with the start of the Third Reich'.[39] This attitude, stemming from an understandable desire to reject the perversion of German culture under the Nazis, was opposed by most of the active anti-Fascists. They pointed out that it ignored the efforts made by the anti-Hitler artists since 1933 and negated the possibility of using the humanist cultural traditions of the German people in the anti-Fascist struggle.[40] At the same time the creations of the past were also seen as sources of inspiration for present-day efforts; the question of heritage was not only the concern of great artistic works but also of modest informal performances, like the impromptu musical soirées:

> When we sing together in the evening, the difference between the Viennese and the Berlin way of saying 'I' doesn't matter . . . Even those who are afraid that every German song has to be a Hitler song, join in with us when we start up the *Song of the Peatbog Soldiers* or when we sing other marching or youth songs . . .[41]

From such experiences the impulses were found to renew the anti-Fascist fight in the cultural field. The close relationship between the cultural traditions of the past and their continuation in internment was reflected in the juxtaposition of performances of classical writers with topical cabaret, which featured in most camp entertainment programmes, or even, as in this example from Onchan Camp in the Isle of Man, with writings by the internees themselves: in October 1940, Peter Ihle and Erich Freund presented extracts from the works of world-famous authors from Aristotle to Thomas Mann under the title 'In Praise of Freedom', while later in the same week Freund also read a selection of poems by the 26-year-old Kurt Barthel (Kuba).[42]

If the respect for German culture was interpreted in different ways, so too was the problem of how to handle attitudes towards the harsh realities of camp life. The senselessness of their enforced confinement obsessed many émigré artists, especially amongst the painters and poets. John Heartfield commented that some of the pictures produced by those in Canadian internment were 'pervaded with a pessimistic tone',[43] whilst an impressive poem, again from Canada, also reflects this feeling of abandonment:

> They stand still by the fence. Sweeping softly
> The evening sinks behind the distant town.
> The quiet songs they are singing
> Are like bright flowers on a forgotten grave.
> They see the bayonets flashing on the barbed wire.
> In the wind many silent longings drift across the field
> To women, who sit in empty rooms
> And wait for them out there in the world.
> Did they weep for long when they had to go?
> In that sad departure how much remained unspoken -
> How often did the boy in his barely conscious
> Senses ask uneasily after his father.
> Then the shrill siren shrieks loud and harsh from the yard.
> The last look waves a greeting to the town in the cast
> Then the prisoners' feet shuffle to roll-call.
> Night is here. And before the gates treads the heavy step of the sentry.[44]

It was understandable that many artists should concern themselves with their immediate surroundings; the danger was that in concentrating on camp reality alone they could easily lose sight of the wider perspective. To avoid this the active anti-Fascists stressed the importance of dealing directly with the world outside the barbed wire. The demand for special treatment and a return to normal life was, according to Freimut Schwarz, one of the main themes of internment art and literature, for despite the imprisonment there remained 'a kind of dialogue between the internees and the . . . authorities, which was never quite broken and finally led to their release'.[45] Such an approach did not always meet with approval or understanding:

> The criticism often raised about art in interment is that its concern with themes [Other than those of camp reality] represents a flight from the present. This is unjustified; most of the positive achievements arose in an atmosphere of strong moral dissatisfaction . . . Internment remained [for the anti-Nazi refugees] bitter and unsatisfactory, but far stronger was their determination to participate in the reality on the other side of the barbed wire. Hence the 'flight' from the narrow reality of the internment camp to the reality of the outside world.[46]

This determination led inevitably to active support of the war effort, especially after the entry of the Soviet Union into the war. If the

formation of a Pioneer Corps in Huyton Camp by a nephew of Sig-
mund Freud was felt by many not only to be an underhand way of
avoiding deportation but a denial of the rights of the German
refugees to fight against Hitler as equals,[47] the desire to give active
support to the anti-Fascist struggle was never lost. This is reflected
both in the content of interned art – such as Carlo Pietzner's large
painting 'Coventry', reacting to the senseless destruction of that historic English city [48] – and in the context, such as the participation of
actors and musicians in 'Aid for Russia' concerts.[49] This influence is
also noticeable in artistic representations of camp life, like Max
Zimmering's poem 'Tower of Refuge' or a drawing from Canada
which strongly impressed John Heartfield:

> . . . most of the [works] . . . betrayed the unshakeable determination
> best expressed in the words: 'Nothing will nor can grind us down!' A
> drawing seemed to me to characterise this attitude. It could be seen
> in an outspread camp newspaper. A long path, leading deep into the
> distance, fenced in on both sides by high barbed wire. In the fore-
> ground we saw, stooping and with heavy steps, a prisoner walking.
> On the back of his uniform the large red mark which the inmates of
> Canadian camps have to wear. At the end of this long path of suffer-
> ing, a radiant sun is shining. This drawing seemed to me a symbol for
> us all.[50]

Internment Theatre

Within such a situation, theatre was particularly suited both to assist
in combating defeatism and isolation and to encourage a more
responsible and outward-looking attitude. Its collective nature –
both in the production process and the method of reception – helped
the internees to create a communal spirit; its *immediacy* discouraged
the tendency towards introspection or hopelessness; the synthesis
involving other art forms in set and costume, musical accompaniment and literary texts supported the sense of common purpose; and
its facility for dealing directly with the social and political issues
which most concerned the interned population made it a key element
in sustaining morale. An impressive range of theatre performances
took place in the camps: one-man shows, Punch and Judy, revues,
sketches, readings from the classics, as well as the regular productions of short plays or even full-length dramas. In Farnham Camp,
on the other side of the Atlantic, the internees put on more than ten
theatre and cabaret productions during their 13-month stay; in
Hutchinson Camp, on the Isle of Man, seven full-length plays were
staged in 1941 alone, and in the women's camps there at least two
plays and numerous informal performances were organised. Only in

the transit camps were productions limited, mostly to smaller-scale cultural events, although at least two original and important performances emerged in Huyton.

The most unusual theatre venue, however, was between decks on the transport ship *Dunera,* taking 2,500 internees to Australia. Recitals from the works of Goethe, Schiller and Heine together with more modern authors like Kästner, Tucholsky and Weinert were complemented by the setting up of an Austrian cabaret club, the 'Interndl' – named after the popular London émigré theatre, the Laterndl.[51] Here, as elsewhere, the main aim was to counter the heavy physical and psychological pressures of a prison existence, particularly aboard a vulnerable floating target in the midst of war: 'The driving-force behind these activities was only to a small extent the desire for self-gratification; it was much more what I would call a sense of social responsibility.'[52] Thus Max Zimmering saw the contribution of the theatre activists in internment, and it was usually those artists who, like him, had already been involved in refugee organisations like the Kulturbund or the Austrian Centre who initiated such performances.

Whilst those on dry land did not have to rely for their material quite so exclusively on 'what existed in the heads of the thespians, could be drawn out of the memories of literary colleagues or retained by writing it down on toilet paper with smuggled-in pencils',[53] the problem of suitable texts was still acute. Where a writing talent existed amongst the internee population, he or she was encouraged to produce work for the stage: in Huyton, Kuba created an original drama; in Australia, regular writers' evenings were arranged, and Max Zimmering provided many of the sketches for the ever-popular revues; in Canada, Paul Dornberger wrote two new plays. Other performances were based on adaptations from favourite books which had survived the many searches and adventures undergone by the internees since their arrest. Occasionally, material sent by friends and supporters back in England, like the FDKB's 'Kunst und Wissen' which regularly reproduced short scenes and sketches, proved suitable for production. More rarely, a sympathetic camp commander was willing to assist in acquiring play-texts. Even so, the selection was very limited and dependent on chance. The importance placed by the anti-Fascists on obtaining suitable plays is shown in a letter written by Wilhelm Koenen from Canadian internment to Thomas Mann in New York requesting copies of dramas, including Brecht's *Fear and Misery of the Third Reich.* [54]

The lack of scripts did not, however, prevent the development of a lively theatre scene in almost every camp. Although the concrete conditions varied from place to place, the general circumstances under which productions took place were similar everywhere. A satirical account of the process is provided by Gerry Wolff, later a leading performer in the GDR but then a member of the Hutchinson Camp drama group:

> It's very simple: you take 1. producer; 2. several copies of a play; 3. a dozen or so people suitable to act the parts; 4. technical staff (actually you can dispense with that but it looks well); 5. draw money from the immense funds of the theatre groups for [paints], costumes, etc.; 6. get a quietly situated hall for rehearsals and 7. get to rehearsing.[55]

Of course, as Wolff knew only too well, the reality was very different with – personnel apart – everything in short supply. To compensate for this lack, a great deal of imagination and improvisation was needed, and the delight in experimentation was, as Freimut Schwarz noted, one of the most important and productive features of the camp theatres.[56] This applied in particular to the creation of sets and other technical effects: in Huyton, great pleasure was taken in the stage curtain with the traditional laughing and crying masks surrounded by barbed wire – cut out of gold and silver paper and stuck on an ordinary black blanket.[57] In Australia, a stage workshop was organised which provided a splendid set for R.C. Sherriff's *Journey's End* 'where at the end the trenches collapsed to perfection'[58] and in Canada, the internees constructed their own stage and devised an original way of portraying God in the 'Prologue in Heaven' to Goethe's *Faust:* 'A piece of board was removed from the false ceiling in the recreation hut and an actor installed above it under the roof; the Divine Voice came booming through the gap.'[59] Such effects, created out of virtually nothing by the painters, sculptors and craftsmen in the camps, made a great impression on their fellow inmates. The technology in the Australian production of *Faust* does, though, seem to have got slightly out of hand: 'If [the] 'Hallelujah' didn't have quite the desired impact, this lay in the disruptions from which the scene suffered, particularly the unsuccessful lighting effects. Where the required impression cannot be obtained with existing, let alone non-existent, means such experiments should be avoided.'[60]

In general, however, the theatre practitioners in internment seem to have accepted the limitations of their situation, and the technical input in most productions provided an enriching contribution. Even then, the onus was placed chiefly on the skills of the actors, amateur and professional, including veteran performers of the London refugee stage like Josef Almas, Gerhard Hinze and Erich Freund, and newcomers like Wolff and Michael Mellinger. As well as enthusiasm and talent, great versatility was demanded as is shown by

Otto Tausig, who in Hutchinson Camp within the space of a few months appeared in the title role of *Schwejk,* as Dr Bull in *The Man Who Was Thursday,* as Daja in *Nathan der Weise,* as Franz in *Die Raüber,* and as Mrs Barthwick in *The Silver Box.*

This last role highlights a particularly delicate area – the portrayal of the female characters. Where possible this was avoided by putting on plays with all-male casts, such as *Journey's End,* or by keeping the character off-stage, as in the Canadian version of *Faust:* 'The absence of a suitable boy to play Gretchen caused a trickier problem. It was decided to present her voice only. When Faust first meets her in church, and later in her home, she was simply heard, through an open door. It was not hard to cast a suitable falsetto voice to speak her lines.'[61] in other cases, where an appearance could not be avoided, great tact and restraint were needed. In Hutchinson, the director, Fritz Weiss, succeeded in sending 'women' onto the stage 'who did not arouse the slightest feeling of embarrassment which could so easily arise from such masquerading',[62] and Jacques Bachrach seems to have had a similarly sensitive approach in Australia. In Canada, on the other hand, where the 'women problem' was particularly acute and homosexuality a real if temporary issue,[63] the appearance of 'stage females' often made a dubious impact, especially when the effect was heightened by elegant dresses put together from old sugar sacks by a specialist tailor, and make-up obtained through the auspices of a friendly camp commander: 'With open mouths and staring eyes many internees sat through the performances, never letting their attention drop from the 'female' performers. One of these amateur actors thought to have some fun out of his success. He carved wooden shoes with thin, very high heels and strutted about the camp, wiggling his behind.'[64]

Another general worry for the theatre groups was the organisation of rehearsal space, as the recreation rooms, lounges and other possible locations were seldom free with, as Wolff comments, 'somebody ... sure to [be playing] ping-pong ... and four pianos ... going at the same time.'[65] The premiere of *Journey's End* in Australia, for example, had to be postponed for a few weeks because the mess-hut was being used for Jewish holiday celebrations.[66] Rehearsal possibilities, despite the large amount of free time available, were thus rather restricted: for the last week of the production of *Of Mice and Men* in Hutchinson only twenty hours could be set aside, including time for costume calls and dress rehearsals.[67] But despite these difficulties, the theatre performances were high points in internment life, awaited by the camp population with great expectancy, even if some of the accompanying manifestations were less desirable:

Whether it was an expression of enthusiasm for the theatre or the result of 'whisper campaign' which preceded the [premiere] – in any case good seats could fetch on the black market up to ten shillings. It should be emphasised that tickets had been produced without expense by potato print and distributed in equal numbers to the barracks with democratic fairness. But even here well-to-do connoisseurs and snobs who had to experience the première under any circumstances from the front row.[68]

Even this could not diminish the effectiveness of the camp productions, reflected not only in the critical reviews in the camp newspapers but also in the huge popularity which the performers enjoyed amongst their fellow inmates: 'No public is so grateful as that behind barbed wire. We, the members of the camp stage, became popular overnight.'[69]

'Septembertage' in Huyton Camp

The temporary nature of most of the internment camps in England was a strong factor in determining the kind of cultural and performance work undertaken there. Most of the events were spontaneous, improvised affairs, often initiated by the younger prisoners who were able to adapt more quickly to this new kind of existence: 'Even in a camp like Kempton Park, the youth group was able to organise concerts cabarets and similar social activities.' [70] Most performances remained at this impromptu level, often centred round individual artists like Hugo Baruch and his spontaneous cabarets.[71]

Open criticism of the state of affairs in the transit centres was usually too risky, so a number of clandestine gatherings were organised where political recitations and sketches were performed. Another way of 'rebelling' against the camp restrictions was discovered at Huyton: one of the cooks found a hidden cider store and, during the regular *Hausabende* which took place in the communities with more spacious living-rooms, he served this up as soup to the prisoners, thus allaying the suspicion of the guards.[72]

It was also at Huyton that two of the most original and ambitious theatrical projects occurred, both involving the young Communist poet who later became a major figure in the literary scene of the German Democratic Republic, Kurt Barthel. Kuba, as he was known, was responsible for the direction of *Böhmische Passion* by Louis Fürnberg, with whom he had earlier run an anti-Fascist theatre troupe in Czechoslovakia.[73] The play depicted recent Czech history through a combination of strong poetic images relating the struggles of the ordinary Bohemian people and highly satirical portrayals of the leading politicians involved. Eugen Brehm, who witnessed at least two productions of the piece, found this mixture of 'art and kitsch' puzzling and even accused Kuba of distorting the original for his own political ends.[74] Apart from the fact that such a mixture had been a feature of the earlier collaboration between Kuba and Fürnberg, this technique of adopting different styles to contrast historical figures with ordinary people is not unique – around the same time in America Bertolt Brecht was toying with a similar idea in his adaptation of Hasek's classical novel which later developed into *Schwejk in the Second World War,* in which a stylised depiction of Hitler is counterpointed by some of Brecht's most lyrical songs. Unfortunately little is known of the production of *Böhmische Passion* in Huyton except that it must have had a cast of at least thirty to forty actors, for Brehm noted almost a dozen leading roles (although some may have been doubled up) as well as a number of speech choirs *(sprechchöre).* This would make it the largest dramatic enterprise undertaken during the internment period.

Whilst Brehm found Fürnberg's play, for all its apparent contradictions, at least intriguing, he dismissed Kuba's *Septembertage* as a 'hurriedly put-together agit-prop play of the smoothest kind, having an impact only on the converted, but being totally incomprehensible for the mass of Jewish internees born in Germany'.[75] A full account of the production in *Freie Deuische Kultur,* the magazine of the FDKB, presented a very different picture: 'In my life I have often visited the theatre and seen many great artists and wonderful productions, but one of the deepest impressions which I have experienced was a production by the Youth Group in Huyton Camp.'[76]

The following description of the play by the anonymous Kulturbund critic supports the impression that we are dealing here with an original and important contribution to the refugee theatre in British exile. The story concerns a group of young people living in the border area of the Sudetenland, the German-speaking part of Czechoslovakia, which was under threat of annexation by Hitler:

Hidden in the woods the youngsters . . . wait on guard . . . In vain [the Nazi Stormtroopers] try to force them out of hiding, the village remains united, they are not found . . . [The boys] have formed a singing group, Das neue Leben (The New Life), and have been performing in the surrounding villages, but now times have become too serious, they want to give up singing, the moment for fighting approaches. Then a telegram calls them to Prague, they are to sing on radio and through this show how for centuries the Sudetenland has

been culturally linked with the Czech land ... (They sing on radio
and the whole country hears them.) But it is too late, the surrender
has already been agreed. They return home but the invasion has
begun. They want to fight ... but the order comes: 'Shooting Forbidden. Lay down your arms.' Now they know they have lost – they
are hunted, they have to flee. But they swear to continue the fight
until the day comes when they can return home.[77]

Clearly the play is more than just a smooth piece of agit-prop theatre, it works on a number of levels. Historically, it presented
experiences that only a year before many of the refugees had
directly undergone themselves – the autobiographical connection is
further underlined by Kuba using the same name, 'Das neue Leben',
as that of the drama group he and Fürnberg had run in Czechoslovakia[78] – and most of the audience had had to face up to the
consequences of a Fascist invasion. At the same time such personal
identification with the immediate past was set in a wider perspective, enabling the internees to draw parallels with their present
predicament especially the frustration of not being able to play a
direct part in the anti-Fascist struggle. And although in the end the
youngsters are defeated, the overall impact of the play comes not
from the uselessness of their efforts but from their determination to
continue the fight against overwhelming odds. This impression
would have been heightened by the presence of many survivors of
these events and the fact that, however belatedly, the Nazi advance
was being challenged by the major international powers.

Underlying the immediate political concern, however, was a
more general theme which occupied German refugee artists in all
places of asylum: the role of art and culture in the struggle against
Fascism. This aspect was treated in *Septembertage* in three ways:
through the plot, the form and the context. The question of *Kunst
oder Waffen?* (Art or Weapons?) is a dominant concern running
right through the play. It is not, though, treated in a mechanical or
dogmatic way but shown dialectically, with the balance between
the two alternatives constantly shifting according to the prevailing
circumstances. At the start, the young people are committed equally
to both: preparing to defend their country at the same time as using
their musical talents to gain support in the surrounding villages; the
more imminent the invasion, the more important their military
preparation becomes at the expense of their music; but when it is
made clear that their singing can also contribute positively to the
anti-Nazi struggle, they seize the opportunity readily; when even
this fails, a last desperate attempt at armed opposition is made;
finally, both art and arms prove useless, though for the future neither is ruled out. Whilst in the story definite choices have to be

made, they are never shown as absolute and any overall conclusions are left open for the audience to debate.

The discussion about the function of art was supported in the action by a number of concrete examples, illustrating the various ways in which it could contribute to the political struggle. Within the overall framework of a dramatic presentation, song, music, poetry, sketches and even classical theatre combined to form an organic entity. The individual elements, whilst often making particular points in their own right, were only fully effective within the total concept. Thus an early inclusion of readings from *Romeo and Juliet* both introduced a thematic parallel to the immediacy of the situation and raised the question of the relevance of more formal art forms to the current struggle; later, the combination of Kuba's poems and Czech folk songs for the radio transmission underlined both what would be suppressed under Fascism and what had survived over the centuries and would continue to survive in exile; and even the broadcast itself was directly linked in the minds of the audience with the German-language programmes being sent by the BBC to the Nazi-occupied regions.

And, of course, the whole production itself represented the triumph of art over the depressing conditions of the transit camps as well as the internees' recent experiences of sudden arrests, attempted suicides and general abandonment. Although the storyline alone cannot fully convey the impact of the live event, a few examples from the review in *Freie Deutsche Kultur* suggest that, in this respect too, something special occurred at Huyton. The build-up to the radio transmission, for example, indicates a sensitive handling of the dramatic presentation: 'The next scene shows us the youngsters in front of the microphone. Nervously they enter the broadcasting station, the technical apparatus makes them shy. They are told what they have to do, their fear falls away and they sing out confidently. In a wonderful montage of poems and folk songs and a sketch they show the unity of their land with Prague.'[79] Another powerful moment was when a sympathetic gendarme gave the youngsters rifles and a machine-gun and showed them how to use the weapons; as one of the boys aimed at the audience, 'the expression of hatred on [his] face [was] shocking'. If the ending seems somewhat sentimental for present-day tastes, the feelings aroused in the audience were appropriately mixed: sadness yet hope, isolation yet togetherness, loss yet gain, defeat yet victory:

> The play ends with a melodramatic poem which Kuba spoke from behind the stage in the dialect of his homeland, the youngsters humming a simple tune, the stage darkened, and the last words were:

'Mein guter alter Aschberg
Wir kummen wieder z'samm.'
'My dear old Aschberg,
We'll meet again some day.'[80]

Probably more than any other production put on by German-speaking refugees in British exile, *Septembertage* encapsulated the totality of their experience, including the will to survive and the hope of returning eventually to a peaceful homeland.

'Thunder Rock' on the Isle of Man

In strong contrast to the limited number of major productions in the transit camps on the mainland of Britain, the theatre activity on the Isle of Man was characterised by the large amount of serious drama performed there, as well as a variety of other live theatre events. The rationale behind such offerings as the Austrian actor Peter Herz pointed out – was not as light-hearted as it may have appeared: 'I tried at the time within my immediate circle to fight against the depressing atmosphere of the camp by forming the 'Stacheldraht Cabarett' . . . through which new hope, fresh optimism and even a little joy could be planted in the hearts of the abandoned internees.'[81] Amongst the many cabaret offerings, individual artists were prominent, like Peter Pojarski, whose *Galgenhumor* is described in Richard Friedenthal's novel *Die Welt in der Nußschale*, and was directed amongst other sensitive targets at the monotonous culinary offerings, the state of camp hygiene, the poor postal service and even the camp authorities. [82] At the other extreme was the bilingual revue *What a Life!*, premiered in September 1940 under the direction of G.M. Höllering – previously a collaborator on Brecht's film of Berlin working-class life, *Kuhle Wampe*, and later to become the owner of the Academy Cinema in London. Originally suggested by the camp commander, the show covered ten aspects of interned existence and was so popular with the British officers that it had to be repeated.[83] Such activities continued even as late as summer 1941, when most internees felt as if they already had one foot outside the barbed wire and camp life had become somewhat nervy'.[84] In August, as part of a cultural programme organised by the 'Popular University', Arthur Hellmer directed the Prologue from *Faust,* an extract from *Wallensteins Lager* was put on, and the mechanicals' scene from *A Midsummer Night's Dream* performed.[85] In November Hans J. Rehfisch even managed to organise a full-scale production *of Julius Caesar* at the Gaiety Theatre in Douglas.[86]

In the women's camps too, regular theatre events took place. In Port Erin, Luise Astmann put on a puppet show, *Geographie und Liebe,* a 'topical island play in classical guise'; [87] traditional 'Weihnacht' celebrations included an ambitious attempt to 'combine a macabre drama with the Christmas story';[88] and even serious plays like the medieval morality, *Everyman,* and a free interpretation of *Turandot* by Maric Reidemeister were attempted.[89] As in the other camps, the concern was not merely to pass the time agreeably; political considerations could also play a part, as in an afternoon cabaret put on by the 'Youth Players' in front of the camp commander, her staff and a judge from the refugee tribunal: 'The important guests shook our hands. The impression they took away with them could only have been of young people, lively and confident, who even here behind barbed wire have not lost courage. What good and beautiful things these people could achieve if only they could be out there again, in freedom.'[90]

The most consistent theatre work, though, was produced in Hutchinson Camp where, under the direction of Fritz Weiss and with an acting company including Tausig, Wolff, Philo Hauser, Erwin Jacoby and – for a time – Paul Dornberger, an impressive series of classical German and modern English and American plays were put on. Following an earlier version of *Schwejk,* of which little is known, the group adapted G.K. Chesterton's mystical novel *The Man Who Was Thursday,* for presentation in the spring of 1941. Subtitled a 'nightmare' by the author, it was a choice hardly conducive to encouraging an optimistic outlook amongst the internees, reflecting as it does the emergence of anarchism at the turn of the century. Whilst Weiss's direction appears to have played down the symbolic mysticism of the original, as in the shifting of the last scene from this rousing call to 'carry on the fight and courageously keep faith with the 'Sunday's villa' to the more prosaic surroundings of Scotland Yard[91] (although this may equally well have been for reasons of practical staging) this production must to some extent have reinforced the sense of abandonment amongst the interned audience. The same could be said of John Steinbeck's *Of Mice and Men,* which had its première in March. This adapted short story about migrant American farmworkers and their dreams of a secure future does, it is true, invite comparisons with the lives of the internees on the Isle of Man, but here too the overall impact must have been somewhat depressing.

Lessing's *Nathan der Weise,* on the other hand, first performed on 21 April, aroused quite different emotions. At a time when many in Britain and elsewhere equated German culture with Hitler Fascism, such a performance of a German classical play in a country of exile was a strong affirmation of the desire to fight for the 'other Germany'. This work in particular, 'the famous play Hitler banned and burned because of its doctrine of humanity and tolerance',[92] had a special place amongst the exiles in Britain and was later performed by the Österreichische Bühne in London. Encouraged by their success with *Nathan,* the Hutchinson company then undertook in June the difficult task of staging Schilller's *Die Räuber.* Unfortunately little is known of this production either, except that it was performed in modern dress with a set designed by Carlo Pietzner, in which because of limited space the wood scenes were played in the auditorium.[93] No details at all survive of an 'excellent production' in July 1941 of Galsworthy's socially critical drama *The Silver Box,*[94] or of *Die Kassetle* by Sternheim.

Luckily, accounts do exist of the production at the end of August 1941 of Robert Ardrey's play *Thunder Rock,* first produced by Elia Kazan in New York in 1939 and later successfully filmed in England with a cast containing many refugee actors (in March 1943 it was also put on by the Austrian exile theatre, the Laterndl). The story tells of a former fighter in the Spanish Civil War, fleeing from the harsh realities of the outside world, who takes on the post of lighthouse-keeper on an isolated rock. During his one-month stay there he is visited by the spirits of those who tried to emigrate following the defeat of the 1848 revolution in Europe; almost a hundred years previously they had been shipwrecked and drowned near this lighthouse. Through his encounter with the ghosts of these refugees, the keeper, Charleston, realises that his withdrawal is only of use to those who want to delay the elimination of oppression and inhumanity. In the end he decides to rejoin the active struggle against injustice.

For the German internees, after nearly two years behind barbed wire, this rousing call to 'carry on the fight and courageously keep faith with the future'[95] highlighted a problem similar to that dealt with in *Septembertage*: the sense of hopelessness arising from the frustration of not being able to participate directly in the anti-Fascist fight. *Thunder Rock* tackled this theme in a very different yet equally effective way, although, as Fritz Weiss rightly emphasised in an introduction to the play in *The Camp,* the situation faced by the internees was not exactly comparable to that of Charleston:

> I believe . . . this particular play gives expression to many of the problems which are so intimately connected with our life here, with this difference: we refugees still interned are not here trying to escape the issue of our times. On the contrary, just like the hero of the play, we have come to the conclusion that it is our sacred duty to go out and fight for a new and better world, for the progress of civilisation.[96]

The relevance of the play was nevertheless unmistakable, and not only to the internees. The officer in charge of the camp, who had originally suggested the play, also recognised its importance in sustaining the morale of his charges: 'I am certain that this performance will have given you ample opportunity to review your own problems in a different light. It is eminently constructive in so far as it refuses to justify the various moods of escapism and depression to which most of us tend to succumb at times.[97]

Although Ardrey leaves the final decision to the individual, he does suggest that the way forward can be found only with the help of others, working together in a common cause. 'I have a feeling I'll be seeing you again some place', says Charleston, handing his duty over to another lighthouse-keeper who to all appearances will undergo a similar transformation to his predecessor's. The stirring effect of the play lay not only in its forceful message but also in the way in which it managed to handle a highly personal conflict within a wider historical setting without losing dramatic clarity. The appearance of the ghosts from the past, for instance, is not shown as a mystical event but as the concrete realisation of the keeper's thoughts, and the theatrical means by which the political confrontation is presented are realistic, credible and entertaining. The choice of the lighthouse as the place of action works equally well on a literal and a symbolic level, and it is ironic that one of the most famous of all German émigrés in Britain, Albert Einstein, should suggest a similar 'place of asylum' for exiled academics: 'Einstein . . . made the suggestion that a place might be found for some of the younger exiled scholars in lighthouses and lightships, presumably as companions of the Keepers, 'where they might think out scientific problems of a mathematical or philosophical nature.'[98]

It is highly unlikely that this suggestion was the startingpoint for *Thunder Rock*, but it does underline the appropriateness of the central metaphor of the drama. The theatre group in Hutchinson Camp greeted with predictable enthusiasm their discovery of this play, which in its later Laterndl production was regarded as 'the most unforgettable experience of our time in the emigration.'[99] Director Weiss was the first to start reading the script:

> . . . behold during the second act I got so enthusiastic that I could hardly control my emotion. I instantly called together those members of the actors' guild which were within easy reach. And never had I experienced such enthusiastic reception amongst our actors. 'We must start with rehearsals immediately, this is the opportunity we have been waiting for', these were only some of the comments. One had in fact the impression that all of us had been released at the same time, so great indeed was the clamour that was going on at that time.[100]

The attraction for the interned refugees was heightened by Ardrey's astute portrayal of the isolated cynic, which corresponded so closely to their own feelings and experiences, as in this example provided by Weiss: 'A friend of mine recently released from internment told me once that he used to build up personages out of his imagination whilst he was held captive in a Nazi camp. He had to give it up, he admitted, for fear of going insane.[101]

The importance placed on this production is indicated by the wide support given to the theatre company, not only by their fellow inmates and the Camp Captain, but even from London by the actor and FDKB patron, Walter Hudd.[102] Gerry Wolff's previously mentioned description of the production process suggests that the build-up to performance involved a number of difficulties, and even Fritz Weiss admitted that 'it has been far from easy to produce a play with ghosts of flesh and blood on a limited stage like ours'.[103] Despite this, the efforts of the participants, amongst whom Wolff as Charleston, Tausig, Erwin Jacoby and the nineteen-year-old set designer, Jochen Weigert, stood out, were rewarded with a huge success. More than all the other plays put on by the Hutchinson drama group, this production justified the fine reputation which the anti-Fascist theatre practitioners built-up during their confinement on the Isle of Man and demonstrated how important their efforts on the cultural front were:

> The work was hard and has cost many anxious moments, but we all without any exception loved the work on this production. And we here, to the greater part refugees from Nazi oppression, are particularly happy to have performed this play, because we feel that, more than any other play before, it gives expression to our needs and problems. We hope that we will soon be able to leave our 'Lighthouse' to go out and help to fight the menace, which is threatening to overcome our civilisation.[104]

Theatre in Canadian Internment

Of all the internment centres, the least documented with regard to the theatre work is Canada, although there are many passing references to a number of interesting plays. The overall impression, however, is that the theatre was less able to establish itself consistently in comparison with other art forms, especially the visual arts. This may have been a result of the lack of community spirit amongst the internees in the face of the extreme difficulties suffered in Canadian internment, even though the anti-Fascists imprisoned there made great efforts to bring about an effective cultural life.

Alongside the many improvised and small-scale performances, including readings from Shakespeare, a commemoration of Stefan Zweig, and a special programme on the anniversary of the occupation of Austria and Czechoslovakia,[105] a wide range of works by serious authors were performed. The most active drama group appears to have been in Farnham Camp under the leadership of Gerhard Hinze, where plays by Goethe, Wilde, O'Neill, Chekhov and others were produced. As in Australia, a reading of *Faust* took place as well as a performance of *Journey's End;* in addition, we find the first scene from *The Importance Of Being Earnest,* Chekhov's *The Marriage Contract,* Eugene O'Neill's *In the Zone* and a parody of Hugo von Hofmannsthal's *Der Tor und der Tod,* entitled *Tropf und Trommler,* written by Fürstenheim, 'whose profession in England had been pig-breeding, which circumstance made his play still better'.[106] Hinze himself attempted to raise the tone with his performance of songs from Brecht's *Dreigroschenoper* (thus earning the nickname of KanonenHinze), and the final event on 2 November 1941, before the internees were at last shipped back to the British Isles, included a rendering of *Abschiedsouper* from Schnitzler's *Anatol.*[107] Elsewhere another Schnitzler play, *The Green Cockatoo,* and a drama about *Oliver Cromwell* were performed, whilst in New Brunswick two interesting productions of pieces by G.B. Shaw occurred. In his discussion of the theatre activities in this last camp, Erie Koch highlighted the difficulties of putting on a full-scale performance:

> Before then they had staged various revues and cabarets ... But a three-act play, with sets, costumes, and original music, required much more. It could only be undertaken if there was some measure of stability; it required that neither the director nor any of the actors and designers would expect to be released to go to the United States or return to England during rehearsals. . . . In short, such a venture presumed abandoning the hopes of attaining imminent freedom, as well as a ready response to [the] imperative 'You'll Get Used To It!'[108]

Nevertheless the production in question, *Androcles and the Lion,* seems to have been an excellent choice with numerous parallels between 'the absurdity of our internment and Shaw's satirical depiction of Christian virtues'.

The other Shaw offering, *Man of Destiny,* a one-act drama about Napoleon, was deliberately performed in German, 'so that the officers would not be offended by Shaw's diatribes against the English'. Koch even suggested that this might have been the main reason for the choice of this rarely performed piece.[109] Another unfamiliar play with an all-male cast was *The First Legion* by the American Emmet Lavery, set in a monastery and including the young Anton Diffring, who later made a name for himself on the British stage. Unfortunately there are no further details of two original plays written by Paul Dornberger, *The Last Chance* and *Der junge König.*[110]

'Hay Days' in Australia

If Canada appears the most literary-orientated amongst the centres of interned drama, the most overtly political was surely Hay Camp in the Australian outback. There the émigrés were left more or less to themselves, without the continual comings and goings as on the Isle of Man, or the constant confrontations with Nazi prisoners-of-war as in Canada. In addition, there seems to have been a higher proportion of experienced anti-Fascist theatre artists, most of whom had already appeared on the stage of the Kleine Bühne (Little Theatre) in London. These formed the nucleus of the drama group, as Max Zimmering remembered:

> Perhaps it was just an accident, perhaps those of us in Hut 36 had found ourselves together because 'like and like' attract one another – whatever it was, amongst the two dozen inhabitants of our hut there were . . . a painter (Hans Abarbanell), three actors (Josef Almas, Leo Bieber and Hugo Schuster), a man who adapted himself to anything, dramaturg, prompter, prop-man, etc. (that was my brother Siegfried) and finally myself as versifier. We also had our share of promising young talent . . . Of course, the guild from which our Camp Theatre sprang up was not confined to our residence. Actors, singers, musicians and not least writers and journalists were to be found in other huts.[111]

From Hut 36 the ambitious cabaret programme, *Erinnerung an Europa,* a revue in twelve scenes, was organised at the end of 1940 under Almas's direction with texts from Max Zimmering, Jacques Bachrach and Dr Wilhelm Russo, and a set by Abarbanell. This first production developed directly from the need to combat the worst consequences of isolation and confinement amongst the internees:

> Its content attempted to lift the fate of the internees out of the individual consciousness and to place it in the great events of Europe, to give them, despite a global situation which seemed far from rosy, hope for a better future and at the same time to show that – even here in the Australian steppes, behind barbed wire and far from their home in Europe – they were in no way out of circulation or to be regarded as dead.[112]

This confrontation with the moral and spiritual degeneration, which the interned existence brought with it, was not only treated in this revue by confronting the audience with reminders of the positive aspects of their European past; it was also done by criticising the personal attitudes of the camp inmates. This aspect was emphasised by Max Zimmering in his Prologue to *Erinnerung an Europa:*

> You, friends, who've gathered round this stage,
> In short scenes we'll present to you
> With modesty yet humour too
> The great things of our great new age.
>
> Perhaps so great, though, all is not,
> As in this camp where we survive,
> Yet still we should for greatness strive,
> To help to ease our heavy lot.
>
> We play much more than just a game,
> For through the action intertwined
> A piece of truth you each should find
> To help you nearer to your aim.
>
> You each will see within this play
> Yourselves as critically perceived;
> Be warned, though, do not be deceived
> By digs and jibes, it's just our way.
>
> Who sees himself, whose look turns grim
> And leaves complaining with a curse,
> Of him his friends will think the worse:
> Self-criticism's not for him.[113]

The biting yet constructive criticism which underpinned the revue as a whole did not prevent it from becoming an enormous success. The 'experts' declared it 'in the best traditions of the pre-Hitler German and Austrian cabaret' and, out of a camp population of a thousand, 1,500 seats were taken for the four performances.[114] To satisfy the demand for light-hearted yet high quality entertainment, a second programme, *Hay Days,* was put on, and as late as New Year 1942 Kurt Sternberg organised a *Snow White Revue.*[115] Other events included recitation evenings of classical and modern writers and a series of 'Autorenabende der Camp-Bühne', dedicated both to encouraging new literary and poetic talent and to sustain the contact between the larger community and the individual'.[116]

This concern to provide a broader perspective is also seen in the numerous efforts to promote traditional European culture, though Rolf Stein's adaptation of *Schwejk* provoked – much to the disgust of the rest of the camp – 'a protest from an Austrian monarchist who maintained his sense of allegiance to the Hapsburgs right into the Australian wasteland'.[117] The highpoint of the classical offerings was undoubtedly Bachrach's production of *Faust.* Divided into two separate evenings, Part One of Goethe's masterpiece, apart from the omitted 'Walpurgisnacht' scene, was performed as a 'kind of playreading', some scenes being acted out 'properly', others merely suggested. Despite the mixture of theatrical approaches, this 'novelty in the history of the stage' – a *Faust* performance behind barbed wire – seems to have been an interesting and thought-provoking effort: '. . . Speakers and listeners alike showed themselves equal to the only-slightly shortened version and many scenes achieved very vivid effects.'[118] For this production, which attracted six hundred spectators, Ernst Hermann Meyer sent specially written musical accompaniments out from England![119] But above all it was the actors who formed the basis of the success, with Almas outstanding in a number of roles, including one somewhat unusual characterisation:

> Marthe Schwerdtlein is still rather a problem for a male speaker. And when this speaker is of such quality as Josef Almas, you forget totally that the casting of this role is an emergency solution. Of course he is more convincing in the stud or on the Easter walk as the speaker of Wagner, even without costume or make-up the figure of the desk-bound student of limited horizons appears true to life.[120]

In the title role Bieber was also excellent, Bachrach's 'happiest entrance' as Mephistopheles was in the students' scene, and Gretchen 'whom we can't really afford to have in any proper sense' was played impressively and with tact by the young Michael Rittermann. It was also Rittermann who directed the last major production at Hay Camp, *Journey's End*. Sherriff's popular play was written in 1919 under the immediate impact of the senseless staughter of the First World War but was not performed in London until 1928. Even if the *Camp News* felt it had a very pro-British tendency and showed 'the fairness of the British character'[121] – a rather ironic sentiment for the interned anti-Fascists – the real strength of *Journey's End* lay in its critical attitude towards the traditional officer elite in the British army, who up till then had been portrayed as heroically patriotic. Sherriff 'demystified' these heroes in order to bring out the brutality and senselessness of war. Michael Rittermann pinpointed the importance of this production for the camp population: 'Each of the internees, with the exception of a few quite young inmates, could of course remember the First World War; for this reason the play had a tremendous sense of reality for everyone who saw it. This was the reason for our great success in the camp.'[122]

Like their colleagues in the English transit camps, in the boarding-houses of the Isle of Man and the barracks in Canada, the members of the Camp Bühne in Australia were also able to show that even under the worst conditions of internment, culture – and the theatre in particular – had a major role to play. Rittermann summed up the feelings of all those, both performers and spectators, who experienced the numerous live performances behind barbed wire: 'The work on this production was wonderful and gave us all endless satisfaction. It was for a camp public unaccustomed to live entertainment enormously valued. We had a great success with it and this understandably delighted us all.'[123]

Notes

*Most of this article is adapted from my unpublished Ph.D. thesis, *Die Rolle des Theaters des 'Freien Deutschen Kulturbundes in Großbritannien' im Kampf gegen den deutschen Faschismus (1938–47)*, Section ii: 'Die Theatertätigkeit der deutschen anti-faschistischen Emigranten während der Internierungsperiode (Mai 1940 Ende 1941)', Berlin (GDR), 1972. Additional material supplied by Günter Berghaus. Translations from German undertaken by myself are indicated by an asterisk.

1. 'West Middlesex Gazette', quoted in *This England: Selections From the 'New Statesman, Column, 1934–68*, Harmondsworth, 1969, p. 65.
2. From an interview with Gerry Wolff, Berlin, 30 November 1971.
3. D.N. Pritt, *The Autobiography of D.N. Pritt*, Part One: 'From Right to Left', London, 1965, p. 236.
4. Mentioned by the English MP Eleanor Rathbone, in a debate in the House of Commons on 10 July 1940; quoted in Norman Bentwich, *The Rescue and Achievement of Refugee Scholars*, The Hague, 1953, p. 30.
5. Julius-Bersti, *Odyssee eines Theatermannes*, Berlin (West), 1963, p. 177.*
6. Pritt, *Autobiography*, p. 236
7. Letter from Wharf Mills, July 1940, quoted in *Arbeitsbericht der Sozialkommission des FDKB in Großbritannien*, London, June 1941.*
8. 'Somewhere in England', a poem written by Kuba in Prees Heath Camp, 1940, published in *Neue Deutsche Literatur,* January 1961, p. 46.*
9. H.N. Brailsford in *Reynold's News*, 14 July 1940; quoted in F. Lafitte, *The Internment of Aliens*, Harmondsworth, 1940, p. 92.
10. *Aus Port Erin*, a stenographed pamphlet, Isle of Man, 16 September 1941.*
11. *Frauenruf*, the illegal weekly paper of the Rushen Women's Internment Camp, Port Erin and Port St Mary, Isle of Man, September 1940, p. 1.
12. From an unidentified pamphlet on *Women's Internment Camps*.
13. ibid.
14. Max Zimmering, 'Zwei Zigaretten', in *Der gekreuzigte Grischa*, Rudolstadt, 1969, p. 10.* According to Michael Rittermann the main reason for this harsh treatment on board the *Dunera* was the anti-Jewish attitude of the commander in charge of the troops. Apparently he was later court-martialled and demoted for this. See interview with Michael Rittermann, London, 18 August 1988.
15. See D.N. Pritt, *Erinnerungen an Wilhelm Koenen*, London 10 December 1965, pp. 3–4 (translated into German by Emmy Damerius-Koenen); Erich Milistatt, 'Kämpfer aus St.Helens" *Neue Deutsche Literatur,* November 1966, pp. 41 ff.; *Stacheldraht,* interned newspaper, Farnham, Canada, November 1941, p. 3.

16. Quoted in Freimut Schwarz, 'Kulturarbeit in den englischen Internierungscamps', in *Kunst im Exit inGroßbritannien 1933–45*, Berlin (West) 1986, p. 283.

17. Jan Petersen, 'Panik', in *Geschichten aus neun Ländern*, Berlin and Weimar, 1964, p. 180.*

18. 'Prees Heath', in *Freie Deutsch Jugend* (London), 1 October 1941.*

19. Lafitte, *Internment*, p. 118.

20. Walter A. Berendsohn, *Die Humanistische Front*, 11. Teil, Worms, 1976, p. 98.*

21. See Max Zimmering, 'Kunst hinter Pfählen', in Außbau, vol. 3, 1948, p. 254.

22. See Erie Koch, *Deemed Suspect*, London, 1980, p. 152.

23. Louise Leonhard, 'Frauen im Internment Camp', *Die Zeitüng* (London), 1 July 1941, p. 3.*

24. ibid.*

25. *See Stacheldraht*, Nov. 1941, p. 2; *Zeitspiegel* (London), 18 April 1942, p. 5.

26. Rudolf Steiner, Kunst und Künstler im Camp', *Camp News* (Hay Camp), Australia 1940.*

27. See Koch, *Deemed Suspect*, p. 153.

28. 'F.K.' (Franz Krämer?), 'Kultur', *Stacheldraht*, November 1941, p. 5.

29. ibid.

30. Freimut Schwarz, 'Kunst hinter Pfällen', *Freie Deutsche Kultur* (London), February 1942.*

31. John Heartfield in *Camp Art in Canada*, publicity brochure for an art exhibition organised by the FDKB in London, 1941.

32. See Berstl, *Odyssee*, p. 181; Lafitte, *Internment*, p. 118; Zimmering, *Aufbau*, p. 254.

33. *FDKB-Arbeitsbericht*.

34. Zimmering, Aufbau, p. 254.*

35. *Aus Port Erin*, 16 September 1941.

36. Lafitte, *Internment*, p. 106.

37. Petersen, 'Panik', p. 178.*

38. Zimmering, *Aufbau*, p. 256.

39. ibid.*

40. See ibid.

41. 'Prees Heath'.*

42. *See Onchan Pioneer*, 20 October 1940, p. 3.

43. Heartfield, *Camp Art*.

44. A.B., *Abend der Gefangenen*, in the possession of Ernst Hermann Meyer.*

45. Schwarz, *Kunst im Exit*, p. 283.*

46. Schwarz, Freie Deutsche Kultur.*

47. See Eugen M. Brehm, 'Meine Internierung', Exit, no. 2, 1986, p. 48.

48. Schwarz, *Freie Deutsche Kultur*.

49. See 'We want to fight alongside the democracies' *Freie Deutsche Kultur*, December 1941.

50. Heartfield, *Camp Art*.*

51. See Zimmering, 'Politische Bühne im Exil', in *Der gekreuzigte Grischa*, pp. 61–62, and in *Aufbau*, p. 254.

52. Zimmering, *Aufbau*, p. 254.*

53. Zimmering, 'Politische Bühne im Exil', p. 61.*

54. See letter from Wilhelm Koenen to Thomas Mann, November 1941 in the possession of Emmy Damerius-Koenen.

55. Gerry (Wolff), 'To produce a play', in *Camp Hutchinson Youth* (Isle of Man),

1 September 1941; also in translation in Zimmering, 'Politische Bühne im Exil', pp. 66–67.

56. See Schwarz, *Kunst im Exit*, p. 285.
57. See 'Theater in Huyton', *Freie Deutsche Kultur,* December 1940.
58. Hugh Rank, 'Our Prisoners of War', *Radio Times* (London), 27 November-3 December 1982, p. 98.
59. Koch, Deemed Suspect, p. 154.
60. Dr Wilhelm Russo, '"Faust" auf der 'Camp-Bühne', in *Camp Neus,* Dec. 1940.*
61. Koch, *Deemed Suspect*, p. 154.
62. Zimmering, 'Politische Bühne im Exil', p. 66.*
63. See Koch, *Deemed Suspect*, pp. 157 ff.
64. Petersen, 'Panik', p. 180.*
65. Wolff, 'To produce a play'.
66. *See Camp News*, 16 April 1941.
67. See rehearsal plan written on back of programme for *Of Mice and Men,* 6 March 1941, in the possession of Erwin Jacoby.
68. Zimmering, 'Politische Bühne im Exil', pp. 63–64.*
69. ibid, p. 64.*
70. Lafitte, *Internment*, p. 118.
71. See Michael Seyfert, 'His Majesty's Most Loyal Internees', in *Gerhard Hirschfeld (ed) Exile in Great Britain:* Refugees from Hitler's Germany, Leamington Spa, 1984, p. 180.
72. See Brehm, 'Meine Internierung', p. 49.
73. Hansjörg Schneider, 'Exil inder Tschechoslowakei', in *Exit in der Tschechoslowakei, in Großbritannien,* Skandinavien und Palästina, Leipzig, 1980, p. 119.
74. See Brehm, 'Meine Internierung', p. 51.
75. ibid.*
76. 'Theatre in Huyton', Freie *Deutsche Kultur,* December 1940.*
77. ibid.*
78. See Schneider, 'Exil inder Tschechoslowakei', p. 119.
79. 'Theater in Huyton', Freie *Deutsche Kultur,* December 1940.*
80. ibid.*
81. Peter Herz, 'Die Kleinkunstbühne 'Blue Danube' in London 1939–54', in *Österreicher im Exil 1934–45* Vienna, 1977, p. 451.*
82. See Richard Friedenthal, *Die Welt in der Nußschale,* Munich, 1956, pp. 136 ff.
83. See Seyfert, 'His Majesty's Most Loyal Internees', p. 181.
84. Zimmering, 'Politische Bühne im Exil', p. 65.*
85. See programme for 'Auf der Fest-Wiese', Isle of Man, in possession of Nina Freund.
86. See Hans J. Rehfisch, 'Zeittheater', in *Gebrannte und Gebannte,* FDKB pamphlet, London, May 1942, p. 23.
87. *Frauenruf* (Isle of Man), Sept, 1940, p. 3.
88. 'Frauen im Internment-Camp', *Die Zeitung,* 1 July 1941, p. 3.
89. Programme of *Turandot* by the Ailsa Craig Group, Isle of Man, in the possession of Emmy Damerius-Koenen.
90. 'Lita, 'Youth Players in Port Erin', *Aus Port Erin,* 19 Sept. 1941, p. 2.*
91. See programme for *The Man Who Was Thursday,* in the possession of Erwin Jacoby.
92. Programme for *Nathan der Weise,* in the possession of Erwin Jacoby.
93. From the Wolff interview.

94. See Zimmering, 'Politische Bühne im Exil', p. 65.
95. R.P., '"Leuchtfeur" im Laterndl', *Einheit* (London), 13 Apr. 1943, p. 20.*
96. Friedrich Weiss, 'Thunder Rock', *The Camp* (Isle of Man), 1 Sept.1941.
97. 'Appreciation of the Camp Captain', *The Camp*, 1 Sept. 1941.
98. Bentwich, *Rescue and Achievement*, p. 14.
99. H.H., "Thunder Rock', *Freie Tribüne* (London), 31 March 1943, p. 6.*
100. Weiss, 'Thunder Rock'.
101. ibid.
102. See 'Appreciation of the Camp Captain', *The Camp*.
103. Weiss, 'Thunder Rock'.
104. ibid.
105. See letter from Dr Freund in *Zeitspiegel*, 13 June 1942, p. 8.
106. 'Culture', *Stacheldraht*, November 1941, p. 7.
107. See 'Our Farewell Party', *Stacheldraht*, November 1941, p. 12.
108. Koch, *Deemed Suspect*, pp. 153–4.
109. ibid., p. 154.
110. See Wilhelm Sternfeld and Eva Tiedmann, *Deutsche Exil-Literatur 1935–15*, Heidelberg, 1970.
111. Zimmering, 'Politische Bühne im Exil', p. 63*.
112. Zimmering, *Unsterbliches Lachen*, a partly published manuscript, Dresden (undated), p. 11.
113. ibid.*
114. See Zimmering, 'Politische Bühne im Exil', p. 63.
115. See Seyfert, 'His Majesty's Most Loyal Internees', p. 182.
116. See Steiner, 'Kunst und Künstler in Camp'.
117. Zimmering, *Unsterbliches Lachen*, p. 14.*
118. Russo, 'Faust'.
119. From an interview with Ernst Herrnann Meyer, Berlin, 2 March 1971.
120. Russo, 'Faust'.
121. 'The Campman's Diary', *Camp News,* 30 March 1941.
122. Interview with Michael Rittermann, 13 August 1988.
123. ibid.

CHAPTER 8

THESPIS BEHIND THE WIRE, OR ENTERTAINMENT IN INTERNMENT – A PERSONAL RECOLLECTION

GEORGE W. BRANDT

The summer of 1940 . . . Dunkirk . . . France had fallen. In Britain, German and Austrian nationals were rounded up and interned: a footnote to the war that has been largely forgotten. Except of course by the people involved – like me for instance. To misquote Goethe after the Battle of Valmy, 'Ich bin dabei gewesen'.

What a mixed bunch of people we were behind the barbed wire! Recent and not so recent Jewish refugees from Nazism, affluent or down-and-out, orthodox or atheist; anti-Fascists involved in the anti-Hitler struggle, including some International Brigaders; and random stragglers in this century's population shifts – Czechs, Dutchmen, stateless persons; flotsam like that pathetic group of lit-tle old German barbers who had been working in England for decades but never bothered to get themselves naturalised.

Nearly half a century later, the experience has lost its sting. In retrospect it seems 'not too bad' – as indeed it wasn't compared to the real horrors of the war. It didn't feel too good at the time though, being put away by what one thought of as one's own side.

These hundreds and hundreds of very diverse people cooped up in a small space generated a good deal of friction; a good deal of intellectual energy as well. Some of this energy went into all sorts of performances. The camp show became an important feature of life, as is apt to be the case among wartime prisoners.

My first show was the one I witnessed at Huyton, Liverpool. I had been delivered there by solo transport with my very own armed escort sometime in June 1940 (I forget the exact date). The camp was a recently completed housing estate which had had barbed wire and watch towers thrown around it before any tenants had moved in. We were the first inhabitants. Every square inch of floor space in the empty houses was taken up by suitcases and bodies. It was a hot summer, that summer of the blitzkrieg in the West, so we spent as many hours as possible out of doors, in the streets and backyards of the estate, meeting, arguing, trying to find our bearings. Shortly after arriving I was told there was going to be a camp show.

I went along to this open-air event which happened in the afternoon or early evening, I forget which. A large platform, some five feet high, was surrounded on three or maybe all four sides by a large audience, standing tightly packed like Elizabethan groundlings. The show was a series of cabaret-type turns. A piano, I seem to recall, was the only item on stage. Music was, of course, a feature of all camp shows. Among the inmates there was a formerly well-known composer of *Schlager* who had written a new or adapted an old song for the occasion. He played and sang it and invited the audience to join in. Pleased to be doing something together, we did. I cannot for the life of me remember any of the other turns except for this one: two comedians reading out the current news from a huge sheet of paper. As they went down each column they made their satirical points about the world at large and our situation in particular. Having gone down four columns they looked and looked for another one, couldn't find it and then announced, 'There isn't any Fifth Column here!' This term, coined by Franco to describe his secret supporters in besieged Madrid, was on everybody's lips at the time; the Germans had used Fifth Columns in their attacks in Holland, Belgium and France. We enthusiastically agreed that we were no Fifth Columnists; the declaration was, of course, aimed mainly at the British army personnel watching the show. Strictly speaking it wasn't the whole truth. The vast majority of internees were –passively, or in some cases very actively, opposed to Fascism; but there *was* a Nazi element in the camp as well. They weren't very hard to spot. Flushed with hopes of an early German victory they hardly bothered to disguise where they stood.

If that show had given the inmates a sense of solidarity it wasn't to be for long. Overseas transports were shortly to wrench them apart again. Australia was one destination, Canada another; as the prisoners lined up for trans-shipment they didn't know where they were bound. In July I was sent to Canada on the notorious Ettrick which made the Atlantic crossing in convoy in ten days. My first resting-place was Camp L just outside Quebec City, on the same Plains of Abraham where General Wolfe had defeated the French

181 years earlier. Camp L held 793 inmates. Once we had settled down in our huts, some cultural activities started up. The first was an art exhibition. The commandant, Major Wiggs (affectionately referred to as 'Piggy-Wiggy') was impressed. The camp turned into a buzzing hive of art critics.

Next, a camp show was organised. Again, this wasn't a play but another mixed bag of offerings, a *bunter Abend*. Unlike the Huyton show this was an indoor event set in the dining-hut. Tables, ranged side by side at one end of the hut, made a stage. Was there a curtain? I don't recall. Uprights (were they upsided tables? Fibreboard or wooden planks? I don't remember) masked entrances left and right as well as, set far back, upstage centre. The lighting was rudimentary: on or off.

There were some musical turns – of course. Löffler squeezed his accordion – we had heard him practising for hours in our hut before. A professorial juggler who kept juggling even during the Atlantic passage displayed his skill. I had co-authored and directed a piece which poked fun at the internal camp government – a meeting of self-important hut fathers – in which well-known camp characters were lampooned. At the end of the sketch, the committee members suddenly tilted backwards and vanished behind the table at which they had been sitting.

One number was for the car only – just a radio set placed on stage. Voices were piped in from backstage, comic turns in English and German. One of these was the inevitable Hitler imitation. We were well served by an Austrian who could do a Führer speech at the drop of a hat, guttural accent and all. A line from the Führer's own vocabulary – 'Es ist mein fanatischer Wille ... sticks in my memory. But what was he feeling fanatical about? I just don't remember.

A sketch I wrote and acted in was a duologue between a Canadian soldier and an internee who consistently talked past each other. This, too, pointed out among other things that we weren't Nazis in improbable disguise. Since Piggy-Wiggy and other officers graced the show with their presence it seemed a good opportunity for putting them straight. They seemed pleased with the efforts of 'their' internees.

A few days later some of us received an amazing invitation, or rather order. We were to play some items from the show again – outside. Outside the camp! It seemed too good to be true. Through the wire on one side we had a panoramic view of the Plains of Abraham sloping down to the majestically wide St Lawrence; on the other side we saw the turrets of the Chateau Frontenac Hotel peeping over the crest of the hill that bounded our horizon. Would we be getting a chance to see this *terra incognita* at close quarters? We got ready that evening, hearts pounding. Would we be playing at the Chateau? A private venue? A theatre?

Disillusionment was instantaneous. We were marched not outside the camp, but only out of the inner compound, just a few paces down the road – and there we were, in one of the soldiers' huts. We were to entertain the troops. What a let-down! We went into a huddle to decide what to do next. But since we wanted to prove that we were friendly rather than enemy aliens, friendly we'd better be. We performed. To be honest, the reception we had was OK. Undemonstrative but OK. We got a cup of coffee each and some slices of buttered toast.

There were other events in Camp L. The actor Gerhard Hintze did not actually perform any roles as such but he gave recitals of poetry and, if I recall rightly, passages from plays. His *bühnendeutsch* diction was flawless. For a group of men speaking every known dialect of German (and Austrian), listening to Hintze was more than a pleasure, it was an education. His exquisitely manicured pronunciation was the height of verbal elegance.

In October 1940 the population of Camp L was split up again. A great many of us were transferred to Camp N, outside Sherbrooke, Province of Quebec, where later we were joined by transports from other camps. Unlike our first stopping-off place, Camp N was totally unprepared. It was simply a group of railway repair sheds encrusted with many years deposit of soot, offering only minimal toilet or other facilities. This is not the place to describe our initial resistance, followed by the long slog of making the place fit for human habitation: that story has been told authoritatively by Erie Koch in his book *Deemed Suspect* (Toronto 1980). Once we had dug ourselves out of the debris, the desire for entertainment returned. Music was pre-eminent: concerts by the violin virtuoso Gerhard Kander, piano recitals by John Neumark (or Newmark) and the Hindemith pupil Helmut Blume, who was later to become the Dean of the Faculty of Music at McGill University.

But of course *bunte Abende* or cabarets, though more difficult to set up than music recitals, also happened from time to time. One that comes to mind in particular is the New Year's Eve celebration 1940/41. I was in charge of arranging it, I wrote some of the numbers, acted in it and served as MC. The venue was a good deal more spacious than our dining-hut in Camp L. The mess-hall which was our 'theatre' in Camp N was an enormous railway shed which could hold the entire camp population of 736 men. We rigged a proper stage – timber was readily available – in one corner of the hall, with a small backstage area and some pretence of stage lighting. We got up our basic wardrobe from the clothes we had among ourselves without, as far as I can recall, getting any official help (but I may be doing the authorities less than justice here).

The show had some musical items, of course. There was a comedian who translated some Yiddish expressions into the camp authorities' official jargon. There was a sketch (in English, not in German) in which a top-level British government committee deciding internment policy was portrayed. Needless to say, they were pompous nincompoops.

Suddenly the show was interrupted – an internee in solitary confinement (a punishment actually used for some offences) was brought in to participate in the celebrations. He was in a wooden cage so that his confinement would continue. On closer inspection this figure dressed in the internment uniform with the large red spot on the back of the jacket proved to be a lifesize doll.

I gave a reading of Goethe's *Der Erlkönig* in the grand manner of Hintze, who was no longer with us (he had been sent to another camp from Camp L). This affectionate parody kept being interrupted by announcements and digressions; a man with a deadpan expression entered, stood close to me and just stared; the recital collapsed like Chico Marx's piano. The concluding lines:

> Erreicht den Hof mit Müh und Not,
> In seinen Armen das Kind war tot.

were timed – no, not timed, improvised – to come as a crashing anticlimax. Some lifelong friendships were to spring from that ten-minute skit.

At the end of the show I appeared in a cheesecloth outfit and after cutting a few capers addressed the audience thus:

> Schnell wie der Wind – husch! – bin ich da,
> Die allerschönste aller Feen.
> Ich nenne mich Aspasia
> Und flitze her auf Silberschwingen,
> Durch leichte Lüfte leicht getragen,
> Gar wunderlieblich anzuschen.
> Von dunklen, zukunftsschwangren Tagen
> Will ich euch goldne Botschaft bringen . . .
> Ich sage euch die frohe Märe:
> Noch eh des Jahres Kreis verflossen,
> Ist euch der Stacheldraht erschlossen.
> Fast jeder von euch macht Karriere,
> Und mehrere sind Millionäre . . .

> Swift as the wind – whoosh! – here I am,
> Of all the fairies the most fair.

I'm called Aspasia and I come
A-fluttering on silver wings,
On gentle breezes gently borne,
Wholly delightful to behold.
Of dark and fateful days to come
I bring you golden prophecies. . . .
I give this happy news to you:
Ere the year's circle is complete
The wire will disgorge you all.
You'll most of you have big careers,
With some becoming millionaires . . .

As a general forecast this wasn't too far out. Many of us were to be
released in the course of 1941; some at any rate were to do well in
their subsequent lives. But Aspasia made a number of rather more
specific and indeed fanciful forecasts about the future of certain
well-known camp characters. These in hindsight have turned out to
be less than reliable. The end of the recitation coincided with midnight.

Doch still! Tut's Mitternacht nicht schlagen?
Hör ich nicht, wie die Stunde kracht?
Dann kann ich froh: 'Es ist vollbracht!'
Von Neunzehnhundertvierzig sagen.
Beschissen war's! Darum hurra!
Es leb' des Neujahrs Mitternacht!
So spricht die Fee Aspasia,
Die drauf sich auf die Socken macht.

But soft! Is that not midnight's ring?
Do I not hear the hour boom?
So I can cheerfully declare
Of Nineteen Forty: 'It is done!'
A shitty year! Well then – hooray!
Long live the New Year's Midnight hour!
Thus speaks the fay Aspasia
Who makes a speedy getaway.

I must admit that Camp N never rose to the actual production of a
play, not with live actors anyway. There was, however, a full-length
puppet show. An experienced puppeteer enlisted a group of enthu-
siasts to build a miniature theatre complete with a cast of
marionettes in order to put on the puppet play of Doctor Faustus.
We didn't have a text – but what of it? The script of this traditional
play was reconstructed from memory, with new songs and music
added. For Faust's visit to the Duke of Parma, a very attractive
minuet was written by our resident composer Fritz Grundiand, alias
Freddie Grant. (His camp song, *You'll Get Used to It,* was

subsequently adopted by the Canadian Navy as its theme song.) The puppets were beautifully made. When Kasperle, Faust's manservant in the puppet play, conjured up devils from hell by citing spells from his master's book of magic, the demons that appeared were marvellously fantasticated. One of them had an extensible neck which could stretch halfway across the stage and then shrink back again. A group of puppeteers was trained to a respectable level of competence. For the performance, actors and singers were seated in the wings. I spoke the title role. There was some music – I forget now whether it was only a piano or strings as well. The minuet was danced very handsomely.

Other camps did in fact mount complete stage plays, notably Camp B at Little River in New Brunswick. They performed the other *Faust* – Goethe's version. In the Prologue in Heaven the voice of God (who remained invisible) came through a hole in the false ceiling from which a tile had been removed. Shaw was a popular author in Camp B. Both *Androcles and the Lion* and *The Man of Destiny* were staged, the latter in German so as not to provoke the Canadian officers with Shaw's anti-English gibes. The part of the mysterious lady was performed by Anton Diffring, who was later to make a name for himself in such British films as *The Colditz Story, I Am a Camera, Fahrenheit 451* and *Where Eagles Dare.* Another ambitious production was Schnitzler's *Der grüne Kakadu.* The play's large cast was no deterrent where manpower was freely available, and the number of female roles was mercifully limited. I should add that I am indebted to Eric Koch for this information about Camp B; I wasn't there myself.

There is no cause to praise these theatrical activities beyond their merits. They served the needs of the moment and that was enough. They were effective morale boosters for participants and spectators alike. Some of the former may have been pointed in the direction of their future careers. For the latter they left memories that cast a rosy glow over an unpleasant episode in their lives. These memories, as the writer of this is only too well aware, are growing fainter and fainter as time moves on.

CHAPTER 9

THE MUSES IN GULAG

ALEXANDER SOLZHENITSYN

It was an accepted saying that *everything is possible* in Gulag. The blackest foulness, any twist and turn of betrayal, wildly unexpected encounters, love on the edge of the precipice – everything was possible. But if anybody should ever try to tell you with shining eyes that someone was re-educated by government means through the KVCh – the Cultural and Educational Section – you can reply with total conviction: Nonsense!

Everyone in Gulag was re-educated – re-educated under one another's influence and by circumstances, re-educated in various directions. But not even one juvenile, let alone any adult, was re-educated by means of the KVCh.

However, so that our camps might not be like 'dens of depravity, communes of brigandage, nurseries of recidivists, and conductors of immorality' (this is how Tsarist prisons were described), they were equipped with such an appendage as the Cultural and Educational Section.

Because, as said by the then head of Gulag, I. Apeter: 'To the prison construction of capitalist countries, the proletariat of the U.S.S.R. counterpoises its cultural (and not its camp – A.S.) construction. Those institutions in which the proletarian state enforces deprivation of freedom . . . can be called prisons or by some other name – it is not a matter of terminology . . . These are places where life is not killed off but, instead, gives forth new shoots . . .'[1]

I don't know how Apeter ended. There is great likelihood, I think, that they wrung his neck, too, in those very places in which, as he said, life gives off new shoots. But it is not a matter of terminology. Has the reader now understood what the main thing was in our camps? *Cultural* construction.

And for every need an organ was created, and multiplied, and its tentacles reached out to every island. In the twenties they were called PVCh's – Political Educational Sections – and, from the thirties on, KVCh's. They were supposed in part to replace the former prison priests and prison religious services.

Here is how they were organised. The chief of the KVCh was a free employee with the authority of an assistant to the chief of camp. He picked out his own instructors (the norm was one instructor to 250 wards), who had to be from 'strata close to the proletariat', which meant, of course, that intellectuals (the petty bourgeoisie) were unsuitable (it was more decent for them to be swinging a pick), so they recruited as instructors thieves with two or three convictions, urban swindlers, embezzlers and seducers along with them. And so it was that a young fellow who had kept himself sort of clean and who had got five years for rape with mitigating circumstances might roll up his newspaper and go off to the barracks of the 58s to lead a little discussion on 'The Role of Labour in the Process of Correction'. The instructors had a particularly good outside view of that role because they themselves had been 'released from the productive process'. Similarly such socially friendly elements made up the *activists' group of the KVCh*. But the activists were not released from work. (They could only hope in time they would be able to 'do in' one of the instructors and take over his job. This created a generally friendly atmosphere in the KVCh.) In the mornings the instructor had to see the zeks off to work; then he would inspect the kitchen (i.e. he would be well fed), and then he would go and catch up on his sleep in his cabin. He would be ill-advised to tangle or touch *the thief ringleaders* because, in the first place, it was dangerous, and, in the second place, the moment would come when 'criminal cohesion would be transformed into a productive cohesion'. And at that point the thief ringleaders would lead the shock brigades into storm assaults. And so, for the time being, let them, too, just sleep it off after their night-long card games. But the instructors are constantly guided in their activity by the general overall thesis that cultural and educational work in the camps is not cultural and educational work 'with unfortunates', but cultural and productive work with a knife edge (we just can't get along with that knife edge), directed against it: against the 58s. Alas the KVCh 'does not have the right to arrest' (now this was such a limitation on its cultural opportunities!) but 'could make a request to the administration' (which would not refuse!). And besides, the instructor 'systematically presents reports on the mood of the zeks.' (He who has an ear to hear, let him hear! At this point the Cultural and Educational Section delicately shades into the Security Section. But this is not spelled out in the instructions.)

However, we see that, carried away by our quotations, we have grammatically slipped into the present tense. We have to disappoint the reader with the fact that the matter concerns the thirties, the finest, most flourishing years of the KVCh, when a classless society was being built in the country, and when there had not yet occurred the awful outburst of class struggle that did not occur the moment the society was achieved. In those glorious years the KVCh expanded into many important appendages: the cultural councils of those deprived of freedom; cultural and educational commissions; sanitary and living conditions commissions; shock-brigade staffs; inspection posts for fulfilment of the production and financial plan, etc . . .

And how variegated and varied were the forms of work! Like life itself. Organisation of competition. Organisation of shock-worker movements. Struggle for fulfilment of the production and financial plan. Struggle for labor discipline. Storm assaults on the liquidation of hold-ups. Cultural crusades. Voluntary collection of funds for aeroplanes. Subscription to loans. 'Voluntary Saturdays' for strengthening the defence capabilities of the country. Exposure of fake shock-workers. Conversations with malingerers. Liquidation of illiteracy (they went unwillingly). Professional and technical courses for camp inmates from among the workers (the thieves pushed hard to learn to be drivers: freedom!). And fascinating lectures on the inviolability of socialist property! And simply reading the newspapers aloud! Evenings of questions and answers. And 'Red Corners' in every barracks! Graphs of fulfilment of plans! Statistics on goals! And what posters! What slogans!

In this happy time the Muses soared over the gloomy expanses and chasms of the Archipelago – and the first and highest muse among them was Polyhymnia, the muse of hymns (and of slogans):

> The brigade that excels gets . . . praise and respect!
> Do your shock work – get time off your sentence!

Or:

> Work hard – your family waits for you at home.

You see how clever this is psychologically! After all, what do you have here? First: if you have forgotten about your family, this will start you worrying about them, and remind you of them. Second: if you are intensely alarmed, it will calm you down; your family exists and has not been arrested. And in the third place: your family does not need you *just for your own sake*, but needs you only through conscientious camp work. Lastly:

Let's join in the shock assault in honour of the seventeenth anniversary of the October Revolution!

Who could resist that? Then there were theatricals with politically relevant themes (a little bit from the muse Thalia). For example: the servicing of the Red Calendar! Or the living newspaper! Or propaganda mock trials! Or oratorios on the theme of the September Plenum of the Central Committee in 1930! Or a musical skit, 'The March of the Articles of the Criminal Code' (Article 58 was a lame Baba-Yaga)! How this brightened the life of the prisoners and helped them reach upward towards the light!

And the recreation directors of the KVCh! And then the atheistic work too! The choirs and glee clubs (under the shade of the muse Euterpe). And then those propaganda brigades:

> The shock-workers swing their shoulders,
> Hurrying with their wheelbarrows!

You see what bold self-criticism this is! They were not even afraid to touch on the shock- workers! In fact, it was quite enough for a propaganda brigade to come to a penalty sector and give a concert there:

> Listen, listen, River Volga!
> Night and day beside the zeks,
> On the site stand the Chekists!
> What that means is: never fear;
> The workers have a strong, strong arm,
> The OGPU men are Communists!

And all the party workers and in particular the recidivists would throw down their playing cards and rush off to work immediately!

And there were other measures as well: a group of the best shock-workers would visit a Strict Regimen Company or a penalty isolator and take a propaganda brigade with them. At the beginning the shock-workers would reproach and shame the malingerers, explain to them the advantages of fulfilment of the work norms (they would get better rations). And then the propaganda brigade would sing:

> Everywhere the battles call
> And the Moscow-Volga Canal
> Conquers snow and cold!
> And then with total frankness:
> And so that we'll live better
> In order to eat, in order to drink –
> We have to dig the ground better!

And they invited all volunteers not only to return to the compound but to transfer immediately into a shock-workers' barracks (from the penalty barracks), where they would be fed right on the spot! What an artistic success! (The propaganda brigades, except for the central one, were not released from work themselves. They got an extra portion of grits on the days of their performances.)

(. . .) In the fetid, oxygenless atmosphere of the camps, the sooty flame of the KVCh (hut) would sputter and flare up, casting the merest glimmer. But people would be drawn from various barracks and from various brigades even to this little flame. Some came with a direct purpose: to tear paper from a book or newspaper to make a smoke, to get paper for a petition, or to write with the ink there. (Ink was not permitted in the barracks, and here, too, it was kept under lock and key; after all, ink can be used to forge rubber stamps!). And some came . . . just to put on airs: See how cultured I am! And some . . . to rub elbows and chatter with new people, someone other than their boring fellow brigade mates. And some came . . . to listen to the others and report to the 'godfather'. But there were others still who didn't themselves know why they were inexplicably drawn there for a short evening half-hour, tired as they were, instead of lying on their bunks, allowing their aching bodies to rest a little.

These visits to the KVCh brought the soul a mite of refreshment in imperceptible and unobvious ways. Even though those who stopped by were altogether the same sort of hungry zeks as the ones who stayed sitting on their brigade multiple bunks, here they didn't talk of rations, nor of portions of cereal, nor about norms. People here didn't talk about the things that made up camp life, and therein lay a protest of the heart and some relaxation for the mind. Here they talked about some kind of fabulous past which just could not have existed for these grey, famished, bedraggled people. Here, too, they talked about the indescribably blessed, free-moving life out in freedom of those fortunates who had somehow succeeded in not landing in prison. And those people also talked about art here, sometimes so magically!

It was as if someone, when an evil spirit was raging, had drawn on the ground a weakly gleaming and foggily flickering circle – and it was just about to go out, but as long as it hadn't you could at least imagine that within that circle, for those half-hours, you were not in the power of the evil force.

Yes, and then, too, someone would sometimes be plucking at a guitar. Someone would be softly singing – a song that was not at all the kind permitted on the stage. And something would stir within you: Life . . . exists! It exists! And, looking happily around you, you, too, would want to express something to someone.

(. . .) We shall never now be able to arrive at any judgement of the full scale of what took place, of the number who perished, or of the standard they might have attained. No one will ever tell us about the notebooks hurriedly burned before departures on prisoner transports, or of the completed fragments and big schemes carried in the heads and cast together with those heads into frozen mass graves. Verses can be read, lips close to the ear; they can be remembered, and they or the memory of them can be communicated. But prose cannot be passed on before its time. It is harder for it to survive. It is too bulky, too rigid, too bound up with paper, to pass through the vicissitudes of the Archipelago.

(. . .) And yet at the same time the Archipelago provided a unique, exceptional opportunity for our literature, and perhaps . . . even for world literature. This unbelievable serfdom in the full flower of the twentieth century, in this one and only and not at all redeeming sense, opened to writers a fertile though fatal path.[2]

Millions of Russian intellectuals were thrown there – not for a joy ride: to be mutilated, to die, without any hope of return. For the first time in history, such a multitude of sophisticated, mature, and cultivated people found themselves, not in imagination and one and for all, inside the pelt of slave, serf, logger, miner. And so for the first time in world history (on such a scale) the experience of the upper and the lower strata of society *merged*. That extremely important, seemingly transparent, yet previously impenetrable partition preventing the upper strata from understanding the lower – pity – now melted. Pity had moved the noble sympathisers of the past (all the enlighteners!) – and pity had also blinded them! They were tormented by pangs of conscience because they themselves did not share that evil fate, and for that reason they considered themselves obliged to shout three times as loud about injustices, at the same time missing out on any fundamental examination of the human nature of the people of the lower strata, of the upper strata, of all people.

Only from the intellectual zeks of the Archipelago did these pangs of conscience drop away once and for all, for they completely shared the evil fate of the people! Only now could an educated Russian write about an enserfed peasant *from the inside* – because he himself had become a serf.

But at this point he had no pencil, no paper, no time, no supple fingers. Now the jailers kept shaking out his things and looking into the entrance and exit of the alimentary canal, and the security officers kept looking into his eyes.

The experience of the upper and the lower strata had merged – but the bearers of the merged experience perished. And thus it was that an unprecedented philosophy and literature were buried under the iron crust of the Archipelago.

(. . .) The most populous of all the groups that visited the KVCh . . . were the participants in amateur theatricals. This particular function – directing amateur theatricals – still belonged to the aged and decrepit KVCh, just as it had when it was young and vigorous.[3] On individual islands of the Archipelago, amateur theatricals rose and disappeared in alternating ebb and flow, but unlike the tides of the sea, this did not take place with regularity but in fits and starts for reasons known to the chiefs but not to the zeks, and perhaps because the chief of the KVCh had to make a mark in his report once every six months, and perhaps because they were expecting someone from up top.

Here is how it was done at the remote camps: the chief of the KVCh (who was never ordinarily seen in the camp compound anyway, everything being managed for him by a prisoner instructor) would summon an accordionist and tell him: 'Here's what! Round up a choir![4] And see to it that it performs in a month's time.' 'But Citizen Chief, I don't read notes.' 'What the hell do you need with notes! You just play a song everyone knows, and let the rest sing along.' And so the recruiting of a choir was announced, sometimes along with a dramatics group. Where were they going to practise? The KVCh room was too small for this, they needed a more spacious one, and, of course, there was no clubroom at all. Ordinarily the usual domain for this was the camp mess halls – constantly stinking with the steam from gruel, the odour of rotten vegetables and boiled cod. On one side of the mess halls was the kitchen, and on the other side either a permanent stage or a temporary platform. After dinner the choir and the dramatic circle assembled here. (The surroundings were like those in the drawing by A.G.——n. Except that the artist has depicted not their own local amateur stage group but a touring 'culture brigade'. The last dishes are about to be gathered up and the last-leggers are about to be kicked out – and then the audience will be let in. The reader can see how cheerful the serf actresses are.)

How was one to coax the zeks to join in the amateur theatricals? For out of perhaps five hundred prisoners in the compound there might be three or four genuine amateur singers – so how was one to put together a choir? Well, the main bait in mixed camp compounds lay in encounters at the choir! A.Susi, who had been appointed choirmaster, was astonished at how rapidly his choir grew, so much so that he could never fully rehearse them in any single song. New participants kept coming and coming. They had no voices. They had never sung before. But they kept begging, and how cruel it would have been to refuse them, to ignore their newly awakened thirst for art! However, many fewer choir members turned up at the actual rehearsals. (The reason was that participants in the amateur theatricals were permitted to move about the compound, to and from rehearsals, for two hours after the bed curfew. And so they used these two hours to wind up their own affairs.)

And it was not unheard of for things like this to happen: just before the performance the only bass in the choir would be sent off on a prisoner transport (the transport and the performance were handled by different departments). Or the choirmaster – the same Susi – was summoned by the chief of the KVCh and told: 'We very much appreciate that you have worked so hard, but we can't let you perform at the concert, because a 58 doesn't have the right to lead a choir. So get a replacement ready; waving your arms around isn't like having a voice – you'll find someone.'

And there were those for whom the choir and the dramatic circle were not merely a place to meet someone – but rather a counterfeit of life, or maybe not a counterfeit, but a reminder, instead, that life despite everything still exists, that it does go on existing. From the warehouse they would one day bring rough brown wrapping paper from cereal sacks – and it was handed round to write parts on. A time-honoured theatrical procedure! And then, too, there was the distribution of roles! Who would be dressed in what? How to make up? How interesting it would look! On the night of the performance one could take a real mirror in one's hand and see oneself in a real dress from freedom and with rouged cheeks.

It was very interesting to dream about all that, but good Lord, the plays! What kind of plays they had there! Those special collections, inscribed '*For Use Only Inside Gulag*!' Why ... 'only'? Not 'both for freedom and also for Gulag', but instead ... 'only inside Gulag'. What this really meant was that it was such twaddle, such pigs' swill, that out in freedom they wouldn't swallow it, so pour it out on us! The stupidest and least talented writers deposited their most loathsome and rubbishy plays here! And if anyone wanted to put on a farce by Chekhov or something else, where was he supposed to find a play? It could not be found even among the free people in the whole settlement, and what the camp library had was Gorky, and even then pages had been torn out to roll smokes.

N. Davidenkov, a writer, assembled a dramatic circle in the Krivoshchekovo Camp. From somewhere he got an unusual playlet: it was patriotic and dealt with Napoleon's sojourn in Moscow! (And probably it was on a level with Rastopchin's posted proclamations!). They distributed the roles, and the prisoners rushed to rehearsals with great enthusiasm. So what could interfere now? The main role was played by Zina, a former teacher, arrested after remaining behind in occupied territory. She acted well, and the director was satisfied with her. All of a sudden there was a quarrel at one of the rehearsals: the rest of the women rebelled against Zina's playing the main role. This was not exactly a new situation, and it was one with which a director can ordinarily cope. But here's what the women were shouting: 'It's a patriotic role, and she – Germans on occupied territory! Get out, bitch! Get out, you German whore! Before you get stomped!' These women were socially friendly and also perhaps among the 58s, but not on a charge of treason. Did they think this up themselves, or did the Third Section suggest it to them? The director, in view of his article, was not in a position to defend his actress. So Zina departed sobbing.

And those who had fallen on their faces . . . to punishment block. Sometimes they were not even allowed to enjoy the applause. In the Magadan theatre, Nikishov, the chief of Dalstroi, interrupted Vadim Kozin, a widely known singer at the time: 'All right, Kozin, stop the bowing and get out!' (Kozin tried to hang himself but was taken down out of the noose.)

(. . .) The ensemble of the Moscow Administration of Corrective Labour Camps and Colonies, which went around giving performances in the camps and which had been housed at Matrosskaya Tishina, was suddenly transferred for a while to our camp at the Kaluga Gates. What luck! So now I could get to know them. And perhaps now I would force my way through to them.

What a strange sensation! To watch a performance of professional zek actors in a camp mess hall! Laughter, smiles, singing, white dresses, black frock-coats . . . But what were their sentences? Under what Code articles had they been imprisoned? Was the heroine a thief? Or was she here under the 'universally available 58'? Was the hero here for bribery or for 'Seven-eighths?' An ordinary actor has one reincarnation only – in his role. But here was a double drama, a double reincarnation. First one had to pretend to be a free actor or actress, and only then play a role. And all that weight of prison, that consciousness that you were a serf, that tomorrow the citizen chief might send you to the punishment block for playing your role badly or for a liaison with a serf actress, or to logging, or six thousand miles to Kolyma. What an added millstone that must be – over and above the whole burden the zek actor shared with the free actors – that destructive straining of the lungs and throat in order to force through oneself a mass of dramatised emptiness, the mechanical propaganda of dead ideas?!

The heroine of the ensemble, Nina V., turned out to be there for 58–10, on a five-year sentence. We quickly found a common acquaintance – our joint teacher in the art history department of the Moscow Institute of Philosophy, Literature and History. She was a student who had not completed her course, and she was very young. Abusing the prerogatives of an actress, she spoiled herself with cosmetics and with those vile, cotton-padded shoulders with which all women out in freedom were destroying their beauty at that time. The women in the Archipelago had not suffered that fate, and their shoulders had developed only from hauling hand barrows.

In the ensemble Nina, like every prima, had her own beloved (a dancer of the Bolshoi Theatre), but she also had there her own spiritual father in dramatic art – Osvald Glazunov (Glaznek), one of the senior disciples of Vakhtangov. He and his wife were – and perhaps they had wanted to be – captured by the Germans at a dacha near Istra outside Moscow. They had spent three years of the war in their tiny homeland in Riga, where they had performed in the Latvian theatre. With the arrival of our Soviet forces they had received a tenner each for treason to the big Motherland. And now they were both in the ensemble.

Izolda Vikentyevna Glazunova was already old. It was already hard for her to dance. Only once did we see her in a dance which was unusual for our time, which I myself would have called impressionist, but I am afraid to offend connoisseurs. She danced in a dark silvery costume that covered her completely on a half-illuminated stage. This dance has remained in my memory. Most modern dances are a display of the female body, and that is almost all they are. But her dance was some kind of spiritual, mystical recollection, and reflected in certain of its elements her own belief in the transmigration of souls.

Suddenly, several days later, furtively, the way prisoner transports were always gathered together in the Archipelago, Izolda Vikentyevna was sent off on a transport, torn away from her husband, carried off to oblivion.

Among the serf-owning landed gentry this used to be their own special form of cruelty and barbarism: to separate serf families, to sell off the husband and wife separately. And for that they caught it from Nekrasov, Turgenev, Leskov, and from everyone. But with us this was not cruelty, it was simply a wise and reasonable move: the old woman did not earn her ration, yet she was occupying a staff unit.

On the day his wife was sent off on the prisoner transport, Osvald came to our room (the chamber of monstrosities) with eyes vacantly wondering, leaning on the shoulder of his frail adopted daughter, as if she were the only thing that gave him support. He was nearly insane, and one feared he might do away with himself. Then he fell silent and his head dropped. Then he gradually began to speak, to recall his entire life. He had for some reason created two theatres: because of his art he had left his wife alone for years. He wished now he could relive his entire life differently. . . .

I remember them now as if they were sculptured: how the old man drew the girl to him by the back of her hand, and how she looked up at him from under his arm, without stirring, suffering with him and trying not to weep.

Despite all my efforts, I did not succeed in becoming a member of that troupe. Soon afterwards they left the Kaluga Gates and I lost sight of them. A year later I heard a rumour at the Butyrki that they had been travelling on a truck to one of their regular performances and had been hit by a train. I do not know whether Glazunov was there or not. But so far as I myself was concerned, I once more realised that the ways of the Lord are imponderable. That we ourselves never know what we want. And how many times in life I passionately sought what I did not need and been despondent over failures which were successes.

I remained there in the modest little amateur theatrical group at the Kaluga Gates along with Anechka Breslavskaya, Shurochka Ostretsova, and Lyova G. We did manage to put on something before they broke us up and sent us away. I now recall my participation in that amateur theatrical activity as a lack of spiritual toughness, as a humiliation. The worthless Lieutenant Mironov, if he had found no other distractions and entertainments in Moscow on a Sunday evening, could come to camp in his cups and give orders: 'I want a concert in ten minutes.' And the performers were routed out of bed or torn away from the camp hot-plate if they happened at that moment to be engaged in cooking with relish something in their mess tins. And in a trice we would be singing, dancing and performing on the brilliantly lit stage before an empty hall, in which the only audience was the haughty dolt of a lieutenant and a troika of jailers.

Notes

1. Vyshinsky, pp.431, 429, 438.
2. I will be so bold as to elucidate this thought in its most general aspect. As long as the world has stood, there have always been until now two unmixable strata of society: the upper and the lower, the ruling and the ruled. This is a crude division, like all divisions, but if one classifies among the upper stratum not only those superior in power, money, and social provision but also those superior in education, obtained through either family efforts or their own, in a word all those who do not need to work with their hands, then the division will be almost across the board.

Therefore we can expect four spheres of world literature (and of art in general, and ideas in general). The first sphere: those in the upper stratum portraying (describing, pondering) the upper stratum, in other words themselves, their own people. The second sphere: the upper stratum depicting or pondering the lower stratum, 'the younger brother'. The third sphere: the lower stratum depicting the upper. And the fourth: the lower portraying . . . the lower, i.e., itself.

The upper stratum always had the free times, an excess or at least a sufficiency of means, the education, the training. Those among them who wanted to could always master the artistic techniques and the discipline of thought. But there is one important law of life: contentment always kills spiritual striving in a human being. And as a result this first sphere contained within it many satiated artistic distortions and many morbid and self-important 'schools' – sterile flowerings. And only when writers, who were either profoundly unhappy in their personal lives or had an overwhelming natural drive toward spiritual seeking, entered that sphere as the bearers of culture was great literature created.

The fourth sphere is all the world's folklore. Leisure time here was broken up into tiny pieces – and was available to individuals in different ways. And the anonymous contributions to this culture also came in different ways – unpremeditated, through lucky moments of glimpsing a perfected image or turn of speech. But the actual creators of it were innumerable, and they were almost always oppressed and dissatisfied people. Everything created then passed through selection, washing and polishing a hundred thousand times over, passing from mouth to mouth and year to year. And that is how we have come to possess our golden store of folklore. It is never empty or soulless – because among its authors there were none who were unacquainted with suffering.

The written literature belonging to the fourth sphere ('proletarian', 'peasant') is altogether embryonic, inexperienced, unsuccessful, because individual know-how has always been lacking here. The written language of the third sphere ('looking upward from below') suffered from the same faults of inexperience, but even worse: it was poisoned by envy and hate – sterile feelings which do not create art. It made the same mistake that revolutionaries continually make: ascribing the vices of the upper class to the class itself and not to humanity as a whole, while failing to imagine how notably they themselves inherit these vices. Or else, on the other hand, it was spoiled by servile fawning.

Morally, the second sphere of literature promised to be the most fertile ('looking down from above'). It was created by people whose goodness, striving for the truth, and sense of justice had proved stronger than their soporific prosperity, and whose artistry was at the same time mature and on a high level. But the fault of this sphere was the *incapacity genuinely to understand*. These authors sympathized, pitied, wept, were indignant – and precisely because of this could not *understand precisely*. They always looked at things from the sidelines and from above. They simply could not climb into the pelts of the members of the lower stratum. And any who managed to get one leg over the fence could never get the other over.

Evidently man's nature is so egocentric that this transformation can only take place, alas, with the help of external violence. That is how Cervantes got his education in slavery and Dostoyevsky his at hard labour. In the Gulag Archipelago this experiment was carried out on millions of heads and hearts all at once.

3. The universal concern for amateur theatricals in our country, something on which, incidentally, no small amounts of money are spent, does have some sort of intent, but what? One cannot say immediately. Is it the inertia left over from what was once proclaimed in the twenties? Or is it, like sport, an obligatory means of distracting the people's energy and interest? Or does someone believe that all these songs and skits actually help the required processing of feelings?

4. The political leadership *both* in the army and out in freedom has a superstitious
   faith in the primary indoctrinational significance of choirs in particular. All the
   rest of the amateur theatrical activity could wither, but there has to be a choir! A
   singing collective. Songs could easily be checked out, they were all ours! And
   whatever you sing . . . you believe.

CHAPTER *10*

CABARET IN CONCENTRATION CAMPS

PETER JELAVICH

While the Nazis systematically muzzled cabaret in Berlin after 1933, some of the entertainers who had fled the Third Reich attempted to perform in exile. They had some, albeit limited, success in cities like Zurich, Vienna, Prague, Paris, and London. But in the United States there was no demand for their style of cabaret. Kurt Robitschek's attempt to revive the Kadeko in New York ended in failure. Calling himself Ken Robey, he had better luck as a producer of American-style vaudeville shows. Valeska Gert opened the Beggar's Bar in Greenwich Village in 1938, but it had a very limited clientele. She fared somewhat better when she returned to Berlin in 1950, where she founded the Witch's Kitchen (Hexenküche). Friedrich Hollaender went to Los Angeles, but his attempt to revive the Tingel-Tangel on Santa Monica Boulevard was a total failure, despite the fact that he used English-language texts. Thereafter he made a comfortable living writing music for Hollywood films. In the 1950s and 1960s he again mounted cabaret-revues in Germany, primarily in Munich.

America was inhospitable territory for Berlin-style cabaret, but at least it provided the exiles with a safe haven for the duration of the Third Reich. The European continent was somewhat more receptive to Berlin's émigré entertainers – until the Wehrmacht started marching. In 1943 and 1944 some of the Jewish stars of the twenties mounted shows again, but this time as prisoners in the concentration camps of Westerbork and Theresienstadt. Their story concludes the history of Berlin cabaret.

The Netherlands hosted the two most successful 'Berlin' cabarets in exile, those of Rudolf Nelson and Willy Rosen. Various factors allowed German entertainment to take root there. For one, Holland had long been susceptible to the cultural influence of its neighbour.

Their languages were very similar, so that most Dutch audiences could understand literary nuances and wordplays in German. Moreover, since the number of German artists and writers greatly outnumbered those in the Netherlands, the Dutch could not help but be swamped by Germany's cultural products. In fact, the Dutch were well acquainted with Berlin cabaret since its beginnings. Wolzogen took his Motley Theatre to Amsterdam in 1902, and other touring troupes followed. Holland was especially attractive to German performers in the early twenties, since they could earn hard currency there at a time when the German mark was rendered worthless by inflation. By the end of the decade many of Berlin's stars also became known to Dutch audiences through the medium of film.[1]

Another, very different factor that allowed German cabaret to establish itself in the Netherlands after 1933 was the local tradition of granting asylum. In the early months of the Nazi regime hundreds of Jews, liberals, and leftists crossed the border seeking a temporary or more permanent haven. The Dutch Social Democrats as well as the Dutch Jewish community, which numbered over a hundred thousand, organised relief efforts for the exiles. That was another reason why Berlin's Jewish cabaretists believed they would be welcomed in the Netherlands.

In reality German émigré entertainers faced considerable difficulties as a result of economic and political circumstances. The depression hit Holland particularly hard, and up to 1936 unemployment continued to rise. As the steady stream of refugees strained resources, and native citizens worried that the incoming Germans might compete for scarce jobs, asylum regulations were tightened. In the realm of popular arts, Dutch entertainers feared the competition of the German performers, and their professional organisation (Nederlandse Artiesten Organisatie) regularly mounted protests in the press and with the government against the foreigners. Their opposition forced Willy Rosen's troupe to terminate its stay in Holland in the summer of 1933; it did not return until 1937. Political factors further impeded overly critical cabarets. Dutch politics was dominated by conservative and strongly anti-leftist Protestant and Catholic parties; many of them actually welcomed Hitler's coming to power, inasmuch as they regarded him as a bulwark against 'Bolshevism'. Anti-fascist cabaret thus did not find much sympathy among large sectors of the public. Moreover, the Dutch government did not want to alienate its powerful neighbour, and it threatened to ban performances and even expel troupes that criticised foreign regimes, including that of Hitler.[2]

These factors plagued Ping-Pong, the earliest exile cabaret in

Holland. It opened in Amsterdam in May 1933, and included various performers from Berlin, many of whom had appeared in the Catacombs. Ping-Pong's most prominent members were the chanteuse Dora Gerson, the dancers Chala Goldstein and Julia Marcus, and Kurt Egon Wolff as conferencier; the singer and composer Curt Bry joined the troupe in August. Their numbers included texts by Brecht, Hollaender, Kästner, and Tucholsky, and Marcus often performed dances with an antimilitarist bent. Several conservative newspapers attacked this politicisation of entertainment, by foreigners to boot, and soon the troupe had to blunt its critical edge. By the end of the year Ping-Pong had trouble extending its work permit, so it moved to Switzerland. It returned the following autumn, but was allowed to perform only if it agreed to hire Dutch entertainers as part of its programme. Since these new additions proved to be mediocre, and since most of Ping-Pong's stars (Gerson, Goldstein, and Marcus) had started solo careers, the cabaret soon disbanded.[3]

Another troupe that faced problems was Erika Mann's Peppermill (Pfeffermühle). Founded in Munich in January 1933, that cabaret had to leave Germany in March, and it reconstituted itself in Zurich the following October. The Peppermill was the most political of all the exile cabarets. Although it did not explicitly name Germany or its leaders, its songs and skits consisted of parables that clearly dealt with conditions under Hitler. This led to protests by the German ambassador, and eventually attacks by Swiss Nazis. Fearing for law and order, the canton of Zurich banned its appearance in 1935. The Peppermill then toured other Swiss cantons, and also performed in Czechoslovakia, Belgium, Luxemburg, and the Netherlands. Although it appeared in Holland in 1934 and 1935 without much difficulty, in October 1936 it provoked strong protests by Dutch National Socialists, as well as by local entertainers fearful of the competition. The government accordingly withdrew its license to perform, amid a storm of protest in many newspapers and even the parliament. The troupe moved on to New York in January 1937, where it presented its songs and skits in English. After several weeks it disbanded for good, due to a lack of interest on the part of the American public.[4]

Rudolf Nelson was able to avoid these problems in so far as politics was concerned. He had always been a cautious and astute manager, and after 1933 he fully depoliticised his cabaret. His first stops in exile were Austria and Switzerland, where the Basel *National Zeitung* noted in November: 'The Nelson revue hardly desires to inspire serious thoughts, it wants simply to entertain.' Another Swiss newspaper reported that Nelson 'clings to neutral ground,' and remained 'unconcerned with politics and the economic crisis'. The same apolitical tone prevailed when Nelson brought his troupe to Amsterdam in April 1934 at the instigation of Louis Davids, one of the founders of Dutch cabaret at the turn of the last century. Since Erika Mann's troupe was touring Holland at the time of Nelson's arrival, the Catholic *De Tijd* could compare the two: 'The Peppermill in the Centraal-theater is more thoughtful and literary, while the Nelson revue in the Leidscheplein-theater is more superficial, charming, more entertaining.' The Social Democratic *Het Volk* noted that Nelson offered 'good amusement art; it does not aspire to be more'. Two years later the *Algeineeiz Handelsblad* reported that Nelson's 'idea is that there can be no place for politics on his stage, he exclusively wants diversion to be offered to the visitor who has come there to forget for a moment the sword of Damocles that perhaps has been hanging over his head for the entire day'. Ironically, in November 1936, Nelson's revue included a song that pleaded: 'Oh please, do not be silent, / is not a war in sight?' (Ach, bitte, schweige nicht, / ist nicht ein Krieg in Sicht?).[5] Yet such comments were rare on Nelson's stage, as he generally kept silent on contemporary events. It seemed that he too ignored the sword of Damocles over his own head.

Nelson was able to maintain his troupe in the Netherlands up to the German occupation, not just because he avoided political statements, but also because he provided varied and high-quality entertainment. He changed his programme every two weeks, and mounted over a hundred different revues during his stay in Amsterdam. He regularly performed his old hits from the twenties, and even the Wilhelmine era, but he continually composed new music as well. The texts were usually scripted by his son Herbert; they consisted of sometimes sentimental, sometimes ironic love songs, as well as parodies of film, advertisements, and other cultural and commercial fashions of the day. Much of Nelson's success resulted from the talent of his entertainers. Dora Paulsen was his star chanteuse, and Kurt Lilien his principal comic actor. He also brought other prominent émigré entertainers into his troupe as they decided to leave Germany or (after the Anschluss) Austria. For example, the famous Viennese conferencier Karl Farkas appeared in Nelson's revues in 1938, before he moved on to New York. Although Dutch entertainers occasionally protested that these shows lured away some of their own audience, the government did not intervene because they were genuinely popular with broad sectors of the well-off public. Moreover, no Dutch stage offered the same type or quality of entertainment, so the issue of competition was moot.[6]

A similar venture was Willy Rosen's Prominents (Theater der Prominenten). As its name suggested, it featured well-known actresses, and especially actors. Many of them, such as Otto Wallburg and Siegfried Arno, were known to the Dutch audience from Weimar films. Rosen himself had been a star at the Kadeko. He was one of the few people who both scripted and composed his songs, and performed them while playing a piano. He proudly introduced his numbers with the phrase: 'Text and music by me!' (Text und Musik von mir!). Having been evicted from Holland in the summer of 1933 because of protests by Dutch performers, Rosen toured non-Nazi Europe with his troupe. He also maintained ties to Berlin, since he regularly composed music for Max Ehrlich's shows for the Cultural League of German Jews. The Prominents did not return to the Netherlands until 1937, when they performed at the summer resort town of Scheveningen. That became their home for the next three summers; the rest of the year they performed in Amsterdam, Rotterdam, and Belgium. Rosen mounted several new programmes each year, which featured love songs and numerous comic skits. Like Nelson, he assiduously avoided politics. The programme book for the 1940 season in Scheveningen proclaimed: 'When you want to forget your worries, then come to us, the theatre without politics. (Without politics! For three years we have stuck to that strictly and we want to stay with it.)'[7]

Scheveningen's 1940 summer season had barely begun when politics intruded violently. On 10 May German forces invaded the Netherlands, and the country was conquered in a matter of days. The entertainers who had fled Germany after 1933 were now once again in Nazi hands, under much more frightening conditions. Nevertheless, the occupiers were able to allay outright panic among Holland's Jews by introducing anti-Semitic policies in incremental stages. The delays resulted in part from the Nazis' realisation that their attacks on Jews were highly unpopular with the Gentile population. In February 1941 a near-general strike occurred in Amsterdam and surrounding communities to protest the rounding up of Jews, and the Nazis had to use force to terminate the work stoppage. Within this atmosphere of public solidarity, Rosen's Prominents were permitted to perform in Amsterdam from December 1940 to January 1942. Nelson too continued to mount revues in that city. In November 1941 his troupe was reconstituted as the Jewish Cabaret Ensemble (Joodsch-Kleinkunst-Ensemble). It appeared in the Hollandsche Schouwburg, which was renamed the Joodsche Schouwburg. As in Berlin, only Jews were allowed to attend the performances.

Nelson's revues acquired a new theme song, with words by his son Herbert, that tried to hold out hope for his exclusively Jewish public. The lyrics claimed that 'the great waltzes' and 'the old songs' not only inspired a melancholic nostalgia, but revived a feeling of youth that gave strength to carry on. The refrain then proclaimed:

Life keeps on going, it never stands still.
Life keeps on going, we must follow its will.
Music, our escort, lends wings to our stride.
Life keeps on going, we have hope at our side.

Das Leben geht weiter, es bleibt niemals stehn.
Das Leben geht weiter, wir müssen mit ihm gehn.
Musik als Begleiter beflügelt den Schritt.
Das Leben gcht weiter, voll Hoffnung gehn wir mit.[8]

Such hopes were soon dispelled. Nelson and Rosen gave a final revue together in May 1942. The next month the Nazis began a massive round up of Dutch Jews. Now that the extermination camps in Poland were fully operational, the occupiers could begin instituting their plan of making Holland 'Jew-free' (*judenrein*). With the assistance of Dora Paulsen, his star chanteuse, Nelson and his family were able to go underground and survive the war. Herbert Nelson even managed to perform occasional evenings of opposi-tional cabaret while in hiding, and his father eventually mounted a revue again in Berlin in 1949. Rosen was not so fortunate. Kurt Robitschek, who was trying with little success to revive the Kadeko in New York, had arranged a benefit performance to raise money for Rosen's transatlantic passage, and Rosen had been granted a visa for Cuba and was in the process of procuring one for the United States.

America's entry into the war in December 1941, however, blocked his ability to escape.[9] He thus shared the fate of more than a hundred thousand Jews in Holland. Over the course of several months, the Jews of Amsterdam were assembled at the Joodsche Schouwburg, where Nelson's Jewish Cabaret had performed. Their first stop thereafter was the 'transit camp' at Westerbork.

Ironically, Westerbork had been inaugurated by the Dutch gov-ernment in 1939 as a holding camp for Jewish refugees from Germany. By 1938 the Netherlands had practically halted all immi-gration from the Nazi state, but the atrocities of the 'crystal night' pogrom in November of that year led to public demands to admit a new wave of asylum-seekers. The authorities did not, however, want to make conditions too comfortable for the refugees, in the hope that they would eventually move on to other countries. Thus a holding camp was established at Westerbork, on the desolate moors in the northeast part of the nation. Several hundred German

Jews lived there until July 1942, when the camp was taken over by the SS. Thereafter its population burgeoned to several thousand at any one time, as it became a way station for Dutch Jews being transported to Auschwitz, Sobibor, Bergen-Belsen, and Theresienstadt.[10]

Westerbork holds a troubled place in the history of cabaret because six revues were staged there between July 1943 and June 1944. The numbers were written and composed by Rosen and Erich Ziegler, a musician who had been a long-time member of the Prominents. The stars of the show were Max Ehrlich and Camilla Spira, an operetta singer who had gained fame in Charell's production of *The White Horse Inn* in 1930. She later appeared in many of Ehrlich's shows for the Cultural League of German Jews. Spira left Berlin for Holland in the wake of the 'crystal night' pogrom, and Ehrlich followed in May 1939. They performed with Rosen's and Nelson's troupes until their deportation to Westerbork. The large casts of the camp's revues included Johnny and Jones, a popular Dutch musical duo, but most of the entertainers were German Jews.

Philip Mechanicus, a Dutch journalist whose diary chronicled life in Westerbork noted: 'The revue was a mixture of antiquated sketches and mild ridicule of the conditions and circumstances prevailing at the camp. Not a single sharp word, not a single harsh word, but a little gentle irony in the passing, avoiding the main issues. A compromise.' That characterisation is borne out by the extant documentation on the shows: typed programme booklets, photographs, even film clips. The second revue, entitled *Humour and Melody (Humor und Melodie)*, which opened on 4 September, 1943, was a mixture of mild satire about camp conditions and pure diversion. It began with a 'roll call' (*Appell*) of the cast members on stage, in imitation of the outdoor roll calls of camp inmates. Other numbers dealing with Westerbork were set in the crowded barracks and the infirmary. Yet many scenes were nostalgic looks back at the past: there was a waltz number set in the 1880s and a 'postcoach idyll' from the even earlier Biedermeier era. Other scenes were more modern, such as one that parodied a jazz band. The show even concluded with a 'Girl' number, inasmuch as a skit set in a classroom allowed six 'schoolgirls' to parade in very short skirts. Similarly, the subsequent revue, entitled 'Bravo! Da capo!', included a scene called 'The Westerbork-Girls Dance!' (Die Westerbork-Girls tanzen!). The shows were invariably well-rehearsed, and props and costumes were often elaborate. Mechanicus could rightly note that 'Westerbork has the best cabaret in Holland'.[11]

One might well wonder how it was possible to mount such elaborate shows in the context of a concentration camp. Obviously, it would not have been possible without the encouragement and active support of the camp's SS commandant, Konrad Gemmeker. This rather bland career bureaucrat, who worked his way up office ladders in the Düsseldorf police force and then the SS, was put in charge of Westerbork in October 1942, after three other SS camp commandants had been dismissed in rapid succession for incompetence. Among Westerbork's inmates Gemmeker was a subject of much speculation and confusion. He would regularly give token signs of 'largesse' towards the interned Jews, such as encouraging the cabaret, for which he even allotted large sums for props and costumes. Of course, he too was a beneficiary of the shows, since he was an enthusiast of popular music. On 5 September, 1943, Mechanicus noted in his diary: 'The Commandant was enjoying himself like a schoolboy – blessed are the poor in spirit.'

Etty Hillesum, another inmate who chronicled the camp's life, wrote in a letter two weeks earlier: 'On one occasion he came three times in succession to see the same performance and roared with laughter at the same old jokes each time.' Even Ferdinand Aus der Fünten, one of the most feared Nazis in Holland, who was in charge of the overall deportation programme for Dutch Jews, made regular trips from Amsterdam to attend the Westerbork shows.[12]

Although the performances were immensely popular with the inmates of Westerbork – they were invariably sold out, and tickets were often hard to acquire -they also were highly controversial. Many prisoners saw them as part of a larger strategy of manipulation that ensured the proper functioning of Westerbork – and Westerbork's main function was to fill the weekly quota of 'transport material', the official term for deportees to the Polish camps. Gemmeker was able to remain Westerbork's commandant until the end of the war because he, unlike his predecessors, never failed to meet the quotas and simultaneously to keep order in the camp. His main ploy was a policy of divide-and-conquer, which pitted German Jews against Dutch Jews. Gemmeker favoured Westerbork's 'long-term residents', those German Jews who had been settled there before the Nazi invasion. He granted them preferential treatment in areas such as housing, inasmuch as they could live in small cottages instead of the huge, cramped barracks. More important, Gemmeker appointed some of them to run the camp on a day-to-day basis.

The most important function of Westerbork's German Jewish administrators was to select the names of their fellow inmates who would be sent on the weekly transports, which numbered anywhere from a thousand to three thousand souls. This reflected a widespread tactic: throughout their empire, the Nazis tried to turn Jews against each other, by making some of them responsible for the selection of 'transport material'. Holland was not spared this cynical ploy. The Jewish Council for the Netherlands, formed a Nazis' behest and based in Amsterdam, selected the citizens wh were to be sent to Westerbork. Within that camp, the German Jews selected 'transport material' for deportation to Poland.

Few if any of the inmates knew what awaited them at Auschwitz or Sobibor. They were told that they were being sent to 'labour camps'. Even astute and informed observers like Hillesum and Mechanicus had no inkling of the gas chambers, the fearsome death that awaited most Jews within hours of their arrival at the extermination camps. Nevertheless, all inmates knew that deportation to the east was something to be avoided at all costs. They imagined the Polish camps as places where poor housing, meagre food, and intense physical labour resulted in high mortality rates. Since conditions at Westerbork were relatively tolerable, and above all survivable, it was obviously desirable to prolong one's stay there as long as possible. This gave tremendous power – power over life and death – to those German Jews who drew up the transport lists. In the process, they protected their friends, generally favouring German over Dutch Jews. Mechanicus, who devoted many agonised pages of his diary to the issue, believed that the German Jews were wreaking revenge for the presumed lack of support from Dutch Jews prior to 1940. The Dutch Jews, in turn, became increasingly hostile toward their German co-religionists as the favouritism in drawing up the transport lists became obvious. Mechanicus even feared that if the war were to end and Westerbork be liberated, the German inmates would be massacred by the Dutch prisoners.[13]

Various aspects of the Westerbork revues revealed these tensions. For one, the shows reflected Gemmeker's preference for German over Dutch Jews. Even though the star performers were not 'long-term residents', since they did not arrive in Westerbork until 1943, they were granted the privilege of living in private cottages. Gemmeker would even socialise with some of them, by inviting them to his house and talking with them late into the night. But by far the greatest favour bestowed upon them was exemption from deportation. Becoming a member of the cast was thus a life-or-death matter. Since the revues were performed almost exclusively by German Jews, the performances caused resentment among the Dutch Jews. As early as 27 July 1943, rumours about irregularities and favouritism in the casting reached such a level that Gemmeker became peeved, and issued a proclamation threatening to cancel the shows completely if the bad-mouthing did not stop. The complainers became more circumspect, and the shows continued.

Three months later the greatest reward of all was granted to Camilla Spira, the star of the first two revues: she was pronounced

as made possible by the false testimony of her (Gen-
no claimed that Camilla was not the offspring of her
father. That white lie, combined with a hefty bribe
in Amsterdam, allowed Spira, her Jewish husband,
children to be released from Westerbork. She gave a
formance at the premiere of the third revue. On 18
October ... chanicus noted laconically in his diary: 'Camilla Spira,
the star of the revue, has departed for Amsterdam, Aryanized. A
great loss for the revue.' Mechanicus envied Spira's good fortune,
but he could not be too critical, for several weeks later he himself
tried unsuccesfully to prove that he had an 'Aryan' background. He
noted in his diary: 'There is no disgrace about passing oneself off as
an Aryan, although it is not pleasant to accept a gift from the hands
of the oppressor. The main thing is to get out of his clutches.'[14]

At the same time that the Westerbork revues fuelled the tensions
between German and Dutch Jews, they also played into Gemmeker's hands by acting as a diversionary and quieting force within
a camp whose ultimate goal was the destruction of Dutch Jewry.
This was the heart of the problem, and it provoked numerous
debates among Westerbork's inmates concerning the propriety of
attending the shows. Many prisoners boycotted the revues because
they considered them tasteless at best, and sacrilegious at worst.
After all, the wood for the stage had been taken from the demolished synagogue of a nearby town. Israel Taubes, a survivor of the
camp, noted bitterly after the war: 'On the wooden boards from the
old synagogue of Assen, which were used for the construction of the
stage, the choicest young girls, specially chosen by experts, will
swing their legs to the rhythm of jazz music.' Even more shocking to
many was the fact that the shows were performed in what was normally the registration hall, where newly arrived inmates were
processed, and where one had to go to apply for exemption from
deportation. In the words of Mechanicus, it was 'the same hall
where the transport people are brought, where men sigh and
women and children weep and every week the walls resound to the
entreaties of those who want to escape the awful calamity of being
sent to Poland.'[15]

Etty Hillesum did not attend the premiere of the first revue, but
her letter of 9 July, 1943, revealed great distress:

> It is a complete madhouse here; we shall have to feel ashamed of it
> for three hundred years ... In the middle of this game with human
> lives, an order suddenly comes from the commandant: the *Dien-*
> *stleiters* [Jewish section leaders in the camp] must present themselves
> that evening at the first night of a cabaret which is being put on here.
> They stared open-mouthed, but they had to go home and dress in

their best clothes. And then in the evening they sit in the registration hall, where Max Ehrlich, Chaya Goldstein, Willy Rosen, and others give a performance. In the first row, the commandant with his guests . . . The rest of the hall full. People laughed until they cried – oh yes, cried. On days when the [newly arriving inmates] from Amsterdam pour into the camp, we put up a kind of wooden barrier in the big reception hall to hold them back if the crush becomes too great. During the cabaret this same barrier served as a piece of décor on the stage; Max Ehrlich leaned over it to sing his little songs. I wasn't there myself, but Kormann just told me about it, adding, 'This whole business is slowly driving me to the edge of despair'.

Mechanicus too was loathe to attend the 'unsavoury cabaret shows', but he felt compelled to go, in his capacity as chronicler of Westerbork, for posterity. He vented his own feelings on 17 October 1943, after the opening of the third show, which featured the 'Westerbork Girls': 'Attended the premiere of the new revue yesterday evening. Absolutely packed out. Old numbers that had been refurbished, well acted. A great part of the programme consisted of dancing by revue girls with bare legs. The *Oberstzirmführer* [Gemmeker] present with Aus der Fünten. Went home with a feeling of disgust.'[16]

Israel Taubes reported that there was often a total lack of understanding between 'the majority' who attended the shows and those who refused to go: 'There was earnest and intelligent people who maintained that those doomed to die were not likely to be helped by a boycott, and some might get a little comfort, if only for a few hours. Others, disagreeing, thought that going to the shows was an offence to Jewish self-respect.' Mechanicus too pondered both sides of the issue, which he called 'a psychological mystery. Light music beside an open grave.' He recognised that the inmates, especially the younger ones, craved distractions from their situation. Even before the revues commenced, he noted in his diary: 'People's nerves are at a breaking point. It is a relief, even at Westerbork, to escape from the nervous strain for a moment and break the tension.'[17]

The shows provided such relief, and to the extent that they made life more bearable, they were a welcome attraction to the inmates. Moreover, it seems that the revues sometimes tried to achieve concrete, practical goals. Certain scenes probably attempted to be conduits between the inmates and the camp's commandant, by appealing for good treatment. For example, one number in the second revue had Camilla Spira proclaiming the joys of receiving packages from relatives or friends outside the camp. The importance of the text was highlighted by being spelled out on stage. Since such shipments, which flowed quite freely into Westerbork at that time, were invaluable supplements to the meagre food and clothing rations provided by the camp authorities, the number might have been an indirect means of 'thanking' Gemmeker for the 'privilege' of receiving packages, as well as an appeal not to infringe on that benefit.

Occasionally the performers even expressed a note of defiance. In a photo album presented to Gemmeker by the entertainers, the picture of the package scene bore the commentary: 'Spira is slowly becoming Aryan'. That caption suggested that the official 'Aryanization' of a half Jewish person revealed the sham nature of the Nazis' racial 'science'. Whereas that comment was reserved for the eyes of the commandant, other defiant notes were heard by a larger public. A recurring theme of the second revue was the line: 'When you sit up to your neck in shit, you're not supposed to chirp!' (Wenn man bis zum Hals im Dreck sitzt, hat man nicht zu zwitschern!).[18] Ehrlich's reply was: 'In spite of that, I'm chirping!' (Ich zwitschere trotzdem!). By whistling in the face of adversity, Ehrlich implied that one should resist being destroyed emotionally and psychologically by the demeaning conditions of the camp.

Many inmates believed that the shows provided not only temporary diversion but also gave them the mental strength to carry on. This faith was shared in other, much harsher camps than Westerbork, such as Dachau and Buchenwald. There the maintenance of self-respect and the will to live was often considered a prerequisite for survival; those least likely to survive, it was believed, were the *Muselmänner* (Moslems), the camp jargon for people who had given up all hope. The will to live found its clearest expression in unofficial camp anthems. Two of the most famous were composed by writers associated with cabaret. The 'Buchenwald Song' was scripted by Fritz Löhner, best known as Beda, who had written numerous cabaret skits and hit songs, as well as the libretti for some of Franz Lehar's operettas. Like many of Vienna's entertainers, he was arrested after the annexation of Austria. Transferred to Buchenwald, he wrote a song that was paradigmatic of so many camp anthems. While it evoked the grim conditions, it held up the hope that the day of freedom would surely come. In the meantime:

> Comrade, don't lose courage, keep in step, bear the pain,
> For we all have the will to live in our veins
> And faith, yes faith in our hearts!

> Halte Schritt, Kamarad, und verlier nicht den Mut,
> Denn wir tragen den Willen zum Leben Blut
> Und im Herzen, im Herzen den Glauben!

A similar song was composed in Dachau, where other prominent Austrian entertainers were detained. They included the Viennese comedian Paul Morgan, who had been a co-founder of the Kadeko in 1924, as well as the Austrian conferencier Fritz Granbaum, who had appeared regularly on Berlin's cabaret stages since the days of Nelson's Chat Noir. Morgan and Granbaum performed numerous impromptu shows at Dachau, sometimes with, sometimes without, the knowledge or acquiescence of the guards. Also at Dachau was the young, highly talented Viennese cabaretist Jura Soyfer, who performed the most hard-hitting numbers in the camp and also scripted the 'Dachau Song.' Like Beda's verses, it evoked the brutal conditions – the barbed wire, the armed guards, the cynicism of the promise 'Arbeit macht frei' – and it too ended with a vision of eventual freedom. Its formula for survival was grimmer than Beda's, since it called upon the inmates to become 'steel and stone'. Yet it also urged them to cling to their humanity: 'Remain a human being, comrade, / Be a man, comrade' (Bleib ein Mensch, Kamerad, / Sei ein Mann, Kamerad).[20]

Such songs were extremely popular among inmates, who sang them often and considered them a crutch for survival. Karl Röder, who outlived Dachau, recalled: 'In an incarceration without foreseeable end, whose sole purpose is the mental and physical destruction of thousands of human beings, the flight into unconsciousness becomes the greatest danger ... By means of the manifold performances the world outside could be brought alive and with it the strength to resist ... Seen in this light, the performances were a valuable component of inner resistance, and it is no exaggeration to say that with their help many people's lives were saved.' Be that as it may, the songs did not alter the fate of most inmates. Morgan and Soyfer were transferred to Buchenwald, where they died in December1938 and February 1939 respectively. Löhner was transported from Buchenwald to Auschwitz, where he succumbed to overwork in December 1942. Granbaum died in Dachau in January 1941, shortly after performing on New Year's Eve in an extremely sick and weak condition.[21] It cannot be denied that in Westerbork as well, the revues provided some short-term psychological benefits to many inmates. Yet there too the shows did nothing to change the fate of the detainees.

Even lesser appeals went unheeded: the 'privilege' of receiving packages was curtailed drastically in the autumn of 1943. Above all, the transports kept rolling eastward every Tuesday morning. Insofar as the revues were a palliative, they might even have served the interests of the Nazi commandant, as Mechanicus noted with dismay: 'Man wants to mourn with those who have been struck down by fate, but he feels compelled to live with the living. Is the *Obersturmführer* such a good psychologist that he knows this law

of life and has put it into effect here? Or is he merely a brutal ego-
ist who lets the Jews amuse themselves for his own amusement and
gives them something at the same time? You cannot see the work-
ings of his heart.' Mechanicus' worst suspicion was that it was part
of a deliberately sadistic ploy: 'The henchmen of the *Führer* play a
cat and mouse game with the Jews; they chase them from one corner to the other and take pleasure in their fear and gradual
exhaustion. The henchman at Westerbork mocks and derides them
by laying on a cabaret with light and airy music as a change from
the macabre Tuesday morning transports. And the Jews are not
ashamed to go to the cabarets.'[22]

This dilemma was real, but Mechanicus never lost sight of the
fact that it was the Nazi system which forced Jewish prisoners to
make such inhuman choices. It need hardly be said that the inmates
of Westerbork had no say over their ultimate fate. They could make
only minor choices, such as that regarding cabaret: To play or not
to play? To attend or not to attend? In favour of cabaret, one could
say that at the very least it offered distraction; at best, it might have
provided some amounts of courage, strength, and fortitude. Against
it, a minority of inmates could and did hurl charges of bad taste,
indeed blasphemy: there was no room for light entertainment while
weekly transports to an unknown but doubtlessly terrible fate were
taking place. But beyond the question of juxtaposition, there was
that of linkage. Some inmates could not suppress the thought that
the shows were somehow complicit in the Nazi 'cat and mouse
game'. As we have seen in other, much less threatening contexts,
cabaret's venting of frustration could serve the interests of the powers that be. The reduction of outright anger made Westerbork
function more smoothly, which meant, ultimately, that the transports left with little commotion. But did that tenuous linkage make
the cabarets complicit? The boxcars would have left under any conditions, with their full quotas of 'transport material'. Etty Hillesum
overheard a fellow inmate say: 'Once upon a time we had a commandant who used to kick people off to Poland. This one sees them
off with a smile.'[23] The worst charge one could level against the
Westerbork cabaret was that it was one facet of that smirk.

If the Westerbork entertainers believed they could save at least
their own lives by mounting the shows, most of them were tragi-
cally deceived. The last Westerbork revue, which opened in June
1944, was dominated quite literally by gallows humour. *Totally
Crazy! A Grotesque Cabaret Show (Total verrückt! Groteske
Kabarettschau)* included numbers such as 'The Guillotine' (according to the programme, 'not for people with weak nerves!!'), and
even an operatic parody of Gothic horror plays entitled 'Ludmilla,

or Corpses on a Conveyor Belt' (Ludmilla, oder Leichen am laufenden Band). On 3 August, Gemmeker suspended all cabaret and other types of performance; a month later he announced that Westerbork was being closed. While some trains left for Auschwitz, the stalwarts of the revues – Rosen, Ehrlich, and Ziegler – had the 'honour' of being sent to Theresienstadt. That was merely a diversion. After only two weeks there, Ehrlich and Rosen were sent on to Auschwitz, where they were gassed on 29 September. Only Ziegler survived the camps.[24]

The inmates of Westerbork had long harboured illusions about Theresienstadt. It was considered a 'favourable' camp, much like Westerbork. Mechanicus noted that when the issue of transports arose, discussions centred around 'Theresienstadt, Theresienstadt, Theresienstadt, Auschwitz, Auschwitz, Auschwitz.' Being sent to the former was considered a sign of 'clemency'. Even the means of transport to the two camps were different: those to Auschwitz were the notorious boxcars, those to Theresienstadt were often third-class passenger trains. After the departure of one of the latter in January 1944, Mechanicus mused:

> 'The word "Theresienstadt" has had a magnetic effect on people's minds, like Wengenrode or the Isle of Wight or Capri. Fantastic tales were going the rounds. It was said that life there was so good that the residents were not imprisoned behind barbed wire, but could move freely through the little old fortress town and live in small houses . . . So the tram departed with men and women who took their leave of Holland and their friends with rather heavy hearts, but consoled themselves with the thought that they were going to a place remote from the scourge of war, the cruelty of the concentration camp and the callousness of the slave-driver who is master in Poland. A pleasure train and a little bit of sightseeing.'

Mechanicus was, however, sceptical. He guessed correctly: 'Hitler wants to exterminate the Jews . . . He exterminates them in separate classes, just as a firm of undertakers buries its dead clients according to different categories.' A friend of Mechanicus expressed the matter most succinctly: 'Theresienstadt is the cat's whiskers, but the cat stinks.'

Theresienstadt (Terezin in Czech) was indeed a giant deception. Originally an Austrian garrison town founded in the late eighteenth century, it had less than four thousand Czech inhabitants in 1939. They were moved out in October 1941, and the city was declared a 'ghetto' exclusively for Jews. It became a holding pen with up to 53,000 inmates at a time. They consisted not only of Jews from Bohemia and Moravia, and later Holland and Denmark, but also 'distinguished' Jews from German-speaking territories. These included decorated veterans of the First World War, as well as noted scholars, writers, artists, and musicians. The Nazis had special reasons for creating a supposedly 'model' ghetto at the time that the mass extermination of Jews was entering its most intense phase. In the face of mounting reports of atrocities, the Germans could invite outside commissions, such as those of the International Red Cross, to Theresienstadt in order to counter reports of bad treatment, let alone mass murder, in the camps. In particular, the Nazis could demonstrate that various well-known Jewish personalities, whose disappearance caused concern abroad, were alive and well.

With respect to the Jewish victims, the myth of Theresienstadt likewise served Nazi interests. We have seen that many of Westerbork's inmates were happy to join the transports to Theresienstadt. Throughout Central Europe many Jews willingly signed over their life savings in exchange for a promise of good care in clean, well-furnished, and private rooms; at times the Nazis even touted the locale as a retirement spa – 'Theresienbad'. Even more insidiously, the myth of Theresienstadt could be used to drive wedges within Jewish communities. Those individuals who acquiesced to Nazi policies without complaint could be 'rewarded' with transport there, while those who made trouble were guaranteed a trip to Auschwitz, Sobibor, or Treblinka. Of course, the true nature of the reward became brutally clear upon arrival at Terezin. Compared to Westerbork, the dormitory barracks were more crowded; medical treatment was much more primitive; physical labour was harder and lasted longer; and the food supply was significantly worse, since most inmates of Theresienstadt rarely received the packages that made such a difference in the Dutch camp. These conditions produced a high mortality rate: of the 141,000 Jews sent to Theresienstadt, 33,000 died there of overwork, malnourishment, and disease. Another 88,000 were shipped on to extermination camps, primarily Auschwitz. Like Westerbork, Theresienstadt was essentially a deceptive way station along the path to the 'final solution'.[26]

Despite the harsh conditions, the inmates of Theresienstadt managed to develop an incredibly rich and active cultural life. Recitals and readings began informally in early 1942, even though they were forbidden by the camp authorities. By the end of that year, however, the official policy was reversed, and cultural life was actively encouraged. Throughout 1943 and up to October 1944, when massive transports to Auschwitz decimated the camp's population, Theresienstadt witnessed numerous events of every conceivable type: lectures, poetry readings, recitals, chamber music, symphony concerts, oratorios, even several operas. Cabaret too proliferated, owing to the versatility it had demonstrated throughout its history: it did not require elaborate sets and costumes or extensive scripts, but could be pieced together quickly from diverse sources. Moreover, it could be performed in every conceivable venue. Theresienstadt's numerous cabarets appeared not only in the (very few) performance halls, but also in barracks, attics, courtyards, and infirmary wards. Of the Czech-language cabarets, the most popular was headed by Karel Svenk, who scripted the most critical numbers presented in the camp. The majority of cabarets were performed in German. Several different ensembles were formed by professional entertainers, most of whom hailed from Vienna (Egon Thorn, Hans Hofer, Bobby John, Ernst Morgan, Walter Steiner, Walter Lindenbaum). One notable group was headed by Leo Strauss; despite the second 's', he was the son of Oscar Straus, who had been the in-house composer of Wolzogen's Motley Theatre forty years earlier. Carl Meinhard, one of the 'Bad Boys' of the Imperial era, was likewise interned in Theresienstadt, but he took little part in the ghetto's stage life.[27]

January 1944 saw the arrival of Kurt Gerron, one of Berlin's greatest stars of the twenties. He had appeared in every major cabaret and revue of the time: the Wild Stage, Megalomania, the Kadeko, the revues of Hollaender and Nelson. He had played the role of Tiger Brown at the premiere of *The Threepenny Opera* and the vaudeville director in the film *The Blue Angel*. After Hitler's takeover he moved to Amsterdam, where he directed several successful films, until protests by Dutch film-makers, who disliked the competition, put an end to his involvement. He subsequently appeared in Nelson's and Rosen's revues. Following the Nazi invasion Marlene Dietrich tried to bring him to the United States, but he loathed the thought of emigrating once again, so he turned down the offer. He also rejected the opportunity to go into hiding in Holland, as Nelson had done. As a decorated veteran of the First World War, Gerron trusted the certificate given him by the Germans that supposedly exempted him from deportation. Like all other Nazi promises, it was soon broken. In September 1943 he was sent to Westerbork, where he appeared in the third revue. At the beginning of 1944 he was transported to Theresienstadt.

Whereas Gemmeker often went to the Westerbork revues, Karl Rahm, the German commandant of the Terezin ghetto, rarely attended any of its inmates' performances. Nevertheless, he had seen Gerron on screen and was pleased to have such a famous actor in his camp; he even arranged to have Gerron give a special performance for the SS. Having been shown supposed goodwill at the top, Gerron proceeded to mount the most lavish of the

Theresienstadt cabarets. Known as the Carousel (Karussell), it performed over fifty times, most frequently during June and July 1944. Gerron could draw upon the best talent in the camp. The music was usually arranged, and often composed and played, by Martin Roman. This German musician, another who had arrived in Terezin via Westerbork, was also the leader of The Ghetto Swingers, the Theresienstadt jazz band. Sets for the cabaret were designed by Frantisek Zelenka, who had been a prominent stage designer for the Czech National Theatre in Prague. For his texts Gerron drew on the talents of Leo Strauss and another writer, Manfred Greiffenhagen.[28]

As in Westerbork, the Theresienstadt cabarets led to serious questions of propriety and complicity. The performers could not be accused of entertaining Nazi officers, since attendance by the SS was very exceptional; otherwise, all of the other qualms resurfaced. Performers had a vested interest in their activities, which raised them to the ranks of so-called 'prominents'. This usually guaranteed private sleeping quarters, better food rations, and above all protection from transports. The fact that thousands were constantly being shipped 'to the east' again made many inmates question the propriety of light entertainment. H.G. Adler, a survivor who wrote the most extensive account of Theresienstadt, was thoroughly disgusted by the 'unhealthy to-do' and the 'dissipated thoughtlessness' of the cabarets; he contended that 'human dignity was eroded from the inside out, without the victims noticing it'. Zdenek Lederer, another survivor and chronicler of the camp, contended that the entertainments served Nazi purposes in two ways: by distracting the inmates, and by putting on a facade of leniency for outside inspectors. Lederer argued that 'the Germans were not inspired by generosity when granting cultural freedom to their victims. They only cared for the success of their propaganda stunt and the smooth progress of deportations: cultural freedom would lull the prisoners into a false sense of security and would also provide a harmless outlet for any will to resistance.' Another survivor, Jacob Jacobson, took issue with such sentiments, claiming that it would be unjust to blame the people for using those institutions and, by using them, helping the Nazis indirectly to carry out this manoeuvre of camouflage and deceit'. He claimed that distraction was a psychological necessity for most inmates, a welcome 'counterbalance' to 'horror and despair': 'Just because the danger of deportation was menacing everyone at every moment, the people in the Ghetto had to live as if this danger did not really exist, as if a life of freedom and human dignity was waiting round the corner.'[29]

The surviving texts from Gerron's cabaret allow us to examine the ways in which the shows attempted to cope with the inmates' psychological needs. Although the Carousel presented much old material – for example, Gerron often sang tunes from *The Three-penny Opera* – a number of new songs addressed conditions in Theresienstadt. Leo Strauss wrote most of these lyrics, including the theme song for the cabaret. Likewise entitled 'Carousel', it described life as a 'strange voyage, a journey without a destination' (Das ist eine seltsame Reise, / Das ist eine Fahrt ohne Ziel); only when the turning stopped could you see where you stood. In this confusing world, there was one great need: 'Illusion, oh please, please, illusion' (Illusion, ach bitte, bitte, Illusion). This appeal for illusion, for suppressing the present, characterised many of the Carousel's numbers. Several of them harked back to friendships and romances in the past, and promised that friends and lovers would find each other in the future. The first half of the 'Theresienstadt Viennese Song' (Theresienstädter Wiener Lied) described how the singer and his 'sweetie' (*Schatzerl*) used to rendezvous at the Prater, Vienna's amusement park. In the second half, he sang that he was now in Theresienstadt, while she was 'somewhere in the east'; yet the refrain contended that every night he still met her in the Prater in is dreams, and it held out the hope that they would be reunited there some day. Such numbers, which swept the audience out of the present into an idyllic past and a hopeful future, were evidently very popular. One inmate, Frieda Rosenthal, even wrote Leo Strauss a poem thanking him for his songs, since 'thanks to the dear cabaret' (Dank dem lichen Cabaret), she could forget temporarily about hunger and the travails of the day. In particular, numbers that spoke of 'once upon a time' (Es war einmal) and 'it will be once again' (Es wird einmal wieder sein) stilled the 'longing' in her heart.[30]

Not all of the cabaret's numbers contributed to illusion, however; some of them cautioned against it. That was the case with 'From the Strauss Family' (Aus der Famille der Sträusse). The number essentially described the confusion generated by the numerous, often unrelated composers of that name (Josef; Johann father and son; Richard; and Leo's father Oscar). But punning on the word *Strauss* (ostrich), the song contended that of all the Strausses, the most respected one in Theresienstadt was the ostrich, because it could stick its head in the sand. In general, the Carousel shows treated illusions ambivalently. On the one hand, Leo Strauss recognised that visions of hope were necessary for survival, or at least for maintaining sanity. On the other hand, he realised that certain delusions could be deadly, especially since Theresienstadt itself was a city built upon deception. Perhaps the most popular Strauss text was 'As If' (Als ob), which described Terezin as an as-if city with as-if occupations, as-if celebrities, as-if food, and as-if beds.

Significantly, a note of self-criticism entered the last stanza, which
suggested that visions of a better future might also be as-if hopes:

> Oppressive fate we carry
> As if it were quite light,
> And speak of better futures,
> As if they were in sight.

> Man trägt das schwere Schicksal,
> Als ob es nicht so schwer,
> Und spricht von schönrer Zukunft,
> Als obs schon morgen wär.[31]

Strauss spoke of disillusionment because that was the first, over-
whelmingly shocking experience of all new arrivals in Terezin.
Almost all survivors' accounts describe the horror of the people
who came expecting to find a pleasant town, only to be treated like
animals. Upon reaching Terezin, they had to drag their baggage for
over a mile until they reached what inmates called the 'sluice'
(*Schleuse*), where all of their belongings were promptly confiscated.
Not yet fully disillusioned, many people would request special
accommodations: double rooms, for example, or balconies with
southern exposure. The final, irreversible blow came when they
were herded into the crowded barracks, with their three-tiered
wooden bunk beds. Many inmates, finally realising the massiveness
of the deception, went into shock or deep depression – a condition
that made them prime candidates for the next transport to
Auschwitz. Strauss addressed this phenomenon in one of his most
bitterly humorous songs. It took the form of a dialogue between a
newly arrived lady and a long-term inmate of the camp. The fash-
ionable woman's conceptions of what food, lodging, and clothes she
expected were fundamentally, if wittily, destroyed in the course of
the conversation.[32] What is interesting about the song is that it
made fun of the new arrival, and thus spoke to an audience that was
presumed to consist of long-term residents. In addition to giving this
public a sense of superiority vis-a-vis the newcomers, it suggested
that their ability to survive was a product of their adaptability, their
realism, and even their sense of humour.

Once again, it is hard to speak of 'humour' in the context of a
concentration camp, but the Carousel's songs implied that wit was
one component of survival. Many numbers tried to laugh off the
annoyances of the inmates' lives, such as the seemingly endless
standing in line for meagre food rations. Strauss even wrote a song
on that subject which parodied 'Here Comes the Music', one of his
father's hits at Wolzogen's Motley Theatre forty years earlier. Lilien-
cron's text had described the passing of a military band; now

Strauss's 'Here Comes the Grub' (Die Menage kommt) recounted the hierarchic order in which people were allowed to line up for their servings.[33]

Whereas such songs attempted to come to terms with facts of camp life that could not be changed, other, more serious numbers tried to correct modes of behaviour whereby the inmates hurt each other and themselves. One of the most important of such themes was the prejudice rampant among the Czech, Austrian, and German Jews incarcerated in Terezin. As in Westerbork, the German Jews were perceived to have a superior attitude, and so were resented by the Austrian and Czech Jews; yet the German and Austrian Jews together looked down upon the eastern European prisoners.

Several cabaret numbers combated anti-Semitic prejudices among the Jewish inmates themselves. Many had come from thoroughly assimilated families, and were even baptised. Some of these people not only considered themselves as not Jewish but they despised Jews in general and east European Jews in particular. In Strauss's dialogue between the new arrival at Terezin and the long-term inmate, the former's first complaint was that she was suddenly surrounded by 'Polish Semites'. As conferencier, Strauss would tell the following joke: 'A gentleman who lives in the same room with me said to me today: 'I'm really suffering from a great injustice. Never in my life have I socialised with Jews – and now I'm forced to live in a room with so many Jews.' I replied to him: 'And I suffer from an even greater injustice. In my whole life I have socialised only with Jews-and now I'm forced to live in a room full of anti-Semites.' While Strauss indirectly appealed for tolerance by underscoring the absurdity of anti-Semitism among Jewish prisoners, Manfred Greiffenhagen, the other major lyricist at the Carousel, wrote a song that pleaded overtly for solidarity among the interned Jews, be they Czech, German, Austrian, Dutch, or Danish citizens.[34]

The Carousel thus made serious attempts to alleviate the situation of the prisoners in Terezin. At the very least it offered them distraction, at best it sought to improve their behaviour towards each other. Nevertheless, as in Westerbork, that did not alter the ultimate fate of the inmates, nor did it obviate the fact that the cabaret was part of an elaborate Nazi charade. Indeed, the performances took place most frequently in June 1944, at the height of the notorious 'beautification project' (*Verschönerungsaktion*). In anticipation of a visit by the International Red Cross on 23 June, Theresienstadt's population was mobilised to clean up the town. Facades were repainted, gardens planted, and fictitious shops, schools, playgrounds, and even a bank were concocted. Performances, including those of the Carousel, were spruced up. Worst of all, over seven thousand elderly prisoners were shipped off to Auschwitz, in order to give the city a less crowded look. When the Red Cross observers arrived, they were taken on a carefully choreographed eight-hour tour of the ghetto, which gave them the impression of a peaceful, happy, and culturally thriving community. They did not observe the cabaret, but saw instead a few minutes of Hans Krasa's *Brundibar*, a children's opera that was the inmates' favourite production.[35]

The Nazi officials were so thrilled by the success of their ruse that they planned one final deceit: they decided to use the cleaned-up camp as the backdrop for a propaganda film which would show for all time how well they treated the Jews. The film was cynically entitled *The Führer Presents a City to the Jews (Der Führer schenkt den Juden eine Stadt)*. It was to be Gerron's last work, and his most terrible concession to the Nazis. As a famous actor and film director, he was the most obvious candidate for the project. Since refusal to comply would have meant certain death, he felt compelled to undertake it. He worked out a detailed scenario, and the shooting took place on twelve days between 16 August and 11 September.

The film showed clean barracks, well-equipped workshops, a well-supplied hospital, and several activities that were unthinkable to the prisoners in reality, such as tilling private garden plots or swimming in the nearby river. Naturally, the cultural life of the camp was highlighted: there were clips from *Brundibar*, a symphony concert, and a performance of Verdi's Requiem. Since Gerron was the film's director, his cabaret naturally appeared as well. That segment too underscored the film's duplicity. The Carousel always performed within the ghetto, since the prisoners were forbidden to venture beyond the moats of the former garrison. Nevertheless, the film's cabaret sequence was shot in an open field well beyond the town, to give the impression that the inhabitants were free to roam the countryside.

Alice Randt, a survivor of Terezin, witnessed the filming of the cabaret segment on 19 August. She and hundreds of the other prisoners were told to put on summer clothes, which had been given to them as part of the 'beautification project', and to assemble for a performance of the Carousel, at which ice cream would be served. Most of the inmates were loathe to participate in the filming, since they had been mortified and infuriated by the Red Cross visit. However, they had no choice but to comply; and a chance to walk in the countryside, taste ice cream, and see the stars of the Carousel (tickets for which were hard to come by) certainly sweetened the pain. Under heavy guard the 'audience' was marched to an outlying meadow. What awaited them was disappointment. There was no ice cream, and they heard only short snippets of songs, repeated several times for out-takes; Gerron sang 'Mack the Knife' and the 'Cannon-Song' from *The Threepenny Opera*, among other things. The crowd was supposed to provide images of 'happy spectators'. The shooting was delayed because there were too many blond-haired people in the audience. Since Gerron had been ordered to show only 'Jewish-looking' individuals in the film, he had to await a delivery of more dark-haired prisoners. The whole situation – including the fact that they were surrounded by armed SS guards, just out of camera range – put the spectators into anything but a jovial mood, and Gerron had to work hard to get them to laugh. Randt remembered:

> Whoever looks into the camera, makes faces or speaks into the camera, will be arrested immediately'. Bathed in sweat, Gerron urged us, implored us, begged for discipline, for us to follow orders absolutely. He cracked jokes and made despairing efforts. 'Please, no incidents, don't provoke any use of force!' He begged us urgently: 'Do what I show you, when I laugh, laugh with me!' And he began a contagious, irresistible laugh, during which he wobbled his fat belly, so that we really had to laugh, even though the situation for him and for us was anything but laughable. *Laugh, Pagliacco!* Thus he stood before us, pale, sweaty, laughing loudly, with a wobbling belly. And thus they filmed peals of laughter from three thousand cheerful country dwellers enjoying their glorious summer variety show!

She recalled further that they all returned 'furious' and 'full of shame'.[36] The soundtrack was not added to the film until March 1945, and it was shown to a Red Cross commission on 6 April. By then the fictitious scenes could do little to whitewash the Nazis' crimes, as irrefutable proof of German atrocities was being uncovered daily by the advancing Allied armies. In the fall of 1944, however, clips of Gerron's film had already appeared in the weekly newsreels shown in German cinemas. Images of 'Jewish-looking' people sitting in the Terezin cafe were juxtaposed with shots of fighting German soldiers, and the voice-over proclaimed: 'While the Jews in Theresienstadt dance and consume coffee and cake, our soldiers bear all the burdens of a terrible war, its dangers and deprivations, in order to defend the homeland.' Since German cities were being systematically levelled by bombs at that time, the German spectators could not but have felt resentment at the privileged and protected residents of the idyllic Theresienstadt.[37]

In reality, by the time the clips were shown on German screens, the population of Terezin had been decimated. Having duped the Red Cross commission and shot the film, the Nazis had no further use for their 'model ghetto'. September and October 1944 were the most terrible months in the history of the camp, as almost twenty thousand prisoners were transported to Auschwitz. Among them were Kurt Gerron and Leo Strauss, who died in the gas chambers. Manfred Greiffenhagen was sent on to Dachau, where he perished in January 1945.

Cabaret usually tried to end the evening on an upbeat note. In part, that was commercially astute: it sent the audience home in a 'feel-good' mood. It would be possible to give this book a 'happy end' as well. After all, Friedrich Hollaender and Rudolf Nelson not only survived the war, they even mounted cabaret shows and revues in the Federal Republic. Werner Finck and Erich Kästner, who had remained in the Nazi state, also contributed to West Germany's post-war cabaret scene. The more leftist entertainers and veterans of the agit-prop movement gravitated toward the German Democratic Republic, which developed a distinctive cabaret culture of its own.

But those later developments cannot blind us to the fact that an entire era of Berlin cabaret had come to a tragic end by 1945. *Kabarett* in the Federal Republic and the GDR was quite unlike that of the previous eras: it was less showy, and much more focused on political themes. By contrast, the Wilheimine and Weimar tradition of cabaret was an unstable but vital combination of satire and parody dealing with love, fashion, art, and – at times – politics. This mixture constantly shifted in response to Germany's volatile political, cultural, and economic climate. The genre was strained to the limit in the concentration camps, and it was there that Berlin cabaret died. It perished not because it could not cope with the inhuman conditions; it managed to retain a blend of art and entertainment, of humour and seriousness, even in those impossible circumstances. Berlin cabaret died because the Nazis murdered so many of the human beings who sustained it – women and men, writers and composers, actors and musicians, professionals and amateurs, entertainers and audience.

Notes

1. For Dutch interest in German cabaret before 1933, see Jacques Klöters, 'Denk vandaag met aan morgen: Cabaret en revue in Duitsland en Nederland', in Kathinka Dittrich et al., eds., *Berlin Amsterdam: Wisselwerkingen* (Amsterdam:1982), 168–77. The remainder of the article (177–85) surveys German cabaret in Holland from 1933 to 1944. For general studies of the German exile experience in Holland, see Kathinka Dittrich and Hans Würzner, eds., *Die Niederlande und das deutsche Exil, 1933–40* (Königstein: 1982); and Klaus Hermsdorf et al., *Exil in den Niederlanden und in Spanien* (Frankfurt am Main: 1981).

2. On the initial Dutch response to the Nazi regime, see Harry Pappe, 'Die Niederlande und die Niederländer', in Dittrich and Würzner, *Die Niederlande*, 18.

3. See Jacques Klöters, 'Momente so, Momente so: Dora Gerson und das erste Emigranten-Kabarett 'Ping-Pong', in Dittrich and Würzner, *Die Niederlande*, 174–85.

4. See Hermsdorf, *Exil in den Niederlanden*, 74–76; and Klöters, 'Denk vandaag niet aan morgen', 180–81.

5. *National Zeitung*, 19 November 1933; *Zürichsee Zeitung*, 5 December 1933; *De Tijd*, 3 May 1934; *Algemeen Handelsblad*, 11 September 1936; song quoted in ibid, 19 November 1936.

6. For an account of Nelson's revues in Amsterdam, see Klöters, 'Denk vandaag niet aan morgen', 178–80.

7. '4 Jaar Theater der Prominenten,' in programme booklet, Theater der Prominenten, Lutine Palace, Scheveningen, Seizoen 1940, copy in Nederlands Theater Instituut. For an account of the Prominents, see Klöters, 'Denk vandaag niet aan morgen', 181–82.

8. Herbert Nelson, 'Das Leben geht weiter', reprinted in Kühn, *Deutschlands Erwachen*, 206.

9. Rosen's attempts to reach the United States are recounted by his widow, Elsbeth Rosen, 'Mein Mann Willy Rosen,' in Will Meisel, *Willy Rosen: 'Text und Musik von mir'* (Berlin: 1967), 6.

10. For accounts of Westerbork, see J. Presser, *The Destruction of the Dutch Jews*, trans. Arnold Pomerans (New York: 1969), 406–64; and Jacob Boas, *Boulevard des Misères: The Story of the Transit Camp Westerbork* (Hamden, Conn.:1985). The most direct and complete accounts are diaries and letters by two inmates who eventually perished in Auschwitz: Philip Mechanicus, *Year of A Jewish Prisoner as he waits for Auschwitz*, trans. Irene Gibbons (New York: 1968); and Etty Hillesum, *An Interrupted Life: The Diaries of Etty Hillesum, 1941–43*, trans. Arnold Pomerans (New York: 1983), and *Letters from Westerbork*, trans. Arnold Pomerans (New York: 1986). See also the account by Israel Taubes, 'The Persecution of Jews in Holland, 1940–44: Westerbork and Bergen-Beisen', typescript, Jewish Survivors Report, Documents of Nazi Guilt, no. 2 (London: Jewish Central Information Office, 1945). For further reflections on the Holocaust in the Netherlands, see Louis de Jong, *The Netherlands and Nazi Germany* (Cambridge, Mass: 1990), 1–25.

11. Mechanicus, *Year of Fear*, 146, 89. Typed programme booklets for five of the six revues are located at the Rijksinstituut voor Oorlogsdocumentatie, Amsterdam. The photographs, from an album documenting 'Humor und Melodie' that was presented to Gemmeker, are housed in Yad Vashem, Jerusalem.

12. Mechanicus, *Year of Fear*, 147; Hillesum, *Letters*, 136.

13. For Mechanicus' discussion of the hostilities between Dutch and German Jews, and his plans to assuage them, see *Year of Fear*, 30–33, 101, 104, 113, 120–24, 147, 151, 175, 183, 191, 218–19, 239, 246.

14. Mechanicus, *Year of Fear*, 176, 202. For Gemmeker's socialising with the entertainers and other favours, see ibid., 99; and Hillesum, *Letters*, 133, 136.

15. Taubes, 'Persecution of the Jews in Holland', 26; Mechanicus, *Year of Fear*, 46.

16. Hillesum, *Letters*, 89; Mechanicus, *Year of Fear*, 103 176.

17. Taubes, 'Persecution of the Jews in Holland', 27; Mechanicus, *Year of Fear*, 147, 22.

18. Ehrlich's line is quoted at the beginning of the photo album of 'Hunior und Melodie' presented to Gemmeker; Mechanicus also refers to it, ibid., 147.

19. Beda, 'Buchenwald-Lied,' in Kühn, *Deutschlands Erwachen*, 309. For an early account of performances at Dachau and Buchenwald by a former inmate, see Curt Daniel, 'The Freest Theatre in the Reich: In the German Concentration Camps', *Theatre Arts*, 25 (1941): 801–7. The origins of the first camp anthem,

composed at Börgermoor ('Wir sind die Moorsoldaten'), are recounted in Wolf-gang Langboff, *Die Moorsoldaten* (1935; reprinted Halle: 1986), 165–86.

20. Jura Soyfer, 'Dachau Lied', in Kühn, *Deutschlands Erwachen*, 316–17.
21. Röder is quoted in Walter Rösler, ed., *Gehn ma halt a bisserl unter: Kabarett in Wien von den Anfängen bis heute* (Berlin: 1991), 273. Grünbaum's last days are described by a fellow inmate in Karl Schnog, 'Das Ende eines Spassmachers', in Helga Bemmann, ed., *Mitgelacht -dabeigewesen: Erinnerungen aus acht Jahrzehnten Kabarett* (Berlin: 1984), 285–89.
22. Mechanicus, *Year of Fear*, 159, 100.
23. Hillesum, *Letters from Westerbork*, 136.
24. The murders of Ehrlich and Rosen are mentioned in Max Mannheimer, 'Theresienstadt, and From Thersienstadt to Auschwitz', typescript, Jewish Survivors Report, Documents of Nazi Guilt, no. 3 (London: Jewish Central Information Office, 1945), 8–9.
25. Mechanicus, *Year of Fear*, 152, 154, 230, 230–31, 228.
26. The two most complete accounts of Thesienstadt were written by survivors: Zdenek Lederer, *Ghetto Theresienstadt* (1953; reprinted New York: 1983); and H.G. Adler, *Theresienstadt 1941–45: Das Antlitz einer Zwangsgemeinschaft* (Tübingen: 1955), as well as Adler's volume of primary sources, *Die verheim-lichte Wahrheit: Theresienstädter Dokumente* (Tübingen: 1958). For important recent studies, see Ruth Bondy, *'Elder of the Jews' : Jakob Edelstein of There-sienstadt* (New York: 1989); and Ruth Schwertfeger, *Women of Theresienstadt: Voices from a Concentration Camp* (Oxford: 1989).
27. Cabaret in Theresienstadt is described in Eva Somorova, 'Kabarett im Konzen-trationslager Terezin (Theresienstadt), 1941–45', in *Kassette 5* (1981): 161–69; and Joza Karas, *Music in Terezin, 1941–45* (New York: 1985), 143–56. Karas describes the other musical activities in Terezin. The visual arts are described in Gerald Green, *The Artists of Terezin* (New York: 1969); and in Johanna Bran-son, ed., *Seeing through 'paradise': artists and the Terezin concentration camp* (Boston: 1991). Some of the thousands of children's drawings, and dozens of children's poems that survived their young creators are reproduced in *I never saw another butterfly: Children's Drawings and Poems from Terezin Concen-tration Camp, 1942–44* (New York: 1962).
28. Martin Roman, who survived the camps, mentioned the special performance for the SS in an interview cited in Karas, *Music in Terezin*, 147. The total number of performances by the Carousel is unknown; however, an accounting of per-formances in Theresienstadt made in the summer of 1944 (Yad Vashem, document 064/415) indicates performances almost every other day from 13 June to 2 July, and notes that the troupe had appeared forty-five times by 20 July. For Roman's 'Ghetto Swingers', see Karas, *Music in Terezin*, 151–52; and Kater, *Dif-ferent Drummers*, 177–79.
29. *Adler, Theresienstadt*, 579, 589, 588; Lederer, *Ghetto Theresienstadt*, 126; Jacob Jacobson, 'Terezin: The Daily Life, 1943–45', typescript, Jewish Survivors Report, Documents of Nazi Guilt, no. 6 (London: Jewish Central Information Office, 1946), 12.
30. Typescripts of the surviving Theresienstadt lyrics are housed at Yad Vashem. Almost all of them have been reprinted in Ulrike Migdal, ed., *Und die Musik spielt dazu: Chansons und Satiren aus dem KZ Theresienstadt* (Munich: 1986). For Leo Strauss, 'Karussell' and 'Theresienstädter Wiener Lied', see 59–61, 65–67; and Frieda Rosenthal, 'Dank dem lieben Cabaret', 70–71.
31. Leo Strauss, 'Aus der Familie der Strässe' and 'Als oh', in Migdal, *Und die Musik*, 67–70, 106–8.

32. Leo Strauss, 'Theresienstädter Fragen', in Migdal, *Und die Musik*, 71–74.

33. Leo Strauss, 'Die Menage kommt', in Migdal, *Und die Musik*, 87.

34. Strauss, 'Theresienstädter Fragen', 72; 'Aus den Theresienstädter Conferencen von Leo Strauss', typescript in the archives of Pamatnik Terezin, Herrmann collection, no. 4092/1; and Manfred Greiffenhagen, 'Die Ochsen', in Migdal, *Und die Musik*, 105–106.

35. On the 'beautification project', see Adler, *Theresienstadt*, 162–75.

36. Alice Randt, 'Die Schleuse: Drei Jahre Theresienstadt' (typescript, given to Yad Vashem in 1951), 94–96. For more on the film, see Adler, Theresienstadt, 178–91, and the documentation reprinted in Adler, *Die verheimlichte Wahrheit*, 324–351. The documents indicate that 1800 prisoners were marched to the meadow. No copy of the completed film survives; however, about a half-hour of out-takes are housed in Yad Vashem. The cabaret scenes are not among them.

37. The use of the clips in the 'Wochenschau' is mentioned in Adler, *Die verheimlichte Wahrheit*, 325.

PART IV

THEATRE AT THE FRONT

CHAPTER *11*

BRIGADES AT THE FRONT

JOSEPH MACLEOD

No one man speaks the truth, but all collectively do – PLUTARCH

Perhaps one of the most interesting war developments of the V.T.O was the theatrical 'brigades' it organised. These brigades were a universal feature of the Soviet theatres, and provided a further link between East and West. This impinging of the two was not itself a war development; it had been going on for years, Kipling or no. But war put it in arms against a common threat; and comrades in arms are the closest and most enduring comrades. Because of international Fascism, Europe and Asia fused; and that fusion has an importance for us all, if we have only the wit and honesty to see it.

Immediately the war broke out, the V.T.O. began to organise small concert parties to tour the forces, inviting several leading actors from the Maly, Vahtangov, Theatre of the Revolution, the Children's and other Moscow theatres, who were specially released for the purpose. Opera singers too were included. People's Artist N. N. Rybakov of the Maly was placed in charge. These 'brigades' as they were called performed sketches, one-act plays, recitations, either solo or in production numbers, popular vaudevilles sometimes so long established as to have become 'classic', songs, dances and so on. Their stages were whatever was offered in the shape of lorry platforms, warship decks, forest clearings; and the scenery was tents or sheets.

Instructional units too were formed, a producer, a choreographer, and a chorus-master, to visit and advise amateur groups in the Red Army and the clubs that were to be found wherever members of any of the forces had a few hours' leisure.

The brigades were such favourites that as the first months passed it became clear that much more was needed. Concert parties were regrouped into companies, capable of taking entire works to the fronts, whether classical or contemporary. Two such companies were in operation by the spring of 1942, one of which had in its repertoire the Ostrovsky comedy, *Not all Cream for the Cat*; a new play by Kaverin, *The House on the Hill*, an evening of Chehov, and a straight concert programme. Its producer was Nikolay Yanovsky a former actor of the Vahtangov Theatre. An abridged version of *Russian People* was added in December 1942, as the company toured the Southern and Stalingrad fronts up to April 1943. Yanovsky said he was rather doubtful about giving Red Army men a play so near to their own conditions and lives, although before producing it he had spent a good deal of time on the Kalinin and Central fronts getting to know men and commanders, how they lived, and what they were thinking and feeling. With a gifted company he was thus able to ensure that inner authenticity which Stanislavsky considered to be the essence of a good actor ... and it is significant that Yanovsky followed the Moscow Art Theatre in giving prime importance to the actor. There can be little doubt that this inner authenticity was largely the cause of the intense emotion roused in Red Army audiences by this play. They appear to have been quite remarkably stirred; a tribute not only to the actors, and to the author, but also to the sturdy realistic outlook of the audiences.

Put yourself in the position of a commander, resting with his unit somewhere in the rear. Many of your men have been outstanding for their utter absorption in their job ... to the point of self-oblivion. They have come through alive, so far, by several miracles. Also there may be a particular girl in one of the services whose pluck and resourcefulness in tight corners you and your men have admired, though there is no need to suppose you are unconsciously in love with her, as is the commander in this play. Your mother is back behind the enemy lines in cccupied territory, and you do not know whether she is alive or dead; because as a fine, firm, outspoken old lady who does not count consequences, you are more than doubtful that she has been murdered by the Nazis ... .and in what form of death ?

This will have been a common state of mind among Red Army men whether commanders or not. Yet you will go, and be enthralled by a group of play-actors impersonating yourself in this state of mind, sending the girl on an almost impossible mission because you have to; your fine soldier going to certain death with song and a light heart; your old mother losing control and being dragged out to be hanged. You will be profoundly moved, even to tears; yet it will not be useless emotionalism. The truer the experience, the more you are made aware that there are millions like you, suffering like you and resolute like you. And the play ends with yourself on the stage, shouting, not in an effective curtain line, but in a conclusion drawn by stage logic from the people and the plot, and also in the only possible climax to your own spiritual experience during it: 'Nothing! Nothing, Comrade Major-General; nothing! Only I so want to live, to live a long time. To live till the moment when I see the last of the men that have done this, see them dead with my own eyes. The very last; and, dead. Dead just here, under my feet!'

Russian people, like French people, are more directly and expressively patriotic than the British; but only a person viewing life from an armchair on an island could dismiss this as war propaganda. It is the complete identification of stage and audience. Yanovsky's qualms were idle. The play was in great demand throughout the winter of 1942–3, as the V.T.O. company went with the advancing Russian armies through Kotelnikovo to Novo-Cherkassk and Rostov-on-Don, where performances were given within a few days of the German's withdrawal.

That was a long road, and hard. In the icy winds of the winter steppe on lorries, to act each evening in villages partially or wholly destroyed by the retreating Huns; no food nor water, nor even a roofed-room big enough to perform in, and Red Army men rigging up some half-wrecked barn or store-shed to serve as a frosty theatre, with perhaps a few stoves made from oil drums if they were lucky. But the close relation of stage to audience, and skill and spirit of actors and actresses, made such hardships negligible. Socialist realism made the play important; the spirit of the Soviet peoples shown in it, and their hope and objective, made its performance valuable. Thinking, as well as suffering, showed them what Nazism meant.[1]

Theatre Brigades

If that was the effect of an ad hoc company drawn from several theatres, we can imagine the effect of one composed of fine artists used to playing to each other. And there was hardly a first-class theatre in the Soviet Union which did not organise a similar front-line brigade. Nor was this considered a paragon, or a mere act of 'cheering up the boys'; certainly, not as a means of evading active service in the armed forces. Tarasova, Zuyeva and Dorohin, in a joint letter to the Press in October 1942, wrote: 'Work at the front must be part of our productive work in the theatre'; and again, 'We need systematic excursions to the fighting line with the best examples of our art. We must prepare brigade programmes in the same way as we prepare first nights. . . . We are bound to show front line real high art.'

These stars of the Moscow Art Theatre were not writing vaguely. They were members of an Art Theatre brigade which also included violinist Karevich who played principally Dvorak, a singer, and an accordion player. Joseph Rayevsky, an actor attached to the Art Theatre, was in charge; and they carried the stars' ideas into practice, by showing excerpts from plays by Tolstoy, Chehov, Ostrovsky and Pushkin, and from The Lower Depths. One of the most popular recitations was Lukovsky's topical heroic poem about the defence of Leningrad, delivered by Tarasova with all the power of a skilled actress who had been in touch with audiences for many professional years.

A short tour in the autumn of 1942 was chiefly confined to the Red Air Force, though they stopped at Moscow on their way to the front from Sverdlovsk. In ten days they gave fifteen performances, covering 900 kilometres for the purpose. Often the audience came straight from their machines, clad in the clumsy necessities of an airman's outfit; and Rayevsky sums up their reactions in the happy phrase: 'We were glad that we were able to offer them cultured and joyous relaxation from the strain of battle'.

To this Dorohin added detail: they aimed at keeping 'the aroma of Art Theatre productions, their delicate psychological tissue, deep humanity and austere purity of form'. Then it struck them that in the hard, tense atmosphere of war, this kind of thing might conceivably be out of place and their subtle art unwelcome. In most armies, discipline necessarily knocks personal life into an unresponsible, unresponsive anonymity, peacetime taste is suspended; fatigue and pattern compel conformity; there is no time for comment. Of the Red Army, the Red actor ought perhaps to have known better; but the company had none the less that proud self-distrust which overcomes all good stage artists before a first night. And, as if to test them under the most stringent conditions, their first-night audience was an uncompromising one, 3,000 men and commanders.

The players put on evening dress, because they wanted to show their respect, and day clothes would have been too ordinary. They had to change in the small bus they had. As the tour continued, they forgot little things, like the confined acting areas, the improvised lighting; they lost themselves in the art of acting. Hence, whenever they appeared, in hangars, garages, sheds, or simply forest glades, they received an ovation. The audience clamoured for their favourite scenes, something from *Anna Karenina* or the chief

Vershinin-Masha passage from *The Three Sisters*. Dorohin describes how odd it felt to make a stool and an ammunition chest serve for the salon in Princess Betsy's palace, where Anna first meets Vronsky; or for the Prozorovs' drawing-room. He casts back his mind to the days when the Moscow Arts Theatre found difficulty in getting into their parts at the Paris Exposition des Beaux Arts in 1937, because the Theatre des Champs Elysées had no revolving stage! But acting triumphed even over cannonade rumble and explosions of landmines which rattled the window of the tiny 'stage'. And when it was over the two planes left an aerodrome, one containing the little company, another visitors from a neighbouring Air Force station who had flown over for the show. Or the little bus would go bumping and grunting over shell-pitted steppe or forest ride.

By such visits, by mixing with the virile, active, cultured, thoughtful men of the Red Air Force who would come round after the show and criticise points that had seemed wrong in the performance and stayed to talk about their own lives and experiences; by understanding their hatred of Fascism and how it sprang, like Gorky's, from their intense love of life and of individual humanity, and from the system that had made both possible for them; these fine artists of one of the best theatres in the world acknowledged on their return not only that the venture had been a success, and that they had been wanted, but that they themselves had learned.[2]

The Maly Theatre brigades reported the same. Within nine months in 1942 over a thousand performances were given by various groups of Maly artists. Some in military hospitals, training schools, aerodromes; others, men crawled through communication trenches to attend. One brigade contained Turchaninova, Shatrova, Fadeyeva, Grigorevskaya, Slobodinskaya, five very gallant women. By September 1943 the Maly had organised and sent out its tenth front-line brigade, which included three prominent actors and a vocal quartet. And to be included in the list of stars who had at least once gone on such a tour were People's Artist Sadovsky, People's Artist Gogolyeva, Honoured Artist Mezhinsky (who played Dr.Mamlock in the film of that name), and Stalin-Laureate Ilyinsky. The first two were in a group that toured near Mozhaisk, Maloyaroslavl, and Kaluga in the early summer of 1942. Another group was headed by People's Artist Mihail Lenin, one of whose best performances in peacetime was the Shakespeare-spouting old-style strolling tragedian in *The Forest*. . . . a subtle study, bringing out the Don Quixote in this character, when he takes the comedian on a visit to his aunt and finds himself in a forest of provincial vulgarity, selfishness and human injustice.

It was not all in the open spaces. Sometimes the area was very cramped. At an exhibition of 'The Theatre in Arms' in the foyer of the Maly (December 1942) there was a photograph of Turchaninova reciting to an audience of anti-aircraft gunners in a dug-out. They were sitting on their bunks; she was standing in the narrowspace between them and the log wall. An interesting mental rhythm at this exhibition, one would imagine, as the eye included Repin's portrait of Shchepkin in that very foyer. Or perhaps this had by then been removed for safety.

The reactions of the audience were described by Aksyonov, who headed a brigade early in 1943. On one occasion, he said, the biggest room in a village had been turned into a club. A tent-cloth served as proscenium. Since the would-be audience could not possibly be stuffed into the remaining space, two consecutive performances had to be given. As soon as Aksyonov announced that the actor Ostuzhev was one of the party, the whole of the 'first house' rose to its feet and thundered out its appreciation. Apparently more than a sprinkling of Moscow men were among the audience.

If you will turn back in your mind to the same sort of ovation given to the two Moscow actors at Nizhny in 1812, you will see why this 'reception moved Ostuzhev so deeply that for some time he could not open his mouth. 'No triumph', he said afterwards, 'that I have had in playing Othello can compare with the tremendous joy I felt during that brief moment. I felt that the soldiers of my people needed me.'

Under these circumstances that was no complacent speech of an exhibitionist, still less the pompous hint of a seeker of honours. Ostuzhev was nearly seventy, and loaded with honours. It was a statement of fact, important not so much to him as to the development of human culture. It was the pride of an artist in a land that loved its artists.

Actresses at the Front

From the actresses' angle, too, those Maly tours had a wider importance than just personal sensations. Gogolyeva wrote in her diary on International Women's Day: 'I want to tell all the women of the world: the Fascists shall pay with their blood for all the sufferings of our women, for all the tears of our mothers, for the anguished yearnings of wives and sweethearts. Our turn will come. We shall make the Hitlerites rebuild our demolished factories brick by brick, the razed.villages, the plundered towns.'

Was that a mere outburst of general hate, inspired by a figure on a calendar? No. A day or two previously, after being bombed by a German aeroplane, she had been touring through the remains of a village, and seen bereaved women returning to it; and not more than a mile off was Petrishchevo, where Zoya Kosmodemyanskaya, 'Tanya', now to all time and to all nations with Joan of Arc and La Pasionaria, was tortured and hanged because though little more than a child she was faithful. And that day Gogolyeva had driven with the others down a road under enemy shell-fire. The brigade leader had hesitated, there being women in the party. But the actresses' only wish was to follow the advancing Soviet Army; and they drove on, and through.

These are experiences that deepen and impassion a woman of any age. When there is the organic tie between life and art which exists in the Maly Theatre these entries in an actress's diary become events in theatre history.[3]

Actors in Action

The Vahtangov Theatre had the honour of being the first central theatre whose brigade visited the Front. Strictly speaking, it collaborated with the V.T.O.'s second company. This brigade went to the Tula, Kalinin, South-Western, Stalingrad, Bryansk, and Voronezh sectors, and followed the advance from Rossosh, Kantemirovka, and Valuiki. Its leader was Orolchko. In two months it gave 150 performances, including some within 500 yards of the enemy. One of its most moving experiences was had at Valuiki. There the Fascists during their occupation had closed the school, and planned, if they did not actually contrive, to open it as a brothel. The first time the children re-entered it, a civilised sweetness had been restored to the building by its use by the Vahtangov brigade.[4]

But it was only to be expected that the Central Theatre of the Red Army would bear the honours in some way or other for front-line entertainment. A T.S.D.K.A. brigade holds the record for travel. By June 1942, that is, in eleven and a half months, it had toured the entire Soviet Front, from Bessarabia to Murmansk, giving 855 shows in so doing. On one occasion, it is related, they were in a dug-out about 70 metres from the Finnish trenches, and at the request of their invisible audience they included the singing march which was banned in Finland. Indeed the company discovered talents it did not know it possessed, as each member in continually renovating the repertoire on the march found he had a voice, or could dance, or in some other way improve his performance when travelling did not permit new plays to be rehearsed.

Dressed in camouflage capes, often under fire, the six artists and their leader-producer, Shaps, made their way up the map, in any manner they could, on foot, on horseback, hitch-hiking or boarding munitions trains. As a reward they received decorations from the Karelo-Finnish Government ... military decorations, not civilian ones. They were the first actors to win them, though later many other members of brigades were so decorated ... and a military award for war services is not easily won in the Soviet Union. Nonetheless, Nina Volodko and Zinovieva, the two actresses in this group, were thus honoured with the men. 'For the Fighters of our favourite Central Theatre of the Red Army' said a member of the War Soviet of the Karelian front as he made the awards. It must have been a weird thing sometimes for these Moscow artists driving in sledges through the arctic night under the Northern Lights, and performing sometimes in low earth huts where they could not always stand upright.[5]

Two-thirds of the entire theatre company took part in the theatre's brigades, of which there were eleven in all by the autumn of 1943, regularly visiting the front. Other Red Army Theatres competed with them. At the outbreak of war, the Theatre of the Red Army in the Kiev Special District was playing Lvov and Zholkev. They immediately re-organised themselves as the Theatre of the South-West Front, and mobilised themselves in a column of lorries. They took *A Fellow from Our Town, The Keys of Berlin* (by Guss and Finn) and a concert programme. To this they added, by rehearsing anywhere at any time, *The Armoured Train* 14-69, *Unquiet, Old Age, To be Continued, Partisans in the Steppes of the Ukraine,* and a play by Pervomaisky called *Battle Opening.* This was not a first-class theatre; and it had to acquire its own technique as the months went by. B. Nord reported that it found the way to its technique from the circumstances of playing in the open air by daylight. The audience could follow every move, and the actors, unable to rely much on make-up, had to feel their parts more deeply.

The Red Army Theatre of Central Asia made a three-month tour in 1943 of towns in their region. One of their plays was Rzheshevsky's *Always With Us,* another was *Peter Krymov,* the play that linked front with rear.

The Leningrad House of the Red Army competed too. They sent a party playing mostly Komeichuk's *The Front,* which by January 1943 had reached its 1,500th performance, to the immediate neighbourhood of the Leningrad front. The figure of performances, which looks unlikely, is possible from the shortness of journeys; but it implies a high degree of devotion and indeed of physical endurance. Many of the other Leningrad theatres formed brigades for either front or rear, among them the 'Pushkin' Theatre, which toured the North-West Front, giving sixty-three shows in a month, which included scenes from *Suvorov,* songs, anti-Fascist sketches, and comedy numbers. The Leningrad 'Gorky', too, gave over fifty shows in much the same space of time to sailors, in submarines, coastal batteries, on battleships' decks, and any other stages they could reach by cart, horse, cutter or boat.[6]

Sailors' Actors

This opens the fascinating tale of the Soviet Navy and its entertainment. Each of the Regional Fleets had its own theatre long before the war, based in a port in each case, but spending most of its time in visits. Some account of them is given in *The New Soviet Theatre.* War meant merely an intensification of this work, and danger in the voyages. Enemy dive-bombers could not differentiate between a travelling theatre and any other form of shipping, nor would they if they could. But the companies, many of whom were sailors by training, were proud of that danger; and if I know anything of Soviet citizens, sailor or actor, few will have been content to be passengers during an engagement.

The Northern Fleet had its own tug-boat, in which, laden with props, costumes, simple scenery and all sizes of packing cases, the theatre crept from anchorage to anchorage. Sometimes it landed, was unloaded by marines, and in naval lorries proceeded to the nearest section of the land front, where a marine audience awaited it. *A Servant of Two Masters, Russian People,* and *The Front,* were played in 1943; but there were concerts too. In one trip of nine days, eleven performances and fourteen concerts! But the Northern Fleet also had its amateur groups, helped by the amateur-dramatic section of Northern Fleet House under Captain Chertygin. One eminent production was Virta's play, *My Friend the Colonel,* acted by commanders, navigators, electricians and men of the lower deck together.

A pleasant photograph of a Fleet concert was shown at the *Theatre in Arms* exhibition. The young actress Ivanova on a skerry sitting and playing the saxophone to an audience so close that their bayonets made steel scenery round her.

In March 1942 the Political Direction of the Navy organised the First Black Sea Front-Line Theatre, including People's Artist Rybnikov of the Maly at its head, B. Filippov as director and political chief, and at least three prominent actors. Besides a concert programme they offered Solovyov's *Belugin's Wedding* and Ostrovsky's

Truth is Good a new play by Konstantin Finn about the war, *The Ruza Forest,* and other things. All these had sets by the same artist, V. Miller.

The cream of the Fleet theatres, though, was the one belonging to the Red Banner Baltic Fleet. In the summer of 1941, this was already celebrating its tenth birthday in a ten-day festival. It owed its existence to a chance suggestion of Voroshilov at an amateur Fleet concert, and at first it was amateur. Then it became a branch of naval service for sailors or commanders, like navigating or engineering. Its range broadened and its standard rose. During those ten years it produced thirty-six classical or Soviet plays and gave nearly 2,500 shows. In 1934 the Leningrad producer, A. V. Pergament, became its artistic director, and it reached a high degree of skill and experience in dramatic art, though it never abandoned the simple concert as well. Indeed it may well have been the model on which all the brigades were formed. Certainly it began the war fully equipped for its job.

Nor did it lower the standard. Four or five performances might be given in a single day, with hurried transport from point to point by boat, bicycle or plane. By January 1943 its war performances had reached 3,150. It had casualties. One party ran into an enemy ambush and was wiped out. Actors and actresses often did duty as stretcher-bearers and nurses. Distant outposts were visited in batches of five. On some occasions inaccessible posts listened-in by field telephone. Shows were often interrupted by enemy land raids or sea attacks, and the company broke off to join in the defence. Fourteen members of it, by April 1943, had been decorated for meritorious conduct in action; and one, Mihailov, won the order of the Red Star.

Besides touring the Fleet and the Baltic front, the company spent some time in Leningrad during the siege. Pergament's productions could hold their own with even Leningrad audiences, even in plays like *The Front* and *Oleko Dundich,* which other bodies, less specialised and less harassed in their work, had already done there. But primarily it performed its own local, or professional, themes. In July 1942, while in Leningrad, a new play, *To Meet the Squadron,* was given its first hearing by a young writer named Tevelev (His first name is given as both Mihail and Matyey). This was a war play, basically naval, but including also those fighting the Fascists behind the lines in occupied zones.

Thereafter quite a group of writers made up a collective with this theatre. Agranenko and Stein wrote a naval vaudeville, *Welcome!* Agranenko collaborated with another war reporter, Ilya Baru, in a more serious work, shown in the summer of 1943, *The Earth Bears*

Witness. This was about the Sea Air Arm. Its heroes were two air aces, both Heroes of the Soviet Union. One is a general favourite, and a nice fellow, but hot-headed, ambitious, and always thinking of his own score of enemy machines destroyed. The other is quieter, less self-assertive, but in some ways the more valuable fighter. The central incident is a dog-fight in which the latter joins to keep an eye on his over-daring friend.

During 1943 the Baltic Fleet Theatre added *Wait for Me* and *Admiral Nahimov* to its list. The latter was by Igor Lukovsky. This theatre was also responsible for the reappearance of Vsevolod Vishnevsky as a playwright. Since *An Optimistic Tragedy* Vishnevsky had written several plays, which had been performed at the Vahtangov or Meierhold Theatres and perhaps elsewhere, but little had been heard of them. In 1943, however, collaborating with Alexander Kron, the author of the psychological play, *Depth Prospecting,* and with Alexander Azarov, he brought out at this theatre *Wide Spreads the Sea,* and a new play by himself alone, *At the Walls of Leningrad.* Simultaneous productions of these plays were given by the Kamerny Theatre in Barnaul. In this way the people of Leningrad and their naval protectors on the Baltic were able to experience what was thought of them in the world outside their areas.

But besides their own special theatre, the Baltic Fleet was visited in the usual way by different brigades. For example, in the spring of 1943, the first V.T.O. Brigade spent six weeks among them doing *Wait for Me, The Minor* (the most popular play today of the eighteenth-century Russia dramatist Fonvism) and the two nineteenth-century plays already mentioned as performed by the Black Sea First Brigade.[7]

Poles

Brigades sometimes developed like the theatres of the nationalities from within; in this case from within regiments. This may happen in any army, even in one of non-Soviet nationality.

In summer 1943 the First Polish Division of refugee Poles, named after Kosciusko the Great Polish democrat patriot, left for the front fully trained and equipped. A few months before it had been a group of would-be soldiers and commanders, anxious to free their country from Fascism of all sorts, but having neither the means nor the knowledge. In early May, during their training, there appeared the nucleus of the Zholner Theatre to be: one Polish literary and artistic stage-manager, one Polish producer, one Polish actress. They had no stage, no costumes, no instruments, for a company. In the division that was to be, and ten musicians; also a painter, who professe some materials together and see what he could a so hard together that inside one month they ge ready.

Nataba Vilter has described it: 'In a big clearing the bare grass in front of spectators sitting on the gr a huge semi-circle of plywood with twin borders of re white, and the inscription ТЕАТР ЖОПЙЕРА. This emblem stood as both curtain and *Décor*. From it appeared, a *conférencier*. A soldier. A ne'er-do-weel. A failure. He was greeted with laughter. Enter the Actress. She stood at the crossing of the ways, in front of a signpost bearing a red arrow and a white bayonet, both of which pointed west. They read the direction:'This Way to Warsaw'. They gave strong, simple speeches about the struggle before them, and the victory to come. Then they sang Polish songs. The orchestra played selections of Russian songs. The players recited poems about the concentration camps in Poland, till before the audience stood the images of their tortured brethren there. Then they danced the Polish Kuyavyak. A short sketch followed; and artists and audience joined in a song that had recently been heard in the Division and was well known to it, 'We are the First Division'. In this way the Poles were reminded of dances and scenes familiar since childhood, and felt they were still part of their homeland. They wept. Youngsters and full grown men alike, without being ashamed of their tears. Their emotion was communicated to the actors. The song rang through the forest.'

Propaganda? Maybe. But what would Ben Jonson not have given for such actual matter, such truthful feeling for the writing and witnessing of his propaganda masques?

Not a very high dramatic standard, perhaps; but their task was to find variety in a limited field. Their producer, Krasnovetsky, was alive to this. They kept observant eyes and ears upon the Division, drawing their matter from its daily life and events. In this way they created four new programmes in three months; and kept their audience small (and themselves busy thereby) through visiting different portions of the Division and giving three, or often four, performances a day.

Soon a concert brigade was formed. The range of instruments was not great, but happily Chervinskaya, the actress, had a deep, rich voice; and a solo harmonica later materialised, named Lurye, self-taught but a virtuoso. A jazz band followed and a complete and very popular puppet theatre. In this later the favourite puppets were

ⱼels and their gang, as might have been expected. Their
ⱼre cleverly modelled in stearine (the stuff candles are made
, and said to have been very expressive! The neurotic Hitler had
a fit of hysterics in the course of his usual speech about the greatness
of Nazidom; Goebbels appeared with monkey's tail, hanging
mouth, and so on. But other puppets performed themes from popular romances and poems by Vazhik and L.Pasternak.[8]

Puppets

It should not be supposed that puppet theatres were the prerogative
and delight only of the Poles, nor that the Red Army, whether Polish, Russian, or anything else, wanted or got only serious shows
that would aid their morale. Far, far from it. There was a plethora
of light entertainment in the brigades, including plays, puppet
shows and whole circuses.

Both glove puppets and marionettes on strings are used in the
Soviet Union and there had been two permanent puppet theatres in
Moscow for years, directed by the puppet masters Eugene Demmeny and Sergey Obraztsov. Obraztsov was an Honoured Artist.
With his teams of puppeteers (two for gloves, two for marionettes)
he obtained his own new premises in 1938. Till then this theatre had
travelled clubs and schools in Moscow and district. It was quite a
big concern: ten actresses, nine actors, four pianists, a violinist and
three bayanisti, or accordion players, together with the necessary
band of managers, craftsmen, producers, sculptors and such,
amounting to twelve more. London readers of this book may have
seen a film of Obraztsov's work including his own most-loved act
with a baby, whose life-like noises and movements he succeeds in
soothing to sleep with great care and tenderness.

They used to give two performances daily at this theatre in peacetime, one in the afternoon for children, the other in the evening for
adults, who specially liked *Aladdin's Magic Lamp* and Gogol's fantastic story, *Christmas Eve*. But alas! the fine new premises were
damaged by bomb blast, and the Obraztsov puppets moved to
Novosibirsk.

They took their time on the journey. Indeed they could not do
otherwise; for wherever they were discovered, they had to perform.
Even on the waters of a great river, they were able to restore the
spirits of two thousand small children, evacuees from Moscow,
whom their boat overhauled. What an encounter for the children!
and how right that a boat of puppets should suddenly draw alongside out of nowhere in strange country, should give them a

performance of *The Magic Galosh,* and then putter off down-stream, the music of *Moscow Mine* floating behind them from the orchestra as the children waved goodbye, and caught up the tune ... Moscow mine, land of mine, you are the best!

Five rivers the Puppet Theatre travelled, the Moskva, the Oka; past dairy villages, between raspberry fields, by sandy dunes or dense forests of pine trees or limes or maple-trees, stopping at historic towns, or farming villages, or bright modern mining settlements. Then down the Volga, as the old Russian actors had done with Burlak, but crossing it now, sailing, east of it, over the rampart to a sure welcome in every strange land. Up the Kama, through Tatar country, and up its tributary the White River and so into the heart of the Urals. Surely of all the exodus to the east, this was the most charming and the most acceptable wherever it reached. Not that it was altogether charming for those on it! At the heart of winter even these rivers were blocked with ice; and the puppet theatre then had to tumble onto railways, and make their way by land.

They toured Bashkiria, Central Asia, parts of Siberia, the Kuzbas. The tough, coalminers were fascinated by their pit-head performances. Workers in factories, recruits in Red Army training centres, children and adults, of all races, natives or evacuees, came crowding and went smiling; for it is one of the advantages of puppets that though the ear hears, it is the seeing eye that best appreciates the skill of liveliness in the motions; and the eye is international.

The four teams split into brigades, touring the outlying rear and the advanced fronts. There is a tale of a tank corps. One of the shows had a satirical television act, in which 'puppets' of another kind were represented by dogs, Pétain, Mussolini, Mannerheim and Antonescu. Pétain was a mangy hound who whined while 'Master' was away. The big mongrel Mussolini yelped himself hoarse. The sorely beaten Mannerheim was a very old dog, and groaned in pain all the time, Antonescu, a surly tyke, had his tail permanently between his legs, but most when a certain lean and ravenous Alsatian appeared. However, on this occasion, in the open air as usual, a Soviet aeroplane came into view during Hitler's speech, drowning it. The dog with the funny moustache looked up, followed the plane apprehensively with its eyes, and then scratched himself helplessly with his hind leg. The appreciative roar from the tank men drowned the noise of the departing plane.

In spite of a lack of time, the theatre in the course of 1943 prepared and put on a new show, set in silver, black and red: *King Deer,* a fantasy by the eighteenth-century Italian, Carlo Gozzi, written for the Sacchi troupe. It was claimed that this had not been performed since on the legitimate stage, and only once by puppets, in Vienna. Certainly it had never been seen in Russia. So it was a real novelty to the men at the front when it toured there. Another new production was 'in the heroic style', about Dmitry of the Don. As a rule, the music for these shows was written specially . . . in the case of *King Deer* by a woman, Alexandrova. Operettas were included too: *On the Roofs of Berlin* and *The American Linnet.*

The Moscow puppet theatre run by Eugene Demmeny had a rather more sophisticated shape to its shows . . . though no less appeal for spectators old or young. It usually opened with a procession of puppets to a special march round, or through, the audience. It usually ended with a dance of Red Army 'Man-puppet' and farmworker 'Girl-puppet'. This theatre favoured the glove form.

A Demmeny brigade on the Leningrad front gave more than 650 performances in five months. It was a topical show, in the sense that it included pamphlet plays about Nazi leaders and their dupes. Thus for *The Strategists* the Moscow artist Bekleshova created portrait heads in 1943, heads that though they were caricatures, were yet credible, especially because the uniformed bodies below assumed life-like poses. Another anti-Fascist playlet was based on a story by M. Tuberovsky called *Fiddlesticks. The Eagle and the Snake* showed mean, inhuman tricks played by Nazi soldiery; *The Appetite of the Wolf,* their crimes and filthy habits. And so, largely with the help of Tuberovsky and another author called A. Flit, a topical repertoire was built up. This was being extended in 1943 to include a revue by the poet Samuil Marshak, *Young Fritz,* and on another theme, *Mitza in Spookland.*

Satirical themes like these were popular; but with puppets fantasy is best of all. *Gulliver's Travels* had been running for years, about fifteen years by 1943. Kipling's *Mowgli* gave opportunity for animal shapes. *The Little Humpbacked Horse,* which had been a tremendous success with all ages on tour, was chosen as the opening play when the Moscow Puppets Theatre returned to the capital in September 1943. But Demmeny told the *Moscow News* that he had found the most wonderful figure for a puppet in Sir John Falstaff, and he was preparing *The Merry Wives of Windsor* as he thought it had all the necessary features for a first-class puppet theme: sparkling development of action, amusing plot, picturesque settings, and clear-cut characters.[9]

Grand Operas and Miniatures

The theatres of miniatures were not unlike the less developed front-line brigades. 'One-act plays, carefully chosen to make a harmonious evening, happy-go-lucky satire, a complete unit of entertainment' – that would describe the work of the Moscow Theatre of Miniatures, which remained in Moscow throughout the war. *No Offence, Short and Sharp,* are rough renderings of two of its show titles, and indicate the contents. Obviously such would appeal in times of strain; and obviously they were mobile. Therefore they were in constant demand at the front and touring the farms of the rear, not standing for very much, perhaps, but gladdening the days of those who came to see. The V.T.O. also organised a special front-line minintures-theatre called Happy Landings. Its matter came almost entirely from local and topical events and remarks; which is indeed the essence of such a show.[10]

At the other end of the scale whole operas were taken to the front. The Fifth V.T.O. Theatre was purely operatic. This set out in September 1942 with an all Tchaikovsky repertoire, including *Eugene Onyegin* complete, scenes from *The Queen of Spades* and *The Little Shoes* and a number of songs and light orchestral pieces. Naturally the properties and scenery had to be easily portable. But the show was a complete one, of a high musical and theatrical standard.

This venture was followed within a month or two by brigades from such units as the Leningrad Little Opera, the Leningrad Kirov (formerly Mariy) Theatre of Opera and Ballet, the Stanislavsky-and-Nemirovich Danchenko Musical Theatre, the Belorussian Theatre of Opera and Ballet, and many others.[11] And just as with the Moscow Art Theatre brigades, the emphasis was on the playing of the drama, and the tables and chairs could be left to look after themselves. So in these simplified but still complex shows the emphasis was on the musical tale and not on its trappings. Skill, beauty, understanding, a sweet voice and a good tune in a tale of human feeling – such things made the fighter's life more worth living, and reminded him of the things he was fighting for.

The Role of the Front Line Brigades

In all armies, after the inhumanity of mechanised battle, during the austere use of human speech for command and discipline, there is a need for words that convey ideas. They may be the humblest and most childlike, in a sentimental story or a funny one; or they may be the finest poetry or the most comprehensive wisdom. But a book does not always suffice. There are too many distractions, and an inert book cannot stir the attention, by itself. Here the live voice of the actor wins. When it is wholly identified with the text, as a good actor identifies it, coming freshly to each word and in a flash giving its exact position and full meaning by tempo, rhythm, or intonation, then the text becomes alive. The text can then stir and hold the attention, however weary the listener. Then that something in the voice is not the personality of the actor, which may differ with the matter read. It is the voice of the thing read. It is a delegate from the culture the fighter is fighting for. So there is nothing wrong in the presence of the word-artist in the firing line. On the contrary, it is right. He was a part of what made the Red Army man fight so well.

With this background to our ideas, we can now consider the vital question, at the root of this chapter: what was the best entertainment the Soviet theatre could give to the men at the front?

A member of a Vahtangov Theatre brigade, A. Gabovich, reported that one time before a performance, a soldier who was obviously speaking for his comrades too, after a discussion as to what sort of show it was going to be, came up and asked, if it would be funny. Gabovich said he sensed that if he had said No, the soldier would still have come to it, but that he was plainly pleased to be told it would be funny.

Another time, Gabovich said, an audience of 3,000 had just completed a very long march and were tired out. The brigade was doubtful if their endeavours would be attractive enough to overcome physical exhaustion. But they need not have feared. Nobody fell asleep and everyone laughed to their and the company's content.

Gobovich makes it clear, however, that front-line audiences did not only nor always want funny shows. This fact is confirmed by Kolesayev, producer to a Maly brigade which included *The Blue Scarf* in its repertoire. 'The fighting man is as interested in classical tragedy as in light sketches', he was reported as saying to the *Moscow News;*[12] and it should be mentioned that *The Blue Scarf* was a very light comedy. Incidentally, it is amusing to notice that during one performance in the evening the lighting failed. The commander ordered all men who had brought their pocket torches with them to move into the front rows, so that by shining them up on the stage the show could go on. The audience thereupon took charge of the production, and every time a 'villain' came on, they light-heartedly plunged him into darkness.

The reason for this readiness to be serious is interesting to speculate about. Front-line audiences are in circumstances of acute emotional strain. They may be listening quietly enough, but they are in full battle-dress and may at any moment be called on to repel an enemy surprise attack. For this they know they must hate their enemy; and for their own sakes they do not want enervating or nostalgic ideas to be enacted before them. This is a very different thing from singing maudlin, homesick or ultra-pessimistic ditties, which merely relieve the spirits and do no harm, in spite of the fact that to read the words of such songs on paper might inspire many an unthinking officer to shoot the culprits for spreading alarm and despondency.

There must be no seconds spent in readjustment to the idea and desire for battle. Yet at the same time they do want to be re-familiarised with and reassured about the ideas of home, peace, culture – for these may in the next few minutes be the drive behind their fighting, the extra drive that turns a good soldier into a heroic one.

And how precious these ideas are to the soldier! Witness the good-humoured attempt which Kolesayev describes of one detachment in the rear, who heard that a Maly brigade was going to another detachment first, and tried to 'capture' it. Others tried all sorts of dodges to keep their visitors with them, by inventing burst tyres, breakdowns, and any excuse to delay a departing lorry.

The task of the 'entertainers' was not easy. Strong, simple, direct emotions wanted satisfying; sentimentality had to be avoided at all costs. Gabovich, a member of a Vahtangov Theatre brigade, was performing in an area cleared of the enemy. One of the turns was a song about an old mother waiting for her soldier son to come back. Among the audience sat a tough old Red Army General, and by his side an old countrywoman from the neighbourhood. Both were in tears. The General afterwards stated that such a song, with its powerful incentive to clear the whole country of the enemy, was worth more than any number of blank cartridges and stage-easy feats of arms. And the company agreed with him.

At the same time the problem was not quite so simple as the one aspect of it which that General solved. Front-line audiences tended to like any sort of a show, sometimes quite feeble ones. That was natural enough. But any playing down to them, any deliberate or cynical or any careless lowering of standards, would have had fatal results. A sentimental performer of even this very same song about the old mother would have aroused indirect, sentimental reactions. These reactions are latent in most people, and if evoked would tend to arouse half-formed feelings of pity, not for the old mother (which would lead to action) but for the listener himself, which would lead to nostalgia, inaction, and a weakening of self-discipline.

Furthermore, a dramatic performance of the right kind is a fuller and more satisfying experience than a solo performance of the right kind. If that same old mother were shown in a play, the range of comment, the spread of life, the importance of the experience would be increased. Plays, therefore, must not be excluded, despite the General. But the experience they offered must be a true one, rousing simple emotions and satisfying them by the comment of the play not indulging feelings of a sentimental kind.

Now two factors enter into every stage performance – the character and outlook of the author on the one hand, and the understanding and skill of the performers on the other. Both these factors must be equal to their task, or the audience will not experience, but dream.

The people on the stage must be convincing as real persons; and their reality must be enhanced by such surroundings as war conditions, the powers of imagination in the audience, and other factors allow. All front-line performances, like all theatrical performances, draw to some extent on the imagination. But to do so to the very great degree required by formalist productions would be both imprudent and dangerous at the front. It would be imprudent, because even in peacetime to appreciate a formalist production requires a mental effort greater than is required by a straight and deep piece of acting; the effort of suppressing human sympathy. And front-line conditions require making mental recreation as easy as possible for the soldier. (If, in a capitalist country, the tired businessman cannot be bothered with the ingenuities of La Compagnie des I5 neither, in a Socialist army, can the tired soldier be bothered with the acrobatics of Meierhold.)

Secondly, it would be dangerous; because emotions aroused by non-real productions are, whatever the mental state of the beholder happens to be, like those roused in a child by a toy. They have little direct connection with reality, and are satisfying only as long as reality does not intrude. But just as when the reality of bedtime intrudes and the toy is taken away, the child cries and storms, not so much because it dislikes the reality of bed (where it can have just as good a dream anyway) as because the particular stimulus to a particular dream-emotion has been withdrawn. So, at the end of a non-real performance, there is left a feeling not of satisfaction but of deprivation; and though the adult spectator does not stamp and roar, he keeps looking back to the dream and resents the reality. He might particularly resent the reality of battle.

So if the front line is to have plays at all, they must be real experiences. And that means the consummate art of a well trained, lifelong actor or actress who knows the world lived in. The better the acting, the fuller the audience's experience. That is why front rank artists enjoy going to the front line.

But it also means that the plays themselves must be true and deep. If they are about the present day, and (as most plays do) show a hero winning through despite great difficulties, then the difficulties must not just melt away before the end of the third act. Because the hero is in a stage situation, they must melt away only as and because he copes with them. Otherwise the event will be worthless to the audience. Reality, and their own difficulties, will intrude too strongly.

And again, if the hero is to be killed, or if he must be unhappy at the end (this will evolve by theatre logic from the circumstances of plot and character), then such a consummation must be related to the real life of the audience. Just as their own personal lives are in wartime bound even more tightly than ever with the whole community, so the result of the hero's personal struggle (and indeed of the struggles of all the people in the play, of whom we are merely taking a hero as representative) must be part of the struggle of the community. Otherwise this experience will be worthless to the audience.

Again, if the play is about the past, then it must not be a romantic dream, with the total of several picturesque details making the past seem more heroic, or more humorous, or more glamorous, than the present.

But if the past is to be enacted in ways that evoke strong, direct emotions, then in what better way than through plays written in that manner by great dramatists or writers of the past? Tolstoy, Ostrovsky, Lermontov, Moliére, Lope de Vega . . . . Yet the performance, too, must be such that these people are real in their own time. Otherwise the audience will dream, not experience. Yet life is complex; and a mere collection of figures out of the past can be made to bear any meaning. If they are to be true, then the comment of the author must be studied and made clear; or else the audience will not understand its own experience. It will not fit in with what they believe they are fighting for.

So it comes about that the stern demands of the front-line audience can only be met by a Socialist-realist theatre and Socialist realism finds a new vindication in battle.

This did not mean that the front-line theatre had to be 'educational' in any narrow sense, quite the reverse. It had to be so attractive, so immediate, that the audience would clamour to come. Singing, dancing, farces and wise-cracks had as much place there as tears or meditations on the greatness of humanity. But these had to be rich, human, full-blooded, worthwhile. There was no place there for sentimentality or snivelling, sanctimoniousness or sneers.

Not every brigade realised this; and not every group was good enough. There was one group from Novosibirsk which journeyed hopefully west but its programme was so bad that it was turned back from Moscow, and ten men who would have been useful citizens in their capacity as militia men made a journey of 3,500 kilometres in vain.

A filial of the Leningrad 'Pushkin' got through to the front with *Forced Landing*. It should have been a bright comedy, full of the joy of life; but they so overacted that the audience would have none of it; and back they went.

Sometimes the concert parties were just a *mélange* of turns put together anyhow and rehearsed in trains. With no unity, and no harmony, the audience soon lost interest. But these were exceptional. The majority set out with a sense of the reality they were going to, and what sort of people in what sort of circumstances would want them. They were, after all, only their peacetime audiences in uniform with some friends. Where the brigade made adjustments to the experience they gained, they became part of the Army. This happened to the Red Army Theatre group, who used local material in some shows; and it also explains the popularity of a Vahtangov Theatre brigade.

Such then were the principles on which the troops were entertained. And understanding these things made the performers able to endure what they did. Splashing through mud that would make an East Anglian fen seem like a tennis court, bumped and bruised in cars and carts with broken springs or none at all, over roads that a fenland drover would jib at, crossing rivers on precarious planks, four shows a day and a hundred miles to cover, sweltering in the sun and the dust, losing themselves in arriving on time but to find their audience gone off on a special mission, not arriving on time, afraid of not arriving at all (and any stage person will know what that means to an artist), nevertheless men, women, and stars alike stuck to the job.

They more than stuck to it, they made it phenomenal. Brigades were not, perhaps, quite an invention of this war. Twenty years previously Moskvin had headed a party of actors touring the Caucasian front. But the figures of this war were astonishing. By August 1942 a hundred and fifty thousand performances had been given; by December, two hundred thousand. By February 1943 Pokrovsky was able to inform the Plenum of the Central Committee of the Union of Art Workers (R.A.B.I.S.) that 260,000 performances had been given by 900 brigades composed of 15,000 workers.

Notes

1. *Soviet War News*, 8 June 1943; *Soviet Theatre Chronicle*, 1943, p. 4, p. 12.
2. *Soviet War News*, 17 November 1942; *Soviet Theatre Chronicle*, 1943, 3, p. 27.
3. *Moscow News*, 16 January 1943; 3 March 1943; *Soviet War News*, 7 January 1943; *Soviet Theatre Chronicle*, 1943, id, pp. 28–30.
4. *Soviet War News*, 8 June 1943, *Soviet Theatre Chronicle*, 1943, 3, pp. 30–31.
5. *Moscow News*, 3 July 1942.
6. *ibid.* 21 March 1942; 30 January 1943; 8 May 1943; *Int. Lit.*, 1942, xi., p. 84; 1943, viii, p. 78; *Moscow News*, 14 June 1942. Nord's account is interesting. My own experience of playing in the open is that the tendency is the other way; the bigger scale, the lack of resonance, the sensation of being a small speck of humanity on show, rather than an assumed personality living in the life of the audience, incline the actor to a 'poster' performance. But then I was never trained in a Socialist Realist theatre. Nord is corroborated by other writers. L. Zhukov, writing of the Front Line Dramatic Theatre under Rayevsky, which was formed from graduates of Rayevsky's and Teleshyova's classes at G.I.T.I.S., says 'The voice has to be forced, a close-up technique has to be adopted constantly, certain details have to be forgone . . . But this kind of thing does not decide the fate of the show. A front-line theatre, which is a special form of our contemporary theatre, makes a definite demand on one thing only: that there should be a relationship of creativeness between the actor and his work, exactness and vividness in the figure created.'
7. *Soviet Theatre Chronicle*, 1943, iv. pp. 12–13; iii, pp. 31–32.; *Moscow News*, 16 January 1943; *Anglo-Soviet Journal*, July 1941, pp. 268–9.
8. ___. ___: 4 November 43.
9. *Moscow News*, 4 November 1943; 2 May 1943 (bis); *Int. Lit.*, 1942, x, p. 79. 1944, vi, p. 77.
10. *Soviet Theatre Chronicle*, 1943, i, p. 6.
11. *Moscow News*, 3 March 1943.
12. M. Bursky, *Moscow News*, 25 June 1943; ibid, 16 January 1943.

INDEX

Agit-prop theatre 26, 102, 192
Anti-Fascist 8, 26, 62, 87, 88, 93, 94, 95, 96, 97, 102, 106, 108, 112, 117
  theatre 100, 108, 110, 138, 174, 180,
Auschwitz 143, 145, 149, 151, 152, 156, 158, 222
Austria 14, 109, 139, 140, 148
Austrian cabaret 97, 111
Austrian Centre 97
Austrian refugees 8, 84, 218

Beethoven 32
Belgium 54, 118, 139, 141, 143, 149, 153, 160
Berlin 94, 104, 137, 138, 139, 141, 142
Blassetti, Alessandro 12, 15
Brecht, Bertolt 4, 35, 46, 48, 97, 101, 104, 109, 139
Britain 8, 54, 59, 64, 84, 86, 88, 89, 104, 105, 106, 107, 117
Buchenwald 2, 148, 149

C.E.M.A (Council for the Encouragement of Music and the Arts) 56–58, 62
Churchill, W. 61
Concentration camps 1, 2, 8, 9, 85, 86, 137, 160, 177

18BL 6, 12, 13–17, 22
ENSA (Entertainment National Service Association) 59, 62, 64

Europe, European 1, 5, 24, 51, 106, 110, 111, 137, 141, 152, 157, 166

Fascism 5, 6, 14, 17, 21, 22, 32, 40, 44, 61, 89, 102, 103, 105, 118, 166, 170, 176
Fascist(s) 1, 5, 6, 12, 13, 16, 17, 18, 19, 21–26, 28, 29, 33, 41, 43, 50, 51, 66, 87, 102, 171, 172, 175,
  Opera 32
  Plays 24
  Theatre 6, 22–26, 29
First World War 23, 54, 112
Frankfurt Opera House 40, 41
France 6, 8, 54, 65–69, 70–73, 75–76, 117–118,

Germany 1, 5, 6, 8, 25, 32–33, 41–44, 46, 47, 49, 54, 87, 92, 101, 106, 137–142
  West Germany 160
Gestapo 3, 77, 87
Ghetto(s), the 2, 3, 151–153, 154, 158, 159
Goebbels, 4, 5, 7, 35, 41, 42, 48, 49, 178
Göring 5, 37, 41
Gulag 1, 8, 124, 131

Hitler, Adolf 4, 5, 7, 8, 37, 38, 46, 47, 85–89, 93, 94, 96, 101, 105, 106, 111, 119, 138, 139, 151, 171–179
Hitler youth 49
Holland 54, 118, 137–144, 151, 153

Italy 1, 5, 14, 17, 18, 21, 22, 28, 32, 33, 42–44

Jews, Jewish 8, 41, 45, 48, 87, 99, 101, 117, 137, 138, 141–148, 150–152, 157, 158, 159
Joan of Arc 7, 65, 67–70, 72, 75–78, 172

London 7, 54, 55, 57–63, 67, 69, 84, 88, 97, 98, 104, 108, 110, 112, 137, 178

Moscow 127, 131–134, 166, 169, 171, 173, 178–182, 186
Moscow Art Theatre 167, 169, 170
Mozart 32
Mussolini 6, 13, 17, 21, 23, 26, 43, 44, 88, 179

National Socialism (Socialist) 5, 7, 35, 36, 42, 46–49, 51, 139
Nazi('s), the 2, 5, 6, 7, 25, 33, 34, 37, 38, 40, 41, 43, 44, 46, 48, 49, 50, 51, 54, 85, 87, 88, 89, 93, 94, 102, 108, 138, 139, 141, 142, 144, 145, 148, 149, 150, 152, 153, 154, 157, 158, 159, 160, 167, 168, 178, 180,
anti-Nazi 74, 85, 95, 102
British supporters 86
civilian prisoners 85
cultural authority 7, 37
musical press 34
occupied regions 103
oppression 84, 108
prisoners of war 110
pro-Nazi 77, 109
state 177, 203
Storm troopers 38, 101

Opera 5–7, 9, 16, 32–38, 40–45, 57, 152, 158, 166, 181
Orwell, George 4

Paris 40, 65–70, 73, 74, 77, 137, 170,
Parisian theatres 68, 78
Peer Gynt 37, 38
Péguy, Marcel and Charles 68, 70–73, 78
Piotrkow 2
Poland 54, 145, 146, 150, 151, 177
Polish 2, 144, 145, 157, 176–178
Propaganda 1, 4–6, 24–30, 33, 42–44, 56, 66–70, 78, 127, 128, 132, 154, 158, 168, 177
Ministry of, 34, 40, 41
Propaganda-staffel 7, 77

Roosevelt 56
Rome 16, 17, 23, 26
Russia (Russian) 1, 6, 8, 9, 25, 28, 96, 129, 167, 168, 176, 177, 178, 179, 180

Second World War 1, 6, 22, 26, 34, 63, 101
Shaftesbury Avenue 55
Shaw, George Bernard 57, 64, 68, 69, 70, 71, 73, 75, 78, 109, 123
Spain 65
Strauss, Richard 16, 37, 40
Strauss, Leo 153–157, 160

Threepenny Opera, the 48, 153, 155, 159
Third Reich 4, 5, 7, 33, 34, 86, 94, 137

UK, the 1
Unity Theatre 55, 58, 60, 62

Wagner 32, 35, 36, 42, 50, 112
Warsaw 2, 177
Weill, K 35, 38, 46
Weimer Republic 34, 35, 41